The Future of Education with AI

Andreas Dengel · Laurence Devillers ·
Koichi Kise · Andrew Vargo
Editors

The Future of Education with AI

Communications of NII Shonan Meetings

Springer

Editors

Andreas Dengel
DFKI GmbH (German Research Center for Artificial Intelligence)
RPTU University Kaiserslautern-Landau
Kaiserslautern, Germany

Laurence Devillers
Interdisciplinary Laboratory of Digital Science
Sorbonne University/CNRS France
Orsay, France

Koichi Kise
Graduate School of Informatics
Osaka Metropolitan University
Sakai, Osaka, Japan

Andrew Vargo
Graduate School of Informatics
Osaka Metropolitan University
Sakai, Osaka, Japan

ISBN 978-981-95-1621-6 ISBN 978-981-95-1622-3 (eBook)
https://doi.org/10.1007/978-981-95-1622-3

This Springer imprint is published by the registered company Springer Nature Singapore Pte Ltd.
The registered company address is: 152 Beach Road, #21-01/04 Gateway East, Singapore 189721, Singapore

Preface

Shonan Meeting 214, *The Future of Education with AI* sought to bring experts from human–computer interaction to discuss the placement of artificial technology (AI) and associated technologies in the future of education, both formal and informal. The meeting focused on both practical implementations of technologies and theoretical impacts on learners and society. As a result of the meeting, the organizers of the workshop facilitated this volume to disseminate the discussions and findings produced during the seminar.

This work was supported in part by grants from JST Trilateral AI "Learning Cyclotron" Grant Number JPMJCR20G3, JSPS Grant-in-Aid Fund for the Promotion of Joint International Research (Fostering Joint International Research) Grant Number 23KK0188, MEXT "Innovation Platform for Society 5.0" Program Grant Number JPMXP0518071489, DFG (Project No. 442581111), and ANR Trilateral AI "Learning Cyclotron" Grant Number LSP n° 237539 (LeCycl, UMR9015) between CNRS-LISN and ANR.

We are grateful to all the administrators and staff which facilitated Shonan Meeting 214 and all of the attendees who participated and added to the lively discussion. We would also thank D. L. Vargo, MILS, MATS, for providing extensive feedback on readability and clarity for all chapters.

Kaiserslautern, Germany — Andreas Dengel
Orsay, France — Laurence Devillers
Sakai, Japan — Koichi Kise
Sakai, Japan — Andrew Vargo

Contents

Introduction: The Future of AI with Education

Andrew Vargo, Koichi Kise, Laurence Devillers, and Andreas Dengel

1 Introduction

The impact of Artificial Intelligence (AI) on education is a frequent topic of discussion within both academia and the popular press. A great deal of focus is directed toward the manner in which AI is disrupting current educational paradigms. This disruption can sometimes be a source of concern among both educational practitioners and the public, but potential solutions aimed at improving the lives of people and enhancing the global standard of living demand a measured and thorough examination. Artificial intelligence is advancing rapidly and researchers need to urgently examine the promise of AI and map out potential avenues for augmenting human intellect and the ability to learn, master, and transfer knowledge. Thus, Shonan Meeting 214 [2] and this volume were titled "The Future of Education with AI." The emphasis on the choice of the preposition "with" rather than "and" is quite intentional. From our point of view, AI is pervasive and will eventually influence, directly or indirectly, all forms of formal and informal education.

In general, this volume looks at education and AI from the viewpoint of the Human–Computer Interaction (HCI) academic community [3]. Although other aca-

A. Vargo (✉) · K. Kise
Osaka Metropolitan University, Sakai, Japan
e-mail: awv@omu.ac.jp

K. Kise
e-mail: kise@omu.ac.jp

L. Devillers
Sorbonne University/LISN-CNRS, Paris, France
e-mail: devil@linsi.fr

A. Dengel
DFKI GmbH (German Research Center for Artificial Intelligence), RPTU University Kaiserslautern-Landau, Kaiserslautern, Germany
e-mail: dengel@dfki.de

A. Dengel et al. (eds.), *The Future of Education with AI*,
https://doi.org/10.1007/978-981-95-1622-3_1

demic domains, such as education or philosophy, have valid points of view and approaches to this topic, we believe that the HCI point of view provides important insight into the practical implementations of AI across modalities. We consider not only the impact of large-language models, but also the many technologies that can affect human learning processes, such as eye tracking, cognitive load sensing, and confidence estimation.

The HCI approach also provides an ethos of human augmentation that is rooted in a fundamental need to understand how humans adopt and work with machines, as well as an understanding of how machines impact individuals and society. There is a belief in this field that machines and systems should enhance the abilities of people instead of simply making tasks easier or even replacing human labor. In order to help create a world in which AI can enrich human intelligence and experience, it is important to understand how these machines and systems work and evaluate the risks they pose to all humans, including children, vulnerable individuals, and marginalized people groups.

This endeavor is a direct product of the Trilateral AI Project: the Learning Cyclotron (LeCycl). LeCycl was a 3-year project led by Professor Andreas Dengel (Germany), Professor Laurence Devillers (France), and Professor Koichi Kise (Japan). The focus of this project was to facilitate a learning ecosystem where human intelligence is amplified via AI. The ecosystem is based on three central learning steps: perception, mastery, and transfer. The perception phase concerns how and where a person absorbs and internalizes new information. The mastery phase describes the process in which the learner improves their skills, deepens their knowledge, and perfects the application of what they have learned. Finally, in the transfer phase, the learner passes on their knowledge by sharing information and processes with others. This not only spreads knowledge, but also consolidates one's own learning process. LeCycl uses sensors to track the physical and cognitive states of learners. This data is used to provide users with personalized feedback and to develop targeted "nudging" techniques to optimally support learning. During the course of the project, three workshops were sponsored or co-sponsored as part of the project, starting with "Delivering Sensing Technologies for Education and Learning" at UbiComp 2022 in Cambridge [5], United Kingdom; "Automated Assessment and Guidance of Project Work" at AI and Education 2023 (AIED'23) in Tokyo, Japan [1]; and "Intelligence Augmentation: Future Directions and Ethical Implications in HCI" at Interact 2023 in York, United Kingdom [4].

Toward the end of the project, the leaders decided to organize Shonan Meeting 214 in March 2024 in order to discuss the placement of these technologies in the real world considering not only the technological aspects, but also the societal aspects of AI technology adoption and adaptation of specific and general technologies. In this book, the workshop participants provide insight into both practical and more theoretical aspects.

This book is organized into two sections, an overview of state-of-the-art AI and related technologies in the education domain, and a section dedicated to the future of AI technologies and education. The former section focuses mainly on using sensing technologies to build evaluative and predictive systems that can be used in both private and institutional learning contexts. Although the technologies included in these chapters are not exhaustive, they are ones that were developed as part of the LeCycl project and showcase the creative arc of the project and how user and group needs are approached in learning contexts. Chapter "Sensing and Actuation for Learning" gives an overview of the sensing and actuation technologies used to estimate a learner's state in order to provide actuation, whereas chapters "AI-Driven Approaches to Knowledge Acquisition and Skill Mastery: an Application to Second-Language Learning" and "Knowledge Transfer with AI" cover specific areas of application, namely, second language learning and knowledge transfer.

The second half of the book examines these and other AI technologies and their place in education and society. Chapter "Skills Training in the Age of AI" looks at the social contract between universities and their students and how artificial intelligence is changing the purpose and scope of skill training, bringing into question the role of tertiary education in the future. Chapter "Affective Computing and the Future of Education" focuses on the future of affective computing in the age of AI, looking at the opportunity that AI presents for making affective computing tractable, while also considering the myriad of ethical and privacy issues. Chapter "Ethics and AI in Education" examines the role of ethics when considering AI in education and calls for the need for interdisciplinary collaboration and more effective education in computer science and sciences in general. Chapter "Beyond the Interface: Augmenting Meta-Skills for Long-Term Cognitive Enhancement" looks at ways that AI go beyond immediate task help and can instead enhance human cognition with lasting impacts. Chapter "Learning in the Loop: AI, Feedback, and the Future of Human Thought" builds upon this and looks at the future of human augmentation by looking at AI as a partner for learning.

Acknowledgements This work was supported in part by grants from JST Trilateral AI "Learning Cyclotron" Grant Number JPMJCR20G3, JSPS Grant-in-Aid Fund for the Promotion of Joint International Research (Fostering Joint International Research) Grant Number 23KK0188, MEXT "Innovation Platform for Society 5.0" Program Grant Number JPMXP0518071489, DFG (Project No. 442581111), and ANR Trilateral AI "Learning Cyclotron" Grant Number LSP n° 237539 (LeCycl, UMR9015) between CNRS-LISN and ANR.

References

1. Abou-Khalil, V., Vargo, A., Manjoumdar, R., Magno, M., Kapur, M.: Automated assessment and guidance of project work. In: Wang, N., Rebolledo-Mendez, G., Dimitrova, V., Matsuda, N., Santos, O.C. (eds.) Artificial Intelligence in Education. Posters and Late Breaking Results, Workshops and Tutorials, Industry and Innovation Tracks, Practitioners, Doctoral Consortium and Blue Sky, pp. 69–73. Springer Nature Switzerland, Cham (2023). https://doi.org/10.1007/978-3-031-36336-8_10
2. Dengel, A., Devillers, L., Vargo, A.: The Future of Education with AI. NII Shonan Meeting Report (214) (2024)
3. MacKenzie, I.S.: Human-Computer Interaction: An Empirical Research Perspective. Elsevier (2024)

4. Neigel, P., Vargo, A., Kise, K.: A summary of the workshop on intelligence augmentation: future directions and ethical implications in HCI. In: Bramwell-Dicks, A., Evans, A., Winckler, M., Petrie, H., Abdelnour-Nocera, J. (eds.) Design for Equality and Justice, pp. 225–231. Springer Nature Switzerland, Cham (2024). https://doi.org/10.1007/978-3-031-61698-3_21
5. Vargo, A., Abou-Khalil, V., Ishimaru, S., Tag, B., Hutin, M., Dengel, A., Devillers, L., Kise, K.: Delivering sensing technologies for education and learning. In: Adjunct Proceedings of the 2022 ACM International Joint Conference on Pervasive and Ubiquitous Computing and the 2022 ACM International Symposium on Wearable Computers. UbiComp/ISWC '22 Adjunct, pp. 263–266. Association for Computing Machinery, New York, NY, USA (2023). https://doi.org/10.1145/3544793.3560373

Sensing and Actuation for Learning

Koichi Kise, Shoya Ishimaru, and Andrew Vargo

Abstract The introduction of AI technology into the field of learning means the introduction into a series of processes, such as learning a person's state, analyzing it, and feeding back the results. Here, the technology to measure and analyze the state of the learner is called "sensing," and the technology that helps to improve the learner's performance through feedback is called "actuation." In this chapter, we give an overview of these technologies and their prospects for the future, focusing on examples of research that the authors have conducted so far.

Keywords Learning · Education · Activity recognition · Sensing · Actuation

1 Introduction

We consider using AI technology to assist the learning process by targeting the learner, a subject who learns in the real world. To do so, we need technology to know and analyze the learner's state (sensing), and technology to improve the learner's state in some sense (action) by feeding back the results of the analysis. In this chapter, we focus on learning with a single learner. Since AI technology is applied to the "learning" behavior of a "learner," the research can be regarded as a field of human behavior recognition. However, unlike running, walking, and other behaviors that are subject to general behavior recognition, the learner's behavior does not involve much movement. Therefore, the state that is the object of recognition is often a mental and internal state such as the learner's interest and level of understanding. The authors have been working on sensing and actuation of "reading" behavior, which

K. Kise · S. Ishimaru · A. Vargo (✉)
Osaka Metropolitan University, Sakai, Japan
e-mail: awv@omu.ac.jp

K. Kise
e-mail: kise@omu.ac.jp

S. Ishimaru
e-mail: ishimaru@omu.ac.jp

A. Dengel et al. (eds.), *The Future of Education with AI*,
https://doi.org/10.1007/978-981-95-1622-3_2

is the basis of learning, and "learning" behavior. We are also working on sensing "Sleeping," which is the basis of the learner's physical condition. In this chapter, we present an overview of our research results in the order of "Reading," "Learning," and "Sleeping" and also describes the future prospects for the development of this field.

2 Sensing and Reading

2.1 Document Image Retrieval: LLAH

The research that led us to work on reading was the development of an algorithm for document image retrieval called Locally Likely Arrangement Hashing. This algorithm retrieves corresponding document files stored in a database from document images captured by a web camera or other means. It is characterized by its high speed and high accuracy in searching large databases, regardless of the camera's position and posture, and the hiding of document surfaces. At the time of development (nearly 20 years ago), a notebook PC was capable of searching 10,000 pages of DB in 100 ms with 98% accuracy. Finally, it became possible to search a DB of 100 million pages in 27 ms with an accuracy of 99%. At the beginning of development, we received questions such as "Why do we have to search from the DB when we have the documents at hand?" In addition to simply being able to search for documents, it is also possible to obtain information on which part of the document is being photographed, making it possible to map the service to various locations on the document [25, 32].

2.2 Reading-Life Log and Mutual Analysis

This technology can be used directly to record which documents you have read. The sensor used can be, for example, a first-person camera. If we have an eye tracker (a device that measures eye gaze) as shown in Fig. 1, we can see where in the user's field of view (the image captured by the first-person camera) the user is looking, and we can determine which words in the PDF document he/she is looking at by coordinate transformation from the camera coordinate system to the PDF document coordinate system. By repeating this process, it is possible to keep track of the documents read and the words read. We call such a function Reading-Life Log (RLL), meaning a life log for "reading." Once RLL is available, various services can be considered. This is explained from the standpoint of what we call mutual analysis.

First, when RLL is collected for a specific person, it is possible to know what kind of documents the person tends to read, what kind of documents the person is interested in, what kind of contents the person finds difficult to read, and so on,

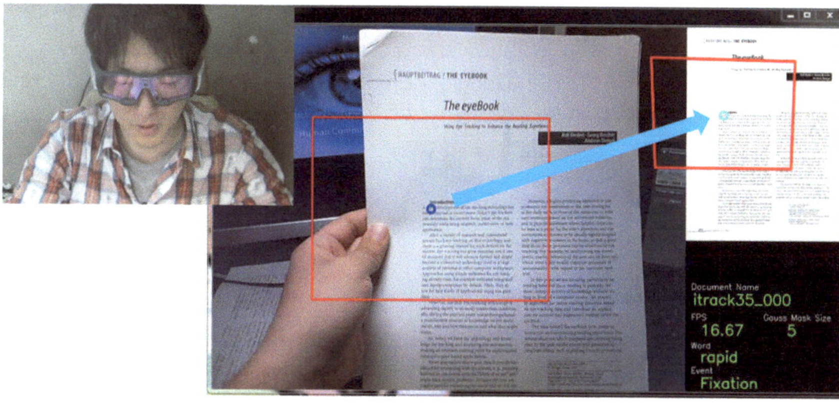

Fig. 1 Reading-Life Log

through the documents. Conversely, if we collect the readings of various people for a certain document, we can accumulate data such as: this part is of interest to many people, this part is difficult to read, or everyone stops reading at this point. This means that we can learn about documents through the reading behavior of people. We call this mutual analysis because we understand people through documents and documents through people. Based on such mutual analysis, we have devised a variety of reading recognition understandings. In the following, we first describe the sensors we have used to collect reading data, and then describe some typical examples of recognition understanding.

2.3 Sensors for Reading Analysis

The typical sensors we have used for reading analysis are shown in Fig. 2. The eye trackers (expensive ones for research (SMI) and inexpensive ones for gaming (Tobii)) and the EOG glasses (J!NS MEME) have played a particularly important role in the analysis of eye movements. Eye trackers are used to estimate where the user is looking. On the other hand, EOG glasses detect the displacement of the eyeball by measuring the skin potential around the eyeball (eye potential; electrooculography (EOG)). Eye movement and blinking can be measured, but unlike eye trackers, information such as where in a scene or on a screen the user is looking is not obtained.

2.4 Multi-layered Analysis of Reading

Using the equipment described above and others, we analyze the readings shown in Fig. 3. The analyses range from quantitative (low level) to qualitative (high level).

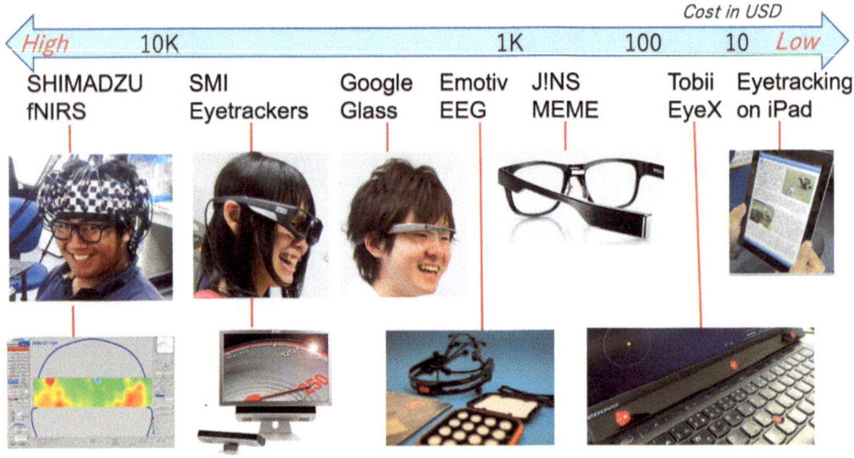

Fig. 2 Sensors used for eye tracking

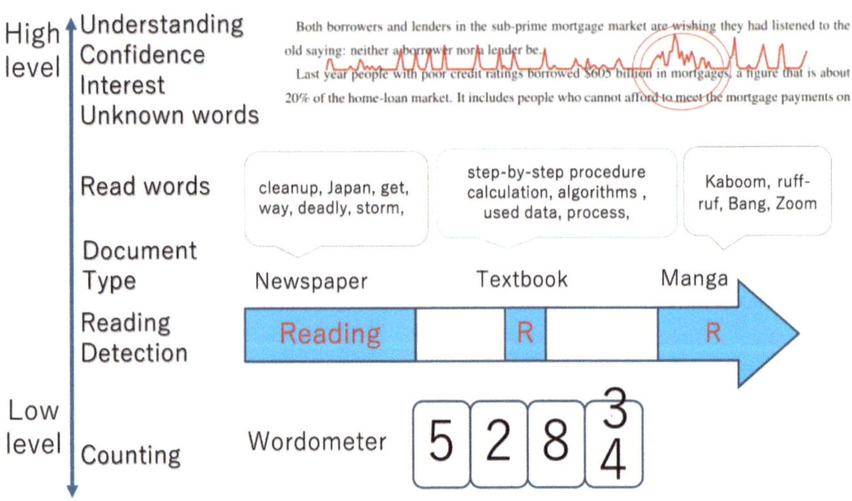

Fig. 3 Multi-layered analysis of reading

Quantitative tasks include the measurement of the number of words read (wordometer) and the measurement of reading time (reading detection). Intermediate tasks include Document Type Recognition and Read Word Logging. Qualitative measurement tasks include unknown word estimation and estimation of the level of understanding. Each of these tasks is described below.

2.5 *Wordometer [3, 15, 21]*

The most fundamental task in reading analysis is to determine quantity. The wordometer is used to determine the amount of reading by the number of words read. This is similar to how a pedometer is used to determine a person's basic physical activity. The wordometer is a pedometer of knowledge. There are two ways to realize the wordometer: using EOG glasses and using a stationary eye tracker. Here, we briefly introduce the one using EOG. The movement of the human eye is usually a repetition of fixation and saccade. As shown in the upper part of Fig. 4, when reading a document, a fine saccade (forward saccade) and fixation are repeated to the right, and a larger saccade (backward saccade) to the left and downward is performed to break lines at the end of a line. The EOG in the horizontal direction changes as shown in the lower part of Fig. 4. The word count estimation can be formulated as a regression problem with the number and timing of occurrences in the forward saccade as input during the backward saccade.

In fact, experiments using the wordometer show that it is possible to estimate with an error of about 10% when the user's own data is not used for training, and with an error of about 3% when the user's own data is used. Just as a pedometer makes people walk more, does the wordometer increases the number of words they read? To answer this question, we experimented with various forms of information feedback to encourage reading [34]. In addition to simply indicating the number of words (number), we used three methods: setting a daily goal (goal), receiving a notification when the time or place where the user regularly reads is approaching (notification), and sharing word count information with other people (peer-pressure). The results

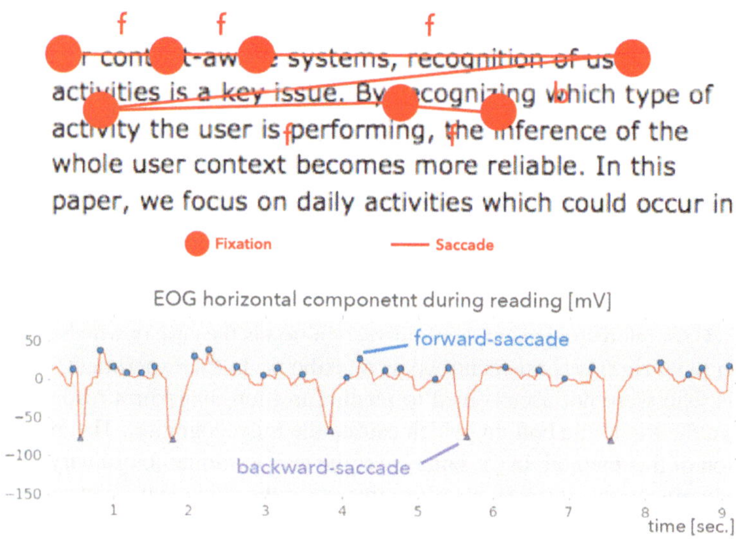

Fig. 4 Wordometer

showed that some people responded well to all of the four methods, while others did not, and that peer-pressure was the most effective among them.

2.6 Reading Detection

Another way to determine the amount of reading is to measure the time of reading. Specifically, the task here is to determine how long the user has been reading. As in the case of the wordometer, the use of EOG glasses makes it possible to detect reading regardless of the medium in which the reader is reading. In addition to EOG, the glasses we used are equipped with an accelerometer and a gyroscope, and the data from these sensors are used to detect reading periods. In order to detect so-called "in-the-wild" readings, i.e., readings for various media that occur freely in real life, rather than artificially produced readings in the controlled environment of a laboratory, a dataset representing such diversity is essential. Therefore, we first worked on the creation of a dataset [17, 36]. Here, we not only labeled the periods as reading/not reading but also added three subclasses of reading: reading Japanese vertical writing, Japanese horizontal writing, and English. A reading detector was constructed using this dataset. The machine learning methods used were SVM, CNN, and CNN with self-supervised learning. The results show that the method with self-supervised learning performs well even with a small number of training samples [18–20].

2.7 Document Type Recognition [22, 31]

Document type recognition recognizes which type of document the user is reading, specifically, a textbook, an article, a novel, a newspaper, a magazine, a comic book, by analyzing the user's reading behavior. We tried two ways of implementation. One is pattern recognition based on the spatial distribution of eye tracking. The other is to classify images captured by a first-person camera. In the former case, the classification is based on the condition that there is a typical reading style according to the document type. Since the distribution of eye gaze reflects the layout of the document, different layouts naturally have different distributions of eye gaze, and thus can be classified. An interesting example of misrecognition is the case in which a magazine (fashion magazine) was misidentified as a textbook. In the experiment, some male students who were not accustomed to reading fashion magazines read the written text from the top to the bottom, which caused the misrecognition. This represents a limitation of this method. In the latter case, the task is similar to ordinary document image classification because it classifies images of the documents themselves. However, it was found that there are cases in which classification cannot be performed simply by looking at the image, for example, it is not possible to distinguish between an article and a textbook effectively because they look similar. This is an example of a case in which the classification cannot be done by simply looking at the image, and an in-depth analysis of the content is needed.

2.8 Recording of Read Words (Reading-Life Log) [2]

The recording of the words read is the Reading-Life Log itself. The system was realized using a wearable eye tracker and a stationary eye tracker. If gaze estimation were perfect, it would be possible to pick out all the words being looked at, but in practice this is not easy because of the error involved. In addition, when a person reads a document, not all letters and words correspond to his/her viewpoint, and he/she may be looking at the document with peripheral vision or may be guessing from the context without looking at the document. A simple way to deal with these problems is to express each word as a probability of being read, taking into account the error in line-of-sight estimation and the extent to which it can be grasped at a time.

2.9 Unknown Word Estimation

An example of a high-level task is unknown word estimation. Specifically, the task is to measure the behavior of reading English sentences and to estimate unknown words contained in the sentences. As for the measurement method, we have developed a smartphone-based method [9, 10] in addition to the eye tracker method [7], as in other tasks. Since eye trackers are currently not available for smartphones, it is necessary to consider other sensing methods. In this study, we developed two methods: (1) a one-line window method and (2) a scrolling method. The one-line window method estimates unknown words by measuring the timing of reading an English sentence through the window that can display only one line of English text and pressing a button to display the next line. On the other hand, the scrolling method is an interface that displays multiple lines centered on a certain line and scrolls through them, estimating unknown words by the amount and timing of scrolling. With these types of unknown word estimation, the user can create a list of unknown words simply by reading the English text and use it separately for learning English. Compared to conventional methods, such as creating a word list by oneself or marking words with markers, this method does not interfere with the rhythm of reading.

2.10 Estimation of the Level of Understanding [28–30]

Finally, we discuss estimation of the level of understanding. This is an estimation of whether or not the user understands the content based on his/her reading behavior.

There are two types of estimation: objective understanding, which is the degree to which the user understands the content (i.e., the degree to which the user can correctly answer questions about the content), and subjective understanding, which is the degree to which the user thinks he/she understands the content. Of these, subjective understanding is directly related to reading behavior. Intuitively, we can say that we think we understand a text when we can read it smoothly and without hesitation, while we feel that we do not understand a text when it is stalled or when we have to reread it. From this perspective, we estimated subjective comprehension by recording and analyzing the reading of a document using an eye tracker, and showed that a certain degree of accuracy was achieved. Subjective understanding, which is treated here, has a strong correlation with objective understanding, but they are not the same. When there is a discrepancy between subjective and objective understanding, specifically, when a person thinks he/she understands something but actually does not, and vice versa, this can cause problems compared to when both understanding levels are in agreement. Since objective understanding can be measured by testing, it would be more useful for users if a support system that takes differences into account could be created. This is also true for "confidence," which will be discussed in the next section, "Learning."

3 Sensing and Actuation for "Learning"

3.1 Confidence Estimation

The first task we discuss in relation to "learning" is confidence in the answers. When we learn something, after acquiring knowledge by reading, we often do exercises to consolidate it and make it usable. There are many possible forms of exercises, one of the most basic of which is the multiple-choice question. Because of the ease of scoring, multiple-choice questions are used in various qualification and entrance examinations, but there is one problem that cannot be avoided: the possibility of guesswork in answering the questions.

Considering this situation, we can see that in addition to the evaluation axis of correct or incorrect answer, there is another evaluation axis of whether the answer was given with confidence or not, and that there are four states depending on the combination of these two axes. While correct answers with confidence that the answer is correct and wrong answers without confidence are frequently observed, the other two states, correct answers without confidence and wrong answers with confidence, require attention.

If the learner answers a question correctly without confidence, he/she may not be able to answer the same or similar question correctly when he/she encounters it in the future. On one hand, since review is usually done in response to wrong answers, the correct answer without confidence is excluded from review, and the problem is left behind. On the other hand, if the wrong answer is given with confidence, the same

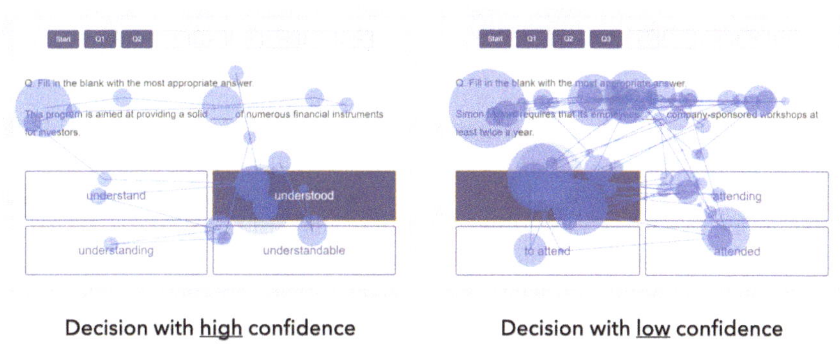

Fig. 5 Four-choice questions and confidence

wrong answer may be repeated in the future. During the review process, the learner needs to be made aware that his/her beliefs are based on incorrect knowledge, and his/her knowledge needs to be revised.

To enable such processing, we are working on confidence estimation. The subject is English language learning. In addition to the multiple-choice questions (specifically, four-choice questions) described above, we used a variety of question types, including word-typing and handwritten words. The sensors used were different for each type: a stationary eye tracker [38] for the four-choice questions, a key logger [24] for typing, a tablet [23] for handwriting, and an arm accelerometer [33] also for handwriting. Here due to space limitation, we only describe the case of four-choice questions.

The four-choice questions here require the selection of the best option to fill in the blanks in the English text. Figure 5 shows an example of a question along with the gaze data for each answer. The circles indicate the location and time length of the fixation (the larger, the longer), and the lines connecting them indicate the saccade. As can be seen from this example, when the user is confident, he/she answers the question without hesitation (left), but when he/she is not confident, his/her line of sight wanders left and right among the question text and options.

We collected labeled data and constructed a method for discriminating the presence or absence of confidence from gaze data by machine learning. As in the case of reading detection, we found that higher recognition performance was achieved using self-supervised learning than using SVM [18].

Next, an experiment was also conducted in which the estimation results were fed back. Half of the students who answered correctly without confidence were added to the review, and half of the students who answered incorrectly with confidence were given a warning during the review to encourage them to revise their knowledge. The results showed that the percentage of correct responses on the test after review was significantly higher than when no feedback was given [16]. This result indicates the effectiveness of confidence aware learning.

3.2 Controlling the Difficulty

It is known that the difficulty level of the exercises must be appropriate for effective learning (about 85% correct is desirable), and neither too high nor too low. In the multiple-choice questions described above, one factor that determines the difficulty level of the questions is the choice of the distractors (the options that represent the wrong answers). The more difficult it is to distinguish the distractors from the correct answer, the more difficult the question will be. Therefore, we also developed a technique to control the difficulty level of a question by appropriately generating distractors. As a result, we were able to maintain an appropriate difficulty level for many users [35].

3.3 Estimation of Cognitive Load

It is important to understand the cognitive load when learning. If the cognitive load is too high, the learner may not be able to continue learning and give up, and if it is too easy, the learner may not be able to continue learning because they do not feel a sense of learning. It is known that the harder the task is, the lower the temperature at the tip of the nose and the higher the temperature at the forehead. Therefore, we attempted to estimate the cognitive load by measuring the face during task execution with a thermal camera. The task we employed in the experiment is the N-Back test: a task in which a number or alphabet is presented randomly for a short period of time, and each time it is presented, the subject recalls the N previous presentations. The experimental results showed that the temperature difference increased as N increased.

3.4 Intelligent Textbook

Using some of the technologies described above, we created an intelligent textbook called HyperMind [11, 12, 14]. As shown in Fig. 6, this system uses an eye tracker and a thermal camera to measure learners as they read the textbook, estimating interest from their gaze, understanding from the passages they read back, and cognitive load from the temperature. The system integrates this information and presents additional material according to the degree of difficulty and interest. This is expected to promote deeper and longer learning.

For services that provide such additional content, the question is who prepares such content and how to relate it to the original content. One way to solve this problem would be to make it easy to prepare content without expert knowledge of HyperMind. To solve this problem, we have developed a system called HyperMind Builder [13] that enables users to prepare contents for intelligent textbooks with simple operations such as Drag and Drop. Using recent generative AI technology, it

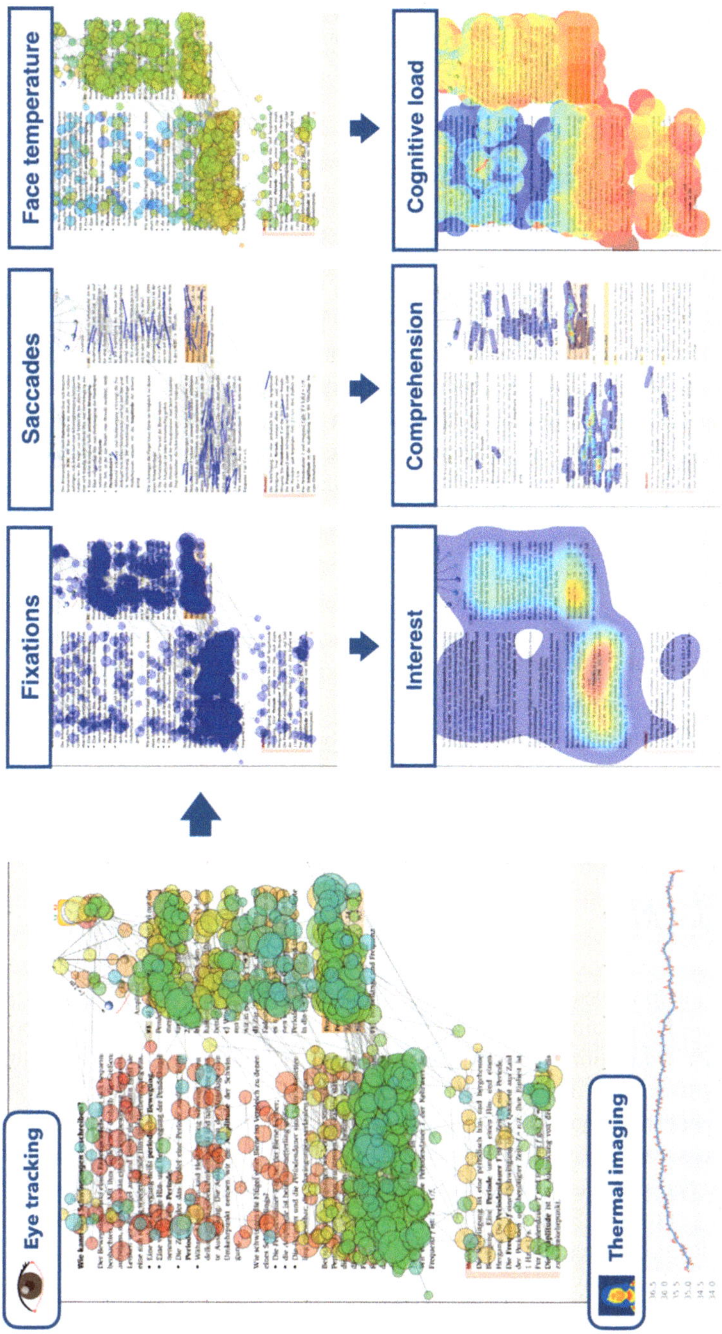

Fig. 6 HyperMind

is also possible to generate additional content on-the-fly. As one example, we have created a system that analyzes eye gaze data and generates simple explanations for difficult-to-understand passages. There are many possibilities for when and what to provide. We are still working to make it better.

3.5 *Learning by Exercising [37]*

This study approaches learning in a different way: Learning by exercising does not mean exercising by answering questions, but rather physical exercise. In general, it is known that aerobic exercise is effective for memory consolidation [4, 6, 8]. Memory tasks performed during moderate-intensity aerobic exercise or after high-intensity aerobic exercise are remembered better than those who do the tasks while just sitting. In this study, an experiment was conducted to demonstrate this. The results show that exercise has a positive effect on memory in many individuals. However, it was also found that the intensity and timing of exercise (before or during the memory task) must be appropriately selected for each individual, showing the need for personalization.

4 Sensing of "Sleep"

Finally, we discuss the measurement and analysis of sleep. Many people may have experienced inefficient learning when they do not get enough sleep. Thus, sleep has an important relationship with learning.

4.1 *Oura Ring*

The first important issue in analyzing sleep is how to obtain sleep data. Polysomnography is used to obtain precise data for medical and other purposes, but the problem is that data acquisition is limited to specialized facilities. For use in learning, it is necessary to acquire data in a real-life environment, i.e., in-the-wild. A promising way to meet this objective is to use wearable sensors. Among them, many ring-shaped sensors have a longer battery life and higher measurement accuracy than watch-shaped sensors. In this study, we use a ring-shaped wearable sensor called the Oura Ring shown in Fig. 7. Although there are up to fourth-generation versions of the Oura Ring, this study uses the second-generation ring, which was available at the beginning of the study, and the third-generation ring, which was released later. The difference lies in whether or not data can be obtained after waking up, but the data acquisition and analysis described below do not use data obtained after awakening. Among the data obtained from Oura Ring, those used in this study are mean heart rate during sleep, maximum heart rate, heart rate variability, total sleep time, deep sleep time, shallow sleep time, REM sleep time, body temperature during sleep, and sleep score. Among these, the sleep score is calculated by the Oura Ring software and indicates the goodness of sleep.

4.2 Data Collection

Oura Ring wearers were recruited from the university's student body. As a result, more than 100 students eventually agreed to participate, and data collection began. This was the result of soliciting participants by calling out to them in classes, etc. Approximately 5–10% of the total number of students applied, and data is still being collected.

Usage of the ring was not universal or consistent. While all users wore the ring at the beginning, many of them stopped wearing it. The analysis shows that about half of the users had worn the ring for less than 200 days, and the rest had worn it for more than 200 days. Half of the users wore the ring more than 70% of the time.

4.3 Relationship to Stress [26]

First, we examined the relationship with stress in order to determine the overall tendency of users without distinguishing between individuals. Participants in the experiment were 103 students wearing Oura Rings. The university has a two-semester system, with final examinations at the end of each semester. Students who participated in the experiment generally took exams at the same time of the semester and had time off. Since students were not forced to wear the ring for the duration of the experiment, as mentioned above, there are missing periods of wearing. We are interested in

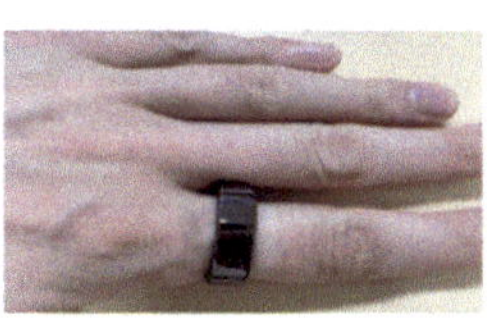

Collected Features	Gen 2	Gen 3
Heart Rate		
Resting Heart Rate (RHR)	√	√
Workout Heart Rate (WHR)		√
Daytime Heart Rate (DHR)		√
Heart Rate Variability (HRV)	√	√
Temperature		
Basal Body Temperature	√	√
Sleep		
Sleep Staging	√	√
Respiration		
Respitory Rate	√	√
Blood Oxygen (SpO2)		√

Fig. 7 The Oura Ring worn on a hand and the differences between Oura Ring generations 2 and 3

whether meaningful data can be obtained in such an environment. Sleep data items related to stress included heart rate (HR) during sleep, heart rate variability (HRV) during sleep, maximum heart rate, and various sleep durations (total sleep time, deep sleep time, and shallow sleep time). In combination with the other results obtained, we found that even without enforcing the use of the ring in the In-the-Wild environment, the collection of data can yield stress trends that are shared by the entire group. Such a framework is easy to implement because privacy issues are not likely to arise.

4.4 Relationship to Fundamental Cognitive Functions

Next, we discuss the relationship between sleep and basic cognitive functions. The three basic cognitive functions are computation, memory (working memory), and reaction. Among the data obtained from Oura Ring, we used sleep heart rate (HR), sleep heart rate variability (HRV), body temperature, and sleep duration (deep sleep duration, shallow sleep duration, and REM sleep duration). As a task, we attempted to estimate the performance of the above cognitive functions from these data.

- Calculation [36]: A two-digit hundred-square sum was used as the calculation. Sixteen participants performed the calculations immediately after waking up for 2 weeks. The results showed that the performance of the participants improved as the amount of time they spent in REM sleep increased. Hundred-square calculation is a calculation task that is well known in Japan, but not so well known in other countries. It is likely that there are not many cases where it has been used for this purpose.
- Working Memory [1]: The standard N-Back test was used to test working memory. In this experiment, nine letters from A to I were presented at random, and N = 3. Twelve participants took part in the experiment immediately after waking up for a period of 2 weeks. The results showed that the higher the HRV, the higher the performance.
- Reaction [5]: We also used the standardized Pychomotor Vigilance Task (PVT) as a test of reaction. This task measures the time required to press a button after perceiving a change. Specifically, we used a smartphone application to measure the time required to press a button after perceiving a change. Normally, the PVT takes about 10 min to complete, but we reduced the time to 1 min because we thought it would be difficult to continue to perform this task in the wild. On the other hand, the PVT was conducted six times a day (immediately after the first through fifth periods of class and after lunch). There were 21 participants in the experiment, and the duration was 3 weeks. The results showed that, as with working memory, an increase in REM sleep time improved performance.

4.5 Gap Between Self-recognition and Measurement [27]

Finally, we discuss the relationship between self-recognition and measurement results. The measurement result used here is the sleep score indicated by the Oura Ring application. This is an overall index of sleep, and a high score is considered good. On the other hand, self-recognition is the answer to the question, "Do you feel that your sleep has improved after looking at the Oura Ring data?" The participants were 22 who wore the ring for 1 or 2 years, and who were willing to answer the questionnaire were considered to be the participants. The results of the questionnaire showed that 15 participants felt improvement and 7 participants did not feel improvement. Comparison of these two groups with actual sleep score trends revealed little relationship between recognized improvement and actual score change. Although a few of those who reported feeling improvement did show an actual improvement in their scores, the majority tended to remain unchanged or even worsen. Four of those who did not feel this way tended to worsen, while the remaining three remained unchanged. Thus, even in an environment where sleep scores are continuously measured and can be viewed, there is a possibility that there is a large discrepancy between self-recognition and measurement results. One of the implications of this discrepancy is that simply showing the measurement results does not lead to effective behavioral changes that improve sleep scores. Conversely, in order to evoke a behavioral change that leads to improved sleep, it is necessary to provide something more than just showing the score as feedback. At this time, the following points should be noted. If there is a large discrepancy with self-recognition, and if the participant is confident in his/her self-recognition, he/she may lose confidence in the data, making it difficult to continue measurement, and if he/she is continually informed of poor results, he/she may lose the motivation to improve. In addition, as in the case of learning, it takes a certain amount of time for the effects of sleep improvement to appear, so it is important to devise ways to keep the behavior change going until then. In the above, we reviewed the results of previous studies on the relationship between stress in groups, basic cognitive functions, and differences in self-recognition. The findings obtained through these experiments are as follows:

- Many students are interested in sleep data.
- Stress and cognitive function can be estimated to a certain degree from sleep data. This indicates the possibility of services based on sleep data.
- On the other hand, due to the discrepancy with self-recognition simply presenting data does not necessarily lead to behavioral change, and an additional mechanism is necessary. At this time, it is necessary to consider individual characteristics.

5 Future Directions

The technologies introduced so far are efforts to apply AI technology to the field of learning, which mainly targets English language learning by individuals. We would like to share our views on some points that are not included in this chapter and that we believe will become important in the future. First, the subject matter of the study. Of the above, HyperMind is related to physics, but the rest of the reading and learning is related to English. While some of the techniques can be used in the same way for different subjects, others are subject dependent. In particular, we believe that qualitative analysis is highly dependent on the subject. How to deal with this problem is an important issue. Next is learning that is not confined to individuals. There are two types of learning: learning among a small number of individuals and learning as a group in a classroom. For learning among individuals, there is the Learning-by-Teaching methodology, i.e., learning by communicating learned knowledge. In our LeCycl project, we are conducting research focusing on this point, which will be reported at another time. On the other hand, there are many interesting themes in learning as a group, such as sensing of the group (e.g., how to acquire the group's gaze data), sensing by the teacher, and so on. Finally, there is the impact of generative AI. Like other fields, it has the potential to be a game changer. Understanding learning data using foundational models and adaptively generating learning content are becoming possible in a way that was only a pipe dream until a few years ago. In addition, the emergence of AI companions that support learners by taking into account their physical condition, such as the quality of their sleep, will help prevent burnout and improve performance.

6 Conclusion

We have described the application of AI technologies to the field of learning, focusing on our research to date. The central issue is how to sense learning behaviors that do not involve large movements, extract necessary information, analyze it, and provide it as effective feedback for learning. As sensors, we focused on the eye gaze, which is commonly important for both "reading" and "learning." In addition, we introduced an example using a ring-shaped sensor for "sleep," which is the foundation for learning. As in other fields, the emergence of generative AI in the field of learning has greatly changed what can be done, and new services are already appearing. We look forward to further developments in this field in the future.

References

1. Arai, S., Vargo, A., Tag, B., Neigel, P., Kise, K.: In-the-wild exploration of the impact of sleep on working memory with a wearable. In: Companion of the 2024 on ACM International Joint

Conference on Pervasive and Ubiquitous Computing, pp. 81–85. Association for Computing Machinery, New York, NY, USA (2024). https://doi.org/10.1145/3675094.3677589
2. Augereau, O., Kise, K., Hoshika, K.: A proposal of a document image reading-life log based on document image retrieval and eyetracking. In: 2015 13th International Conference on Document Analysis and Recognition (ICDAR), pp. 246–250 (2015). https://doi.org/10.1109/ICDAR.2015.7333761
3. Augereau, O., Sanches, C.L., Kise, K., Kunze, K.: Wordometer systems for everyday life. Proc. ACM Interact. Mob. Wearable Ubiquitous Technol. **1**(4), 123:1–123:21 (2018). https://doi.org/10.1145/3161601
4. Chapman, S.B., Aslan, S., Lu, H.: Shorter term aerobic exercise improves brain, cognition, and cardiovascular fitness in aging (2013). https://doi.org/10.3389/fnagi.2013.00075
5. Chowdhury, T.I., Vargo, A., Tag, B., Nishitomi, R., Kise, K.: Exploring the feasibility of a repeated mobile one-minute PVT in-the-wild. In: Adjunct Proceedings of the 26th International Conference on Mobile Human-Computer Interaction, pp. 1–7. Association for Computing Machinery, New York, NY, USA (2024). https://doi.org/10.1145/3640471.3680235
6. Dongen, E.V., Kersten, I., Wagner, I.C., Morris, R., Fernández, G.: Physical exercise performed four hours after learning improves memory retention and increases hippocampal pattern similarity during retrieval. Curr. Biol. CB **26**(13), 1722–1727 (2016). https://doi.org/10.1016/j.cub.2016.04.071
7. Garain, U., Pandit, O., Augereau, O., Okoso, A., Kise, K.: Identification of reader specific difficult words by analyzing eye gaze and document content. In: 2017 14th IAPR International Conference on Document Analysis and Recognition (ICDAR), vol. 01, pp. 1346–1351 (2017). https://doi.org/10.1109/ICDAR.2017.221. https://ieeexplore.ieee.org/document/8270152, ISSN: 2379-2140
8. Hansen, A.: The Real Happy Pill. Simon and Schuster (2017)
9. Higashimura, R., Vargo, A., Iwata, M., Kise, K.: Helping mobile learners know unknown words through their reading behavior. In: Extended Abstracts of the 2022 CHI Conference on Human Factors in Computing Systems, pp. 1–5. Association for Computing Machinery, New York, NY, USA (2022). https://doi.org/10.1145/3491101.3519620
10. Higashimura, R., Watanabe, K., Vargo, A., Iwata, M., Dengel, A., Kise, K.: Estimating unknown English words from user smartphone reading behaviors. IEEE Access **12**, 140223–140234 (2024). https://doi.org/10.1109/ACCESS.2024.3457510
11. Ishimaru, S., Bukhari, S.S., Heisel, C., Großmann, N., Klein, P., Kuhn, J., Dengel, A.: Augmented learning on anticipating textbooks with eye tracking. In: Zlatkin-Troitschanskaia, O., Wittum, G., Dengel, A. (eds.) Positive Learning in the Age of Information: A Blessing or a Curse? pp. 387–398. Springer Fachmedien, Wiesbaden (2018). https://doi.org/10.1007/978-3-658-19567-0_23
12. Ishimaru, S., Bukhari, S.S., Heisel, C., Kuhn, J., Dengel, A.: Towards an intelligent textbook: eye gaze based attention extraction on materials for learning and instruction in physics. In: Proceedings of the 2016 ACM International Joint Conference on Pervasive and Ubiquitous Computing: Adjunct, pp. 1041–1045. Association for Computing Machinery, New York, NY, USA (2016). https://doi.org/10.1145/2968219.2968566
13. Ishimaru, S., Großmann, N., Dengel, A., Watanabe, K., Arakawa, Y., Heisel, C., Klein, P., Kuhn, J.: hypermind builder: pervasive user interface to create intelligent interactive documents. In: Proceedings of the 2018 ACM International Joint Conference and 2018 International Symposium on Pervasive and Ubiquitous Computing and Wearable Computers, pp. 357–360. Association for Computing Machinery, New York, NY, USA (2018). https://doi.org/10.1145/3267305.3267667
14. Ishimaru, S., Jacob, S., Roy, A., Bukhari, S.S., Heisel, C., Großmann, N., Thees, M., Kuhn, J., Dengel, A.: Cognitive state measurement on learning materials by utilizing eye tracker and thermal camera. In: 2017 14th IAPR International Conference on Document Analysis and Recognition (ICDAR), vol. 08, pp. 32–36 (2017). https://doi.org/10.1109/ICDAR.2017.378. https://ieeexplore.ieee.org/document/8270330, ISSN: 2379-2140

15. Ishimaru, S., Kunze, K., Kise, K., Dengel, A.: The wordometer 2.0: estimating the number of words you read in real life using commercial EOG glasses. In: Proceedings of the 2016 ACM International Joint Conference on Pervasive and Ubiquitous Computing: Adjunct, pp. 293–296. Association for Computing Machinery, New York, NY, USA (2016). https://doi.org/10.1145/2968219.2971398
16. Ishimaru, S., Maruichi, T., Dengel, A., Kise, K.: Confidence-Aware Learning Assistant (2021). https://doi.org/10.48550/arXiv.2102.07312, http://arxiv.org/abs/2102.07312 [cs]
17. Ishimaru, S., Maruichi, T., Landsmann, M., Kise, K., Dengel, A.: Electrooculography dataset for reading detection in the wild. In: Adjunct Proceedings of the 2019 ACM International Joint Conference on Pervasive and Ubiquitous Computing and Proceedings of the 2019 ACM International Symposium on Wearable Computers, pp. 85–88. Association for Computing Machinery, New York, NY, USA (2019). https://doi.org/10.1145/3341162.3343812
18. Islam, M.R., Sakamoto, S., Yamada, Y., Vargo, A.W., Iwata, M., Iwamura, M., Kise, K.: Self-supervised learning for reading activity classification. In: Proceedings of the ACM on Interactive, Mobile, Wearable and Ubiquitous Technologies (2021). https://doi.org/10.1145/3478088, publisher: ACM PUB27 New York, NY, USA
19. Islam, M.R., Vargo, A.W., Iwata, M., Iwamura, M., Kise, K.: Evaluating contrastive learning for fine-grained reading detection. In: 2022 12th International Congress on Advanced Applied Informatics (IIAI-AAI), pp. 430–435 (2022). https://doi.org/10.1109/IIAIAAI55812.2022.00091. https://ieeexplore.ieee.org/abstract/document/9894615, ISSN: 2472-0070
20. Islam, M.R., Vargo, A.W., Iwata, M., Iwamura, M., Kise, K.: Exploring sensor modalities to capture user behaviors for reading detection. IEICE Trans. Inf. Syst. **E105-D**(9), 1629–1633 (2022). https://search.ieice.org/bin/summary.php?id=e105-d_9_1629&category=D&year=2022&lang=E&abst=, publisher: The Institute of Electronics, Information and Communication Engineers
21. Kunze, K., Kawaichi, H., Yoshimura, K., Kise, K.: The wordometer—estimating the number of words read using document image retrieval and mobile eye tracking. In: 2013 12th International Conference on Document Analysis and Recognition, pp. 25–29 (2013). https://doi.org/10.1109/ICDAR.2013.14. https://ieeexplore.ieee.org/abstract/document/6628579, ISSN: 2379-2140
22. Kunze, K., Utsumi, Y., Shiga, Y., Kise, K., Bulling, A.: I know what you are reading: recognition of document types using mobile eye tracking. In: Proceedings of the 2013 International Symposium on Wearable Computers, pp. 113–116. Association for Computing Machinery, New York, NY, USA (2013). https://doi.org/10.1145/2493988.2494354
23. Maruichi, T., Ishimaru, S., Kise, K.: Self-Confidence Estimation on Vocabulary Tests with Stroke-Level Handwriting Logs. https://ieeexplore.ieee.org/abstract/document/8892903
24. Maruichi, T., Sakamoto, S., Augereau, O., Kise, K.: Confidence estimation for English word typing by using a key-logger. In: IEICE Conferences Archives IEICE-BioX-513, IEICE-PRMU-514), IEICE–BioX (2018). https://ken.ieice.org/ken/paper/2018031981CO/, publisher: The Institute of Electronics, Information and Communication Engineers
25. Nakai, T., Kise, K., Iwamura, M.: Fast camera-based document image retrieval using local arrangements of feature points. **J89-D**(9), 2045–2054 (2006). https://search.ieice.org/bin/summary.php?id=j89-d_9_2045&category=D&year=2006&lang=J&abst=, publisher: The Institute of Electronics, Information and Communication Engineers
26. Neigel, P., Vargo, A., Tag, B., Kise, K.: Using wearables to unobtrusively identify periods of stress in a real university environment. In: Proceedings of the 2024 ACM International Symposium on Wearable Computers, pp. 17–24. Association for Computing Machinery, New York, NY, USA (2024). https://doi.org/10.1145/3675095.3676608
27. Nolasco, R.H., Vargo, A., Komatsu, Y., Iwata, M., Kise, K.: Perception versus reality: how user self-reflections compare to actual data. In: Abdelnour Nocera, J., Kristín Lárusdóttir, M., Petrie, H., Piccinno, A., Winckler, M. (eds.) Human-Computer Interaction—INTERACT, pp. 665–674. Springer Nature Switzerland, Cham (2023). https://doi.org/10.1007/978-3-031-42286-7_37

28. Sanches, C.L., Augereau, O., Kise, K.: Using the eye gaze to predict document reading subjective understanding. In: 2017 14th IAPR International Conference on Document Analysis and Recognition (ICDAR), vol. 08, pp. 28–31 (2017). https://doi.org/10.1109/ICDAR.2017.377. https://ieeexplore.ieee.org/document/8270329, ISSN: 2379-2140
29. Sanches, C.L., Augereau, O., Kise, K.: Estimation of reading subjective understanding based on eye gaze analysis. PLOS ONE **13**(10), e0206213 (2018). https://doi.org/10.1371/journal.pone.0206213, publisher: Public Library of Science
30. Sanches, C.L., Kise, K., Augereau, O.: Japanese reading objective understanding estimation by eye gaze analysis. In: Proceedings of the 2017 ACM International Joint Conference on Pervasive and Ubiquitous Computing and Proceedings of the 2017 ACM International Symposium on Wearable Computers, pp. 121–124. Association for Computing Machinery, New York, NY, USA (2017). https://doi.org/10.1145/3123024.3123092
31. Shiga, Y., Utsumi, Y., Iwamura, M., Kunze, K., Kise, K.: Automatic Document Type Classification Using Eye Movements and Egocentric Images. D-Abs IEICE Trans Inf Syst (Japanese Edition) **J99-D**(9), 950–958 (2016). https://search.ieice.org/bin/summary.php?id=j99-d_9_950&category=D&year=2016&lang=J&abst=j, publisher: The Institute of Electronics, Information and Communication Engineers
32. Takeda, K., Kise, K., Iwamura, M.: Real-time document image retrieval for a 10 million pages database with a memory efficient and stability improved LLAH. In: 2011 International Conference on Document Analysis and Recognition, pp. 1054–1058 (2011). https://doi.org/10.1109/ICDAR.2011.213, https://ieeexplore.ieee.org/abstract/document/6065471. ISSN: 2379-2140
33. Tanaka, S., Vargo, A.W., Iwata, M., Kise, K.: Confidence estimation via wrist movement. In: Adjunct Proceedings of the 2021 ACM International Joint Conference on Pervasive and Ubiquitous Computing and Proceedings of the 2021 ACM International Symposium on Wearable Computers, pp. 76–77. Association for Computing Machinery, New York, NY, USA (2021). https://doi.org/10.1145/3460418.3479286
34. Tonomoto, S., Iwata, M., Kise, K.: preliminary experiments toward personalized nudging strategies for extensive reading of English. In: Proceedings of CHI2020 Workshop on Detection and Design for Cognitive Biases in People and Computing Systems (2020)
35. Uchida, T., Vargo, A., Kise, K.: Adaptive difficulty adjustment of English multiple-choice questions by generating distractors 105–108 (2023). https://jglobal.jst.go.jp/detail?JGLOBAL_ID=202302258338616874
36. Vargo, A., Ishimaru, S., Islam, M.R., Tag, B., Kise, K.: Obtaining labels for in-the-wild studies: using visual cues and recall. IEEE Pervasive Comput. **21**(1), 9–17 (2022). https://doi.org/10.1109/MPRV.2021.3129500. https://ieeexplore.ieee.org/document/9655316, conference Name: IEEE Pervasive Computing
37. Vargo, A., Ohara, K., Nakai, T., Kise, K.: Just the right amount of exercise: aerobic exercise and memory. In: Adjunct Proceedings of the 2022 ACM International Joint Conference on Pervasive and Ubiquitous Computing and the 2022 ACM International Symposium on Wearable Computers, pp. 126–127. Adjunct, Association for Computing Machinery, New York, NY, USA (2023). https://doi.org/10.1145/3544793.3560346
38. Yamada, K., Kise, K., Augereau, O.: Estimation of confidence based on eye gaze: an application to multiple-choice questions. In: Proceedings of the 2017 ACM International Joint Conference on Pervasive and Ubiquitous Computing and Proceedings of the 2017 ACM International Symposium on Wearable Computers. pp. 217–220. Association for Computing Machinery, New York, NY, USA (2017). https://doi.org/10.1145/3123024.3123138

AI-Driven Approaches to Knowledge Acquisition and Skill Mastery: An Application to Second-Language Learning

Olivier Augereau, Anisia Popescu, Sofiya Kobylyanskaya, and Motoi Iwata

Abstract Speech technology and artificial intelligence (AI) serve as powerful tools for knowledge acquisition and skill mastery. This chapter examines their role in advancing second-language learning (L2) by enhancing both comprehension and production. For L2 speech, AI helps identify pronunciation errors, provides targeted feedback, and fosters native-like speaking abilities. Additionally, tools like eye-tracking enhance comprehension by analyzing reading patterns, predicting language proficiency, and personalizing strategies. Integrating reading aloud with eye-tracking delivers multimodal insights into L2 processing, promoting a comprehensive approach to skill development.

Keywords Knowledge acquisition · Skill mastery · Second language learning · Spoken language · Reading · Eye-tracking

1 Introduction

Artificial intelligence (AI) has emerged as a transformative tool for advancing knowledge acquisition and skill mastery. This chapter focuses on second-language (L2) learning as a compelling example of how AI-driven tools can facilitate complex cognitive processes, support personalized learning, and enhance skill acquisition and

O. Augereau (✉)
ENIB, Lab-STICC UMR CNRS 6285, Brest, France
e-mail: augereau@enib.fr

A. Popescu · S. Kobylyanskaya
LISN, CNRS, Université Paris Saclay, Paris, France
e-mail: anisia.popescu@universite-paris-saclay.fr

S. Kobylyanskaya
e-mail: sofiyakob@gmail.com

M. Iwata
Osaka Metropolitan University, Osaka, Japan
e-mail: imotoi@omu.ac.jp

A. Dengel et al. (eds.), *The Future of Education with AI*,
https://doi.org/10.1007/978-981-95-1622-3_3

mastery. Acquiring a second language is a complex cognitive process that requires learners to integrate new knowledge, refine their skills, and apply them in effectively across different contexts. By leveraging AI-driven tools, learner can receive precise, targeted feedback on key aspects of language learning, such as pronunciation and vocabulary, enabling them to continuously refine their abilities and progress toward native-like fluency. Additionally, advanced technologies provide insights into speaking and reading proficiency, and can be used to personalized learning strategies tailored to individual needs. This chapter explores how a multimodal AI-based approach can measure and evaluate skill acquisition, fostering a holistic and adaptive path to proficiency and mastery.

Learning a second language differs fundamentally from acquiring a native language. The acquisition of first language (L1) develops organically, starting as early as the prenatal stage and continues through childhood, without the need for formal instruction. Babies pick up their native language simply by being exposed to it in their environment. In contrast, learning a second language (L2) usually requires conscious effort, structured instruction, and deliberate practice, especially if the language is acquired later in life.

Since its beginnings in the 1960s, L2 learning research has evolved alongside advancements in linguistics and psychology, as well as the growing influence of technology. Reference [1] outlines several key phases in the development of SLA research over the years: from the early focus on investigating the order and sequence of language acquisition, to the exploration of language transfer and the role of input and interaction, through the cognitive phase in the 2000s, the social turn, and, most recently, the emergence of the sociocognitive approach. In recent decades, technological innovations have further shaped L2 learning, enabling new methods of automatic language assessment and feedback, particularly through the use of digital tools, artificial intelligence, and online communication platforms.

In practice, L2 learning involves developing various skills which generally fall into two main categories: comprehension skills, which focus on language input, and productive skills, which emphasize language output. Comprehension skills include reading and listening. Reading helps learners expand vocabulary and sentence structures, improving comprehension. Listening enhances understanding of pronunciation, accents, and real-time language use. Productive skills encompass speaking and writing. Speaking practice helps learners gain confidence in communication while refining pronunciation and building fluency. Writing, meanwhile, reinforces grammar and spelling, allowing learners to clearly organize and express their ideas.

The process of learning an L2 and its associated skills is further categorized by the Common European Framework of Reference for Languages (CEFR) [2]. This framework defines six proficiency levels: A1 and A2 (beginner), B1 and B2 (independent), and C1 and C2 (proficient). These levels, along with skill descriptors, serve as the foundation for internationally recognized L2 exams, including TOEIC, TOEFL, CAE, and others. In addition to the CEFR, other proficiency scales are widely used for various languages. The ACTFL scale, developed by the American Council on the Teaching of Foreign Languages, and tests like the JLPT (Japanese-Language Proficiency Test) and EIKEN (Test in Practical English Proficiency) cater to specific languages and learning contexts.

In this chapter, we will focus specifically on speech production as a productive skill and reading as a comprehension skill, presented through the lens of using speech technology and AI to support L2 learning. Following this, a dedicated section will explore reading aloud, a complex skill that integrates both reading and speech production with technology. This task requires the combination of two distinct abilities: decoding written text and speech production. To analyze reading aloud effectively, a multimodal approach is essential, utilizing eye movement tracking to assess reading comprehension and speech analysis to evaluate fluency, pronunciation, and intonation. Although this multimodal approach can be challenging, the use of AI and speech technology allows us to leverage each mode to enhance mutual understanding, shedding light into L2 skill development.

The chapter is organized as follows: Sect. 2 discusses speech production mechanisms in L2, focusing specifically on improving pronunciation in a second language. Section 3 explores how eye-tracking technology and AI can assist in assessing comprehension during in silent reading. Section 4 integrates the two skills presented in Sects. 2 and 3, examining reading aloud as a combined practice. We will end the chapter addressing ethical considerations (Sect. 5) followed by a brief conclusion.

2 Spoken Language and Speech Production in Second-Language Learning

Of all the skills involved in learning a second language, speaking is the only one that involves the public display of one's ability. Speech production in a second language (L2) is a complex process that involves various psychological, cognitive, and linguistic skills. A second-language learner is required to find the appropriate words, organize them into correct syntactic structures, while simultaneously attempting to articulate unfamiliar sounds so their interlocutor can understand them.

Assessment of their proficiency includes measures of accuracy, fluency, pronunciation, comprehensibility, and intelligibility. Although there is pairwise correlation between these measures, not all are regarded as equally important, with scholars prioritizing comprehensibility and intelligibility over fluency and native-like pronunciations [3]. Studies have shown that even though foreign accentedness is highly salient (30 ms of speech is enough to reliably distinguish native from L2 accented speech [4]) and can be irritating, it is partially independent of intelligibility [5]. However, native-like productions do bear a role in social and professional settings. Studies have shown that people who speak with non-native accents are often perceived as less competent, less likable, less intelligent and event less attractive than those who speak with more native-like accent [6, 7]. In a meta-analysis of 27 studies, Spence and colleagues [8] showed that having an accented L2 speech has a negative impact on hiring decisions.

With the development of technology in the past decades there is a renewed interest in second-language pronunciation and improving non-native accented speech. A variety of commercial or open-source systems are now available on mobile devices and desktops that propose individualized support, in settings that do not induce anxiety.

In the following subsection we will first go into more detail about second-language pronunciation and then describe the speech technology methodologies for improving L2 speech production.

2.1 Second-Language Pronunciation

Attaining native-like phonetic proficiency in a second language is challenging, especially when the language is learned later in life. Challenges in achieving phonetic proficiency occur at various phonological levels, including the segmental (individual sounds) and the suprasegmental (prosody, fluency) levels. At the suprasegmental level, second-language learners need to master both prosodic features such as rhythm, intonation, and stress patterns as well as fluency features that tap into temporal aspects of speech such as speech rate and hesitation phenomena (filled and silent pauses). At the segmental level, second-language learners encounter various complexities. They must first learn new sounds that may not exists in their native language. For instance, learners of Mandarin need to acquire a three way contrast between voiceless sibilants (dental /s/, alveolo-palatal ɕ, retroflex fricative /ʂ/) [9]. Even when a sound is shared between their L1 and L2, its articulation might differ; for example, the /t/ sound in English is produced with a more retracted tongue tip constriction compared to French. Additionally, learners must adapt to variations in how the same phoneme is realized in different phonological contexts (e.g., position in the word, syllable). In German, for example, voiced final stops (/b, d, g/) are typically devoiced (produced as [p, t, k]), adding further nuance to segmental phonetic learning [10]. In what follows we will focus on segmental L2 phonetic development.

There are several models of L2 speech learning that account for L2 phonetic development. The two most influential are the Speech Learning Model (SLM, [11]) and the Perception Assimilation Model of Second-Language Speech Learning (PAM-L2, [12]). Both models assume the learner acquires the L2 in an immersive L2 dominant environment, however both have been adapted to apply to foreign language classroom settings where the environment is L1 dominant ([13] for SLM and [14] for PAM-L2). The SLM model provides a framework that accounts for both L2 production and perception. The PAM-L2 focuses on perception only, as a precursor to speech production. While the models differ in several aspects such as the level of the learner (PAM-L2: novice; SLM: advanced learner) or the size of the basic phonological unit that is relevant (PAM-L2: articulatory gesture; SLM: position-specific allophone), they converge on two main points: (1) the learning of segmental and suprasegmental features of the L2 is influenced by the similarity of phonetic/phonological characteristics of the native language (i.e., L1 knowledge influences L2 learning) and (2) the role these characteristics play in the learning process changes with time and experience of the L2 (i.e., beginner and advanced learners may differ). The models also assume that the perception–production relationship is not the same in L1 and L2.

A classic example illustrating the first point is the well-documented difficulty of Japanese learners of making a distinction (in both perception and production) between /l/ and /r/ sounds in their L2. Japanese does not have a phonological contrast between /l/ and /r/, the language has a single liquid phoneme / ɾ/ [15, 16]. Depending on their L2 level, the age of acquisition or the position of the /l/ and /r/ in the word, Japanese learners might assimilate the both consonants to their own Japanese liquid / ɾ/ or produce distinct consonants [17, 18]. Similarly, learners of L2 French have difficulties distinguishing between /u/ (*vous* [vu] 'you, pl.') and /y/ (*vu* [vy] 'seen') vowels depending on their L1 and experience with French [19]. While native English speakers that do not have the /u/-/y/ contrast in their language will have more trouble producing the two vowels than L1 German learners that have a similar contrast in German. Similarity with one's native language, however does not necessarily benefit L2 production outcomes. For example, in a study [20] examining the perception of Mandarin lexical tones by naive native speakers of Cantonese, Japanese and English, it has been shown that experience with lexical tones in one's native language does not necessarily facilitate non-native perception. According to the SLM [11] the greater the perceived distance between the target L2 sound from the closest L1 sound, the more likely it is to be learned.

These difficulties present significant obstacles for learners striving to achieve fluency and accuracy in their L2 pronunciation. However, the advent of speech technology and AI offers promising solutions to these issues. These technologies can provide unlimited targeted practice and personalized feedback, enabling learners to identify and correct pronunciation errors more effectively than classic classroom settings. In the next section we will explore the possibilities speech technology offers for learners to achieve proficient L2 pronunciation.

2.2 Speech Technology for L2 Speech Production

Despite studies showing that pronunciation training has a generally large impact pronunciation outcomes (see [21, 22] for meta-analyses), this component is often downplayed or overlooked in second-language classroom teaching. With the advent of new technologies, there is a renewed interest in second-language pronunciation. In recent decades, Computer Assisted Pronunciation Training (CAPT), a sub-field of Computer Assisted Language Learning (CALL); has emerged as a compelling alternative to traditional classroom-based instruction. There a three main advantages to CAPT systems: the large amount of input available, unlimited practice time and the opportunity for individualized feedback. CAPT resources are becoming increasingly more complex, integrating technologies such as automatic speech recognition (ASR) and artificial intelligence (AI). Methodologies range from High Variability Phonetic Training (HVPT, [23, 24]), to ASR comparing learners' to native speakers' speech (dictation applications: [25], Word-Error-Rates: [18]), to phone-level pronunciation error detection (mispronunciation detection and diagnosis method—MDD: [26], parallel native and non-native acoustic models: [27]), to visual feedback tools (articulatory feedback [28, 29]; prosodic feedback [30]). These methods differ in the type of technology they use and in the amount of feedback they provide to the learner.

One of the earliest and most commonly used methods for detecting mispronunciations is the Goodness of Pronunciation (GOP) algorithm [31, 32]. The GOP automatically assesses the pronunciation quality of individual sounds. The algorithm calculates the likelihood ratio of the learner's acoustic phoneme production given the acoustic model for the canonical phoneme. The acoustic models are usually trained for automatic speech recognition (ASR). The training data is usually native speech. Confidence measures are therefore not very accurate and depend on the transcriptions, but can nevertheless provide valuable insights about pronunciation (Ballier et al. 2023; Graham and Roll 2024). Another ASR-based method for detecting pronunciation errors which are specifically tailored to the learner's L1, involves the use of both L2 and L1 acoustic models for specific phonemes [27]. By giving the choice between native and non-native acoustic phone models, which were trained on similar types and amount of data for each language, the ASR system can more accurately identify discrepancies in the pronunciation. This approach allows the learner to understand how their native language influences their L2 speech, thereby providing targeted feedback. The feedback is however limited. Detecting pronunciation errors is one step, but improving pronunciation requires corrective feedback. The provided feedback needs to be understandable and should suggest courses of action for correction. Depending on the how the ASR acoustic models are trained feedback is more or less interpretable. Classical training methods for ASR systems relied on Gaussian Mixed Model–Hidden Markov Models (HMM–GMM) which have manual feature extraction (e.g., ceptral and pitch features). More recent methodologies train acoustic models based on deep neural networks, which learn features from raw input (waveform, spectrogram, etc.), making them harder to interpret. Depending on the level of transparency of the system learners may find the feedback difficult to interpret. However, [33] showed that learners are able to guess what kind of feedback is provided and can therefore rehearse specific pronunciation features. This however requires learners to have a minimal language level.

In contrast, feedback that incorporates visual elements could significantly help learners not just identify but also correct their pronunciation. By providing clear, visual representations of phonetic differences, this approach enables learners to better understand their errors and make necessary adjustments. The following section delves deeper into the concept of visual feedback, and how it could benefit learners' pronunciation skills.

Visual Feedback

While any type of individualized feedback can be useful for L2 pronunciation, feedback that integrates visual components provides more opportunities for learners to understand and correct their pronunciation errors [34]. Two main types of visual feedback are considered here: phonetic visualization and articulatory feedback. Phonetic visualization includes tools such as waveforms, spectrograms, pitch contours and intensity contours to display the acoustic properties of speech. Learners can then compare their own productions to those of native speakers and adjust accordingly. This type of visualization can be hard to interpret without phonetic training, or someone to guide the learner. Articulatory feedback can be more transparent to learners. Articulatory visualizations, such as MRI, ultrasound, or electromagnetic articulography (EMA) based visual feedback, are more intuitive. Learners can either visualize native speakers' tongue postures and copy their behavior, or in more interactive settings see their real-time tongue posture, compare it to native speakers' articulation and adapt their articulation accordingly. Just looking at native speakers' articulation does not guarantee successful interpretation and implementation of articulatory trajectories. Training based on one's own articulation yields better results [35]. Successful training has been found in multiple studies (ultrasound imaging: [36–38]; electromagnetic articulography: [39]). These studies are however lab-based and require learners to be in the room with the equipment. Visualization tools are also important and need to be developed as some outputs of articulatory imagining are not easily interpretable (e.g., ultrasound imaging provides only tongue surface contours but no relation to other reference points like the palate; EMA sensors represent points moving in space). Examples of such tools are the Opti-Speech [40], the VisArtico [41] and other systems [42, 43].

New technology and AI can improve access to such methods through acoustic-articulatory inversion (AAI). AAI consists in reconstructing articulatory trajectories from the acoustic speech signal. Paired with speech synthesis technology [44, 45], it can provide audio-visual feedback to help achieve phonetic targets in L2 phonology. In recent years, deep learning algorithms have become the leading method for both articulatory acoustic inversion [46–48] and speech synthesis [49–51]. Algorithms are trained on real articulatory data recorded in controlled laboratory settings using various imaging techniques (real-time MRI—rtMRI, electromagnetic articulography—EMA, ultrasound tongue imaging—UTI).

AI has made significant advances in assessing and providing feedback to second-language learners, helping them refine their pronunciation. However, further development is needed to create accessible and affordable visualization tools that can reach a wider audience.

In the following section, we will explore another essential aspect of L2 learning: comprehension, with a particular focus on reading in a second language. The review will highlight the complexities of reading processes and introduce eye-tacking as viable method to measure these complexities.

3 Silent Reading in Second-Language Learning

Reading is an important activity for second-language learners as they need to learn new words to build up their vocabulary [52]. Reading exposes learners to new words in context, helping them understand and remember vocabulary more effectively.

Regular reading practice enhances learners' ability to understand and process text, leading to improved comprehension skills. Additionally, it aids in making inferences and grasping linguistic nuances. Furthermore, reading fosters cultural awareness, providing insights into the sociocultural context of the target language, including idiomatic expressions and social norms.

Reading is a cognitive activity: it largely takes place in the mind, and the physical manifestations of the activity will mainly be the eye movements. If we want to build an AI that can help reading, the first steps will be to record the learners' eye movements and to detect if they are reading or doing another activity. If they are reading, we can analyze what they are reading, and how they are reading.

For the past century, psychologists have been using eye trackers to record the reading activity and to analyze in detail how people are reading. Keith Rayner, a pioneer in eye-tracking research, made significant contributions to understanding reading processes [53]. His work, particularly in the study of eye movements during reading, has provided insights into how readers process text, allocate attention, and integrate information. The eye movements is not smooth while reading. It can be seen as a sequence of fixations and saccades [54]. Fixations correspond to the location of where the eyes pause. Their duration reflect the amount of time the reader's gaze is fixed on a specific word or area. Longer fixations may indicate difficulty in understanding or processing the text. Saccades are the rapid movements between fixations. Short saccades may suggest a more careful reading, while longer saccades can imply familiarity with the language.

Our eyes do not stop on each individual word while reading. The fixation duration and saccade length greatly changes depending on the reader's proficiency and the text complexity. Rayner's studies demonstrated how factors such as word frequency, predictability, and sentence complexity influence reading patterns, including fixation duration and saccades [55].

3.1 Eye Tracking Technology

Eye-tracking technology evolved quite a lot since the last decade. Devices are becoming more affordable and more accurate. The three main technologies used for recording eye movements are currently: the stationary video-oculography (SVoG), the mobile video-oculography (mVoG), and the electro-oculography (EoG).

The two first ones are based on active infrared emitters and cameras in order to record pupil movements. The stationary ones can be attached to a computer screen, while the mobile ones are usually attached to the frame of glasses.

EoG relies on electrodes to be in contact with the user's skin near the eye, eye movement is detected as microvoltage between two electrodes. Some companies such as JINS MEME embedded this sensor inside the frame of daily-life glasses. EoG can measure horizontal and vertical eye movement depending on the electrodes positions but it cannot measure the position of the eye gaze. Eye blinks will generate slightly more voltage and can be detected too. VoG can measure the eye gaze position, eye blinks and also the pupil diameter.

Theoretically, VoG can be done with a simple webcam but the quality of the eye gaze position is much lower without infrared lights and cameras [56], which makes reading analysis difficult to perform.

It should be noted that other eye-tracking technologies also exist, but are much less widely used, especially in the context of reading analysis, such as optical [57], acoustic [58], magnetic [59], and electrostatic [60] sensors.

3.2 Processing Eye Gaze Data for Reading Analysis

With the progress of eye-tracking technology, wearable and ubiquitous computing communities tried to develop tools for analyzing reading in daily life. Several challenges arise in order to do this: detecting when the learner is reading versus not reading [61], collecting the read words [62], counting the number of read word and reading speed [63], and ultimately predicting the reader's understanding [64, 65] or even estimating the performance on standardized test of language proficiency such as TOEIC score [66].

EoG can be used to count the number of read words [67], but so far no studies have been done on more detailed reading analysis based on EoG. VoG is the most commonly used technology for reading analysis. A VoG eye tracker can record the raw eye gaze position at a specific frequency.

Detecting fixations can be challenging due to micro-saccades, which are small, involuntary eye movements that occur even when attempting to focus on a specific point. To detect fixations and saccades, several algorithms exist in the literature such as the Buscher et al. algorithm [68], or the Nystrom and Holmqvist algorithm [69]. The Buscher et al. algorithm identifies fixations by analyzing neighboring gaze points that are spatially close to each other on the screen, while the Nystrom and Holmqvist algorithm detects saccades by measuring the angular velocity of eye movements.

The behavior of eye movement should be analyzed by taking into consideration the support type, as well as the language's writing system, which are influential factors of eye movement patterns. The medium can be represented by a text, which can be read horizontally from left to right or from left to right depending on the language. Comic books are another example of reading mediums that combine both textual and visual information and require different visual scanning strategies involving movement from right to left from top to bottom.

Eye movement also depends on the language's writing system. In Chinese, for example, information is densely represented compared to English. While Chinese and English readers show similar ocular behavior in terms of fixation duration and frequency, Chinese readers have shorter saccades than English readers [70].

Siegelman et al. [71] provided a cross-linguistic analysis of eye-tracking behavior based on a multilingual eye-tracking corpora including readers of 13 languages. According to their study, one of the most notable distinctions among languages is the skipping rate influenced by the average word length used in the language. For example, readers of languages using longer words (such as Turkish or Finnish), tend to skip fewer words while reading. On the contrary, readers of languages with shorter words (such as Korean or Hebrew) tend to skip words more frequently.

3.3 Predicting Reading Understanding

Research has demonstrated a strong correlation between reading comprehension and eye movements, such as the time spent on specific words, reading speed, and the number of regressions. The goal of the studies that we report in this subsection is to leverage this relationship to develop systems that can automatically predict a reader's comprehension by analyzing their eye gaze patterns. The typical pipeline consists of three steps: (1) collecting eye gaze data, (2) collecting labels related to the reader's understanding, and (3) training a supervised machine learning algorithm to predict the reader's understanding.

3.3.1 Eye Gaze Data

is collected from several participants while reading several texts. It is important to collect data from readers with different skills in order to capture different reading behaviors. Classifying beginners, intermediate, and advanced readers is a relatively straightforward task. Simple features such as the reading speed can be used for this purpose. But if the task is more subtle, such as predicting the result of a standardized test of language proficiency among a homogeneous group of readers with similar reading skills [66], more detailed features need to be collected. In this case, the features typically used are fixation durations, saccade lengths, regressions, word skippings, eye blinks, etc.

However, all of these features can also change depending on the text complexity: the sentence length, the words frequencies in the language, familiarity with these words and their length, etc. This is the reason why collecting data while reading different texts is also important.

Gathering a diverse range of readers, reading various materials in different contexts, and using multiple types of eye-tracking is essential to develop robust AI that can effectively understand reading comprehension. For this purpose, data sets are crucial, but very tedious to build, which is why they are, unfortunately, not commonly available [72, 73].

3.3.2 Reader's Understanding

can be assessed in two different ways, which we categorize as objective and subjective understanding.

Objective understanding relies on metrics or scores such as answers to comprehension questions, quizzes; or tasks such as rephrasing or summarizing a text. Some can be done automatically [65], while others might need human evaluation. TOEFL, TOEIC, and IELTS are some of the well-known standardized tests for English language as a second language, combining different kind of exercises to assess the learners skill.

Subjective reader's understanding consists of measuring the reader's own personal perceptions. It is usually done through self-assessment questionnaires [64], or by asking which word [74] or which part of a text was difficult to understand, for example. Martínez-Gómez and Aizawa propose a technic for estimating the learners' language proficiency from their eye gaze while reading educational texts [75]. This research achieved a small but significant error reduction in recognizing English language skill as measured by TOEFL or TOEIC (objective understanding), but failed at recognizing self-reported English skill (subjective understanding), probably due to inconsistencies between self-assessment of English ability of the readers.

Indeed, in some cases there can be quite a difference between the subjective and objective understanding: the readers thought that they understood the text but performs poorly to a comprehension test. It can also be the other way around: they performed well to a comprehension test, even they though they did not understand well the text. Measuring the difference between objective and subjective understanding can be interesting from the learning perspective as it might inform about the confidence of the learners about their knowledge. For this purpose eye gaze information can be used for predicting if a learner is answering a quiz without confidence [76] and can be used for detecting overconfidence and underconfidence.

3.3.3 Supervised Machine Learning

models are trained based by inputting the eye gaze data and the reading skill labels. Traditional AI methods will rely on features engineering to extract meaningful features and training models such as Support Vector Machine, Random Forest, XGBoost, and Neural Networks. Finding the best features is a complicated task. Depending on the readers, the text, the language, etc., different features might be more or less relevant. It is possible to train an AI that will perform well for a specific dataset, but will perform poorly on a totally different one.

A more "modern" approach would consist of training deep neural networks with raw eye gaze data. The advantage is to skip the feature engineering part but such methods required very large dataset in order to train the millions or billions of parameters and have not been fruitful yet, mostly due to the lack of available datasets. Some researchers have been successful in using Convolutional Neural Networks on engineered features [74, 77] but not directly with raw eye gaze data.

It worth to be noted that not only using eye gaze information but also adding information about the read text in the model seems to be crucial in order to build more generic models that can be used on text that does not appear in the learning data. For example, the word frequency in a language can be a good indicator about the familiarity that a reader will have with the read word, and the related eye gaze pattern. Indeed, Zipf's Law states that in any given language, the frequency of a word is inversely proportional to its rank in the frequency table [78]. This means a few words (like common function words such as "the," "is," "and") are used very frequently, while most words are used much less often. However, the frequency of a word by itself is not enough to predict the eye gaze pattern of a reader while reading a sentence as many other factors can impact it: phonological complexity, collocated words, etc.

In this section we focus on eye-tracking technology and especially eye gaze data for predicting reading understanding, but with some eye trackers it is also possible to collect pupil dilation [79] or blink frequency [66] . These features can be used for estimating cognition [80], or mental workload [81], so, to some extend it can be used to analyze the reading ability. Other physiological sensors could be used to estimate the reader's mental state [82] or cognitive load [83] such as the electrodermal activity [84], the heart rate variability, the skin temperature, and the brain activity (recorded with an electroencephalogram or functional near-infrared spectroscopy). The problem of using such physiological data is that they tends to perform well in the laboratory conditions but poorly in the wild as they can change depending on the environment and context. For example, the light influences pupil dilation, the temperature influences electrodermal activity, the stress influences the heart rate variability, etc.

3.4 AI Based Reading Services

Analyzing the readers' comprehension can be used to provide different services for themselves, for other readers, for teachers, but also for authors and content editors.

The most straightforward application is to use eye-tracking to predict the reader's understanding: identifying difficult words, phrases, chapters or texts where learners had more difficulties than expected in order to guide them to focus on areas that need improvement. Eye movement can reveal when learners reread specific sections of a text, indicating comprehension challenges. AI can then provide targeted exercises [85] to address specific content or grammatical structures that caused confusion. It can also generate new customized learning situations [86]. In the context of a classroom, this technology can be used to detect the students who struggle the most in order to provide them more help. It can even be used to detect learning disability such as dyslexia [87], Attention Deficit Hyperactivity Disorder (ADHD) [88] or even Autism Spectrum Disorder (ASD) [89].

By detecting the reader's skill and difficult words, it is possible to adapt the text difficulty to the readers. It is the concept behind graded readers. If different versions of a text exists, an AI can select the one which is the most adapted to the reader skills. With the new advances of Large Language Models, we can even imagine to have a tailored adaptation depending on each readers' vocabulary: an AI can rephrase some specific parts of a text to match the reader's skill. This is the idea behind the "vocabulometer" [90, 91]: an application developed to build a model of the readers based on the words they read. The application log the words read by the reader and then the created model can be used to tune a recommendation system in order to suggest texts based not only on the readers' skill but also based on their interest which can be captured by the vocabulary model.

For authors and editors, the reading information of a group of readers will give information about which part of a document is unclear, difficult, or even just skipped by the readers. This reading information can be used for generating document annotations [92]. For example, Cheng et al. generate gray shading, borders, and lines based on reading behavior. Their user study shows that this automatic annotation system helps improve students' comprehension of reading academic papers [93].

Research efforts are underway to develop intelligent textbooks for educators [94]. These intelligent textbooks offer supplementary learning materials and interactions to enhance the learning experience. For example, it can automatically estimating the students' attention [95] or actively ask the reader a question [96].

Without going necessarily deeply in the analysis of reading understanding, simply quantifying reading activity can help to stimulate language learning, in a similar way to how pedometers encourage walking and other quantified self-systems. By tracking metrics such as the reading time or the number of words read [63], the learners could monitor their progress and set personalized goals. Then an application can generate real-time feedback, such as daily or weekly reading milestones or streaks to motivate learners to engage more with the language. This gamified approach, combined with peer comparison can encourage and inspire learners to learn more, while also providing opportunities for mutual support and collaboration, which could make language learning more interactive and rewarding, promoting regular practice and long-term improvement.

To conclude, reading analysis has significantly advanced in recent decades, largely due to eye-tracking technologies. The ability to collect high-quality eye-tracking data using only webcams could revolutionize this field by allowing to collect large-scale data which is necessary to train deep neural networks. Although many research studies achieve high performance in predicting reading comprehension, they are typically constrained to specific contexts: a limited number of readers, a particular language (predominantly English), and specific texts. As a result, the models often lack generalizability to other contexts. Despite these challenges, the potential applications are promising, including personalized feedback for learners, text adaptation based on reading proficiency, and automatic annotation tools for content creators and editors to enhance document quality.

4 Reading Aloud in Second-Language Learning

As discussed in the previous section, eye-tracking have been increasingly used in L2 assessment, for example, assessing reading comprehension level [97] and detecting difficult word while silent reading [74]. It also reflects cognitive load [98], language planning [99] and engagement in the task [100]. Speech patterns at both segmental (phoneme realization) and suprasegmental (prosodic) levels reflect L2 pronunciation specificities depending on speaker's L1 and individual oral production challenges. Disfluencies, such as pauses and hesitations can reflect cognitive load and speech planning [101]. Combining these metrics (speech and eye-tracking) is a promising direction, as it enables both conscious and unconscious processes to be captured [102].

Reading aloud setup allows to combine these two modalities and to account for phonological decoding ability and text comprehension which can be translated by both speech production and eye movement. This experimental setup facilitates the L2 speech analysis, as there is less need for ASR due to the possibility to anticipate the pronounced words. For this purpose, forced alignment of text with speech can be used. However, its performance can be challenged by pronunciation peculiarities and/or by disfluencies, such as truncations, hesitations, repetitions. The reading aloud setup allows to use multimodality by varying the reading medium: for example, by combining textual and visual cues it is possible to account for the role of visual information in oral production and text understanding. Reading aloud experiments are used for the estimation of speakers' L2 level and unknown words [103].

4.1 *Differences Between Reading Aloud and Silent Reading*

When conducting experiments including oral reading, we need to take into account the differences between oral and silent reading. In oral reading, participants typically read slower and need more effort for comprehension compared to silent reading [104, 105]. Consequently, they use longer fixations in oral reading: 275–325 ms compared to 225–250 in silent reading according to [106]. This difference is particularly noticeable among less skilled readers, who read orally at a considerably slower pace [105]. Additionally, participants use regressions for rereading less frequently in oral reading, which is due to the necessity to coordinate their voice with eye movements [ibid.]. Indeed, oral reading is more cognitively demanding than silent reading due to the number of processes involved: semantic decoding, phonological decoding, prosodic realization, and eye–voice coordination. Given that eye movements generally precede articulation, working memory is actively engaged as readers look ahead several words or characters [107].

One of the most commonly used features in reading aloud is the distance between the fixated and the pronounced word. This metric is called eye–voice span and was introduced by [108]. More skilled readers tend to maintain a constant eye–voice span during reading aloud, while less skilled readers fixate on the word being read. [109]. This metric can be automatically calculated using the EyeGotIt sofware [110]. It allows to record the audio, eye movement, to align audio with text, to calculate eye movement features, such as fixations and saccades, as well as to calculate eye–voice span. However, its performance can be challenged by the presence of oral disfluencies (truncations, hesitations, repetitions) and a salient foreign accent that decreases the quality of the speech alignment and consequently influences the eye–voice span calculation. Therefore, when calculating features in a L2 reading aloud setup, one needs to rely on manual correction of audio–text alignment for a better precision.

4.2 Available Corpora in Reading Aloud Studies

A multimodal reading aloud is rarely considered in the literature and, to our knowledge, there are few available corpora including both speech and eye-tracking recordings. One of them is ReadLet [111], a corpus including both silent and oral reading in Italian L1 produced by children and adults. However, the dataset does not include non-native speech. Another dataset was collected in the framework of the LeCycl (Learning Cyclotron) project. It included audio and eye-tracking data of French and Japanese speakers of English, as well as native English speakers [103, 112]. The participants read aloud texts of different levels (beginner, intermediate and advanced), as well as manga (Japanese comic books). Although the corpus is not publicly available, the results obtained on this data paved the way into the possibility of estimating unknown words [103] using a combination of eye-tracking and speech features which will be discussed more in detail in the next section.

4.3 Methods Estimating Learners' Internal States

There are some methods estimating learners' internal states based on their reading aloud behavior. Sabu et al. estimated children's confidence from their speech while reading stories aloud [113]. In this study, pause, speech rate, pitch, intensity, voice quality, and enunciation were calculated as speech features. Based on the obtained speech features, the confidence was estimated using a random forest. Zhang et al. estimated whether children were confident, confused, or hesitant based on their speech while performing a Lego task and talking to their tutors [114]. In this study, various speech analyses such as lexicon, prosody, spectrum, and syntax were performed. The results of these analyses were used to estimate the emotion by a robust classification and regression tree (CART). Thus, speech has been used to estimate confidence, and speech is expected to be effective in estimating unknown words.

4.4 Estimating Unknown Words

Takaike et al. proposed the method estimating whether an unknown word is included in each speech balloon based on the speech and eye gaze information when reading aloud Japanese comics translated into English in 2022 [103]. The use of Japanese comics makes English learning more familiar and joyful, where this direction follows "edutainment" (education + entertainment). Moreover, in comics, eye gaze and speech feature related to short texts can be obtained easily because the short texts distributes in a page. Takaike's method used support vector machine (SVM) as the estimator. For the training of the SVM, the following features were used with sequential backward floating selection (SBFS) [115].

Speech Features First, Mel Frequency Cepstral Coefficients (MFCC) are calculated in the following manner. The 20 dimensions of MFCC are calculated. Then the average of each dimension on the time axis is taken as one feature. Second, we use IBM Watson™ Speech to Text[1] Watson) to obtain speech features considering text information. IBM Watson is an API for transcribing English speech. When speech and text information corresponding to each speech balloon is input to IBM Watson, the output is the result of the transcription, the confidence of transcription (hereinafter called "the confidence"), and the confidence assuming that the result of the transcription is the same as the input text. The confidence are obtained for each speech balloon and each word. The confidence assuming that the transcription is the same as the input text are also obtained for each word. We employ the following values as features: the confidence per speech balloon, the maximum, minimum, and average of the confidence of the transcription per words, and the maximum, minimum, and average of the confidence assuming that the transcription is same as input text per word. Finally, the reading aloud time per speech balloon and the reading aloud time per word are employed as features. The reading aloud time per word is calculated by dividing the reading aloud time per speech balloon by the number of words in the speech balloon.

Eye gaze features First, the number of fixations corresponding to each speech balloon is calculated. Second, the maximum, minimum, and average of the duration of fixation, the maximum, minimum, and average of saccade length, and the maximum, minimum, and average of saccade speed are calculated for each speech balloon and are used as the features. Finally, the gazing time per speech balloon and the gazing time per word are used as features. The gazing time per word is calculated by dividing the gazing time per speech balloon by the number of words in the speech balloon.

Collaborative features of speech and eye gaze The difference between the start time of the reading aloud time and that of the gazing time is used as a feature. Similarly, the difference between the end time of the reading aloud time and that of the gazing time is used as a feature.

[1] https://www.ibm.com/jp-ja/cloud/watson-speech-to-text.

Text features The number of words in each speech balloon and the maximum, minimum, and average of the word frequency are used as features, where the word frequency is strongly related to the word difficulty.

The most effective feature based on the ranking of the SBFS selection is the number of words in each speech balloon. This shows that the text feature is strongly related to unknown words. The following effective features are MFCC, minimum of confidence of IBM Watson per word (speech features), the number of fixations, the average of the speed of saccade, gazing time per speech balloon (eye gaze features), and maximum of word frequency (text features). This shows that the combination of speech, eye gaze, and text features is effective in estimating unknown words.

In this section, we discussed a method of combining eye-tracking with speech characteristics in L2 acquisition research, which can be achieved by using a reading aloud setup. We also provided a detailed example of integrating both eye-tracking and speech features into a machine learning model for estimating unknown words. The results indicate that multimodal feature combinations represent a promising direction for L2 acquisition research, as they represent a more comprehensive view of L2 performance from the point of view of both oral expression and comprehension. Besides the benefits of this approach, it incorporates the challenges of both previously discussed setups—oral production and silent reading—particularly in terms of experimental protocols design and data processing. Indeed, the reading aloud experimental protocols including the recording of multimodal data require specialized, often costly equipment, therefore it is difficult to reproduce this setup in real-time situations for educational purposes. Additionally, data processing, in particular eye–voice coordination, is complex due to the non-native and/or disfluent speech whose analysis often requires manual intervention. These limitations may explain the lack of publicly available multimodal datasets, which could be addressed in future research.

5 Ethical Considerations

Using AI and technology such as eye trackers and microphones for second-language learning raises several ethical considerations. Several frameworks, policies, and core principles for ethical AI have been proposed in the last few years [116–119]. Ethical challenges are frequently associated with AI-based technologies. For instance, the sustainability and environmental impact of training large neural networks are well-documented concerns [120]. Automated technology is also frequently linked to issues of autonomy. AI should support and not replace human interaction. It must at least preserve or even enhance the learner's independence and critical thinking, rather than making them overly reliant on technology.

In this section we will address in more detail the following principles: privacy and security, inclusiveness, autonomy, and transparency.

5.1 Privacy and Security

AI relies on collecting personal data, such as eye movements and voice recordings. Such recordings must be highly protected to prevent misuse: biometric data can be used to identify users and voice can be use to impersonate someone with deepfake techniques. Learners should have a total control over how their data is collected, stored, and used. So a clear and informed consent is essential, ensuring that learners understand what data is being tracked and for what purpose but the learners should also be informed about how AI technologies work, including the potential limitations and benefits of using them in their learning process.

5.2 Inclusiveness

AI systems must be designed to reduce biases in language learning. The main problem is that most of large language model and other AI based on large dataset tends to work well with language broadly available on the internet (English, Spanish, Chinese, French, etc.) for example, but not so much with local and minority languages. AI also tends to recognize well most popular accents but will fail to recognize diverse accents and dialects, which gives privilege to certain groups over others.

When learning a second language (L2), it is important to consider the first language (L1) of the learners, because it influences the learning approach and ease of learning. L1 can affect pronunciation, grammar, and vocabulary due to structural similarities or differences. For example, native speakers of languages with similar syntax to the target language may find it easier to grasp sentence structure. Additionally, certain sounds or phonemes present in the L2 might be challenging if they don't exist in the L1. Understanding these linguistic influences allows instructors (or the AI) to anticipate and address specific challenges. Because of this, AI for learning will also be biased toward dominant languages and cultural references making them less effective for diverse learners.

Access to advanced technology such as eye-tracking, microphone, and AI requires resources that are not accessible to all and limited to a privileged population. The use of this technology for learning will potentially widen existing inequalities.

5.3 Transparency

AI systems used in educational context are mostly based on deep learning approaches. Although this approach provides good performance in a variety of tasks, including L2 level detection [121], deep learning-based methods often lack transparency and explainability. However, these factors are essential for AI models used for learning in general, and in particular for L2 acquisition because they enable the stakeholders to understand, trust, and verify AI decisions, which can help reducing the risk of unintended consequences.

Indeed, explainable models can be used for providing feedback about students' performance, which is beneficial for both teachers and students. A detailed feedback allows one to get a better understanding of students' progress and the aspects to improve, which can help teachers to improve their learning methods and to personalize their approach, while students can benefit from understanding the mistakes they make. In addition, multiple post hoc explanations [122] can help to identify biases in its decision-making and correct them.

Therefore, there is a need of a more transparent and interpretable approach, including rule-based systems and hand-crafted feature extraction [123]. However, manual feature extraction and corrections being time consuming tasks, a hybrid approach can be a promising option.

6 Conclusion

Speech technology and AI have proven to be a transformative tool for second-language learning, providing learners with methods for enhancing both comprehension and productive skills. This chapter highlighted how technology and AI can assist L2 speech production identifying pronunciation errors and providing targeted feedback for pronunciation improvement, supporting learners in achieving more native-like speech. Comprehension skills can also benefit from technological advanced. Eye-tracking during silent reading offers valuable insights into reading behavior, enabling the prediction of language proficiency and providing tailored learning strategies to individual learners. The integration of these approaches, by pairing reading aloud with eye-tracking measures provides further insight into second-language processing and presents a multimodal way to analyze and improve L2 skills in a holistic manner.

The chapter also raises important ethical considerations for the use of AI in educational settings. Issues such as privacy, transparency and ensuring that existing educational inequalities are not exacerbated by the use of AI must be addressed by the international community. Future avenues should include refining AI technologies expanding their affordability and accessibility and incorporating useful adaptive feedback that cater to individual learner profiles.

References

1. Ellis, R.: A short history of SLA: where have we come from and where are we going? Lang. Teach. **54**(2), 190–205 (2021)
2. Council of Europe: Common European Framework of Reference for Languages: Learning, Teaching, Assessment. Council of Europe (2001)
3. Munro, M.J., Derwing, T.M.: Foreign accent, comprehensibility and intelligibility in the speech of second language learners. Lang. Learn. **45**, 73–97 (1995)

4. Flege, J.E.: The detection of French accent by American listeners. J. Acoust. Soc. Am. **76**, 692–707 (1984)
5. Derwing, T.M., Munro, M.J.: Putting accent in its place: rethinking obstacles to communication. Lang. Teach. **42**, 1–15 (2009)
6. Giles, H., Watson, B.M.: The Social Meanings of Language, Dialect and Accent: International Perspectives on Speech Styles. Peter Lang Publishing, New York, NY, United States (2013)
7. Gluszek, A., Dovidio, J.: The way they speak: a social psychological perspective on the stigma of nonnative accents in communication. Pers. Soc. Psychol. Rev: Off. J. Soc. Pers. Soc. Psychol. Inc. **14**, 214–37 (2010)
8. Spence, J.L., Hornsey, M.J., Stephenson, E.M., Imuta, K.: Is your accent right for the job? a meta-analysis on accent bias in hiring decisions. Pers. Soc. Psychol. Bull. **50**(3), 371–386 (2022)
9. Juhász, K.: The acoustic analysis of mandarin sibilants in the production of Hungarian learners of Chinese. In: In Proceedings of 3rd International Symposium on Applied Phonetics ISAPh 2021, pp. 48–52 (2021)
10. Smith, B.L., Peterson, E.A.: Native English speakers learning German as a second language: Devoicing of final voiced stop targets. J. Phon. **40**, 129–140 (2012)
11. Flege, J.E.: Second language speech learning: theory, findings and problems. In: Strange, W. (Eds.) Speech Perception and Linguistic Experience: Issues in Cross-language Research, pp. 233—-272 (1995)
12. Best, C., Tyler, M.: Nonnative and second-language speech perception: commonalities and complementarities. In: Bohn, O.S., Munro, M.J. (Eds.) Language Experience in Second Language Speech Learning: In Honor of James Emil Flege, pp. 13–34 (2007)
13. Piske, T.: Implications of James Emil Flege's research for the foreign language classroom. In Munro, M.J., Bohn, O.S. (Eds.) Language Experience in Second Language Speech Learning. In honor of James Emil Flege, pp. 301–314 (2007)
14. Tyler, M.D.: Pam-l2 and phonological category acquisition in the foreign language classroom. In: A Sound Approach to Language Matters—In Honor of Ocke-Schwen Bohn, pp. 607–630 (2019)
15. Goto, H.: Auditory perception by normal Japanese adults of the sounds "l" and "r". Neuropsychologia (1971)
16. Miyawaki, K., Jenkins, J.J., Strange, W., Liberman, A.M., Verbrugge, R., Fujimura, O.: An effect of linguistic experience: the discrimination of [r] and [l] by native speakers of Japanese and English. Percept. Psychophys. **18**(5), 331–340 (1975)
17. Nagamine, T.: Dynamic tongue movements in l1 Japanese and l2 English liquids. In: Proceedings of the 20th International Congress of Phonetic Sciences ICPhS 2023, pp. 2442–2446 (2023)
18. Popescu, A., Lamel, L., Vasilescu, I., Devillers, L.: An investigation of syllable position /l/ Allophony in l2 English learners using word error rate as an index of phonetic proficiency. In: Proceedings of the 13th International Seminar on Speech Production (2024)
19. Sturm, J.: Phonetics instruction and the /u/-/y/ distinction in French as a foreign language: a preliminary study. In: In Proceedings of the 8th Pronunciation in Second Language Learning and Teaching Conference, pp. 133–143 (2017)
20. So, C.K., Best, C.T.: Cross-language perception of non-native tonal contrasts: Effects of native phonological and phonetic influences. Lang. Speech **53**(2), 273–293 (2010)
21. Lee, J., Jang, J., Plonsky, L.: The effectiveness of second language pronunciation instruction: a meta-analysis. Appl. Linguis. **36**, 345–366 (2014)
22. Saito, K.: Effects of instruction of l2 pronunciation development: a synthesis of 15 quasi-experimental intervention studies. TESOL Quart. **46**, 842–854 (2012)
23. Iverson, P., Hazan, V., Bannister, K.: Phonetic training with acoustic cue manipulations: A comparison of methods for teaching English/r/-/l/to Japanese adults. J. Acoust. Soc. Am. **118**(5), 3267–3278 (2005)
24. Thomson, R.I.: High variability [pronunciation] training (hvpt): A proven technique about which every language teacher and learner ought to know. J. Second Lang. Pronunciation **4**(2), 208–231 (2018)

25. McCrocklin, S., Humaidan, A., Edalatishams, E.: Asr dictation program accuracy: have current programs improved? In: Proceedings of the 10th Pronunciation in Second Language Learning and Teaching Conference, pp. 191–200 (2019)
26. Shahin, M., Ahmed, B.: Phonological-level mispronunciation detection and diagnosis. In: Proceedings of Interspeech, pp. 307–311 (2024)
27. Popescu, A., Lamel, L., Vasilescu, I., Devillers, L.: Automatic speech recognition with parallel l1 and l2 acoustic phone models to evaluate /l/ allophony in l2 english speech production. In: Proceedings of Interspeech, pp. 1015–1015 (2024)
28. Badin, P., Youssef, A., Bailly, G., Elisei, F., Hueber, T.: Visual articulatory feedback for phonetic correction in second language learning. In: Proceedings of Second Language Studies: Acquisition, Learning, Education and Technology L2WS 2010, pp. 1–10 (2010)
29. Engwall, O.: Can audio-visual instructions help learners improve their articulation? an ultrasound study of short term changes. In: Proceedings of Interspeech 2008, pp. 2631–2634 (2008)
30. Bonneau, A., Colotte, V.: Automatic feedback for l2 prosody learning. Speech Lang. Technol. 55–77 (2011)
31. Witt, S.M.: Use of speech recognition in computer-assisted language learning. Phd thesis, University of Cambridge (1999)
32. Witt, S.M., S.J., Y.: Phone-level pronunciation scoring and assessment for interactive language learning. Speech Commun. **30**(2–3), 95–108 (2000)
33. McCrocklin, S.: Dictation programs for second language pronunciation learning: perceptions of the transcript, strategy use and improvement. Koninskie Studia Jezykowe **7**, 137–157 (2019)
34. Bot, K.: Visual feedback of intonation i: effectiveness and induced practice behavior. Lang. Speech **26**(4), 331–350 (1983)
35. Ouni, S.: Tongue gestures awareness and pronunciation training. In: Proceedings of the INTERSPEECH 2011, pp. 881–884 (2011)
36. Gick, B., Bernhardt, B.M., Bacsfalvi, P., Wilson, I.: Ultrasound imaging applications in second language acquisition. In: Hansen Edwards, J.G., Zampin M.L. (Eds.) Phonology and Second Language Acquisition, pp. 309–322 (2008)
37. C., P.L., K., A.T., T, K.: Contribution of ultrasound visualisation to improving the production of the french /y/-/u/ contrast by four Japanese learners. Phonol. Lang. Contact 86–89 (2013)
38. King, H., Ferragne, E.: The effect of ultrasound and video feedback on the production and perception of English liquids by French learners (2017)
39. Suemitsu, A., Dang, J., Ito, T., Tiede, M.: A real-time articulatory visual feedback approach with target presentation for second language pronunciation learning. J. Acoust. Soc. Am. (4), EL382–EL387 (2015)
40. Katz, W., Campbell, T., Wang, J., Farrar, E., Eubanks, J., Balasubramanian, A., Prabhakaran, B., Rennaker, R.: Opti-speech: A real-time, 3d visual feedback system for speech training. In: Proceedings of the Annual Conference of the International Speech Communication Association, INTERSPEECH, pp. 1174–1178 (2014)
41. Ouni, S., Mangeonjean, L., Steiner, I.: Visartico: a visualization tool for articulatory data. In: Proceedings of Interspeech 2012, pp. 1878–1881 (2012)
42. Katz, W., Mehta, S.: Visual feedback of tongue movement for novel speech sound learning. Front. Hum. Neurosci. **9** (2015)
43. Kröger, B., Birkholz, P., Hoffmann, R., Meng, H.: Audiovisual Tools for Phonetic and Articulatory Visualization in Computer-Aided Pronunciation Training, pp. 337–345. Springer-Verlag Berlin Heidelberg (2010)
44. Birkholz, P.: Modeling consonant-vowel coarticulation for articulatory speech synthesis. PLOS ONE **8**(4) (2013)
45. Iskarous, K., Goldstein, L., Whalen, D., Tiede, M., Rubin, P.: Casy: The Haskings configurable articulatory synthesizer. In: Proceedings of the 15th ICPhS, pp. 185–189 (2003)
46. Tobing, P.L., Kameoka, H., Toda, T.: Deep acoustic-to-articulatory inversion mapping with latent trajectory modeling. In: Asia-Pacific Signal and Information Processing Association Annual Summit and Conference IEEE, pp. 1274–1277 (2017)

47. Wu, P., Chen, L.W., et al.: Speaker-independent acoustic-to-articulatory speech inversion. In: ICASSP 2023, pp. 1–5 (2023)
48. Yu, L., Yu, J., Ling, Q.: Synthesizing 3d acoustic-articulatory mapping trajectories: Predicting articulatory movements by long-term recurrent convolutional neural network. In: IEEE Visual Communications and Image Processing, pp. 1–4 (2018)
49. Ribeiro, V., Isaieva, K., Leclere, J., Vuissoz, P.A., Laprie, Y.: Automatic generation of the complete vocal tract shape from the sequence of phonemes to be articulated. Speech Commun. **141**, 1–13 (2022)
50. Wu, P., Li, T., Lu, Y., Zhang, Y., Lian, J., Black, A., Goldstein, L., Watanabe, S., Anumanchipalli, G.: Deep speech synthesis from MRI-based articulatory representations. In: Proceedings of the INTERSPEECH 2023 (2023)
51. Wu, P., Watanabe, S., Goldstein, L., Black, A.W., Anumanchipalli, G.K.: Deep speech synthesis from articulatory representations. In: Proceedings of the INTERSPEECH 2022 (2022)
52. Jenkins, J.R., Stein, M.L., Wysocki, K.: Learning vocabulary through reading. Am. Educ. Res. J. **21**(4), 767–787 (1984)
53. Rayner, K., Pollatsek, A., Ashby, J., Clifton Jr, C.: Psychology of Reading. Psychology Press (2012)
54. Rayner, K., Chace, K.H., Slattery, T.J., Ashby, J.: Eye movements as reflections of comprehension processes in reading. Sci. Stud. Read. **10**(3), 241–255 (2006)
55. Rayner, K.: Eye movements in reading and information processing: 20 years of research. Psychol. Bull. **124**(3), 372 (1998)
56. Wisiecka, K., Krejtz, K., Krejtz, I., Sromek, D., Cellary, A., Lewandowska, B., Duchowski, A.: Comparison of webcam and remote eye tracking. In: 2022 Symposium on Eye Tracking Research and Applications, pp. 1–7 (2022)
57. Li, T., Liu, Q., Zhou, X.: Ultra-low power gaze tracking for virtual reality. In: Proceedings of the 15th ACM Conference on Embedded Network Sensor Systems, pp. 1–14 (2017)
58. Li, K., Zhang, R., Chen, B., Chen, S., Yin, S., Mahmud, S., Liang, Q., Guimbretière, F., Zhang, C.: Gazetrak: Exploring acoustic-based eye tracking on a glass frame. In: Proceedings of the 30th Annual International Conference on Mobile Computing and Networking, pp. 497–512 (2024)
59. Whitmire, E., Trutoiu, L., Cavin, R., Perek, D., Scally, B., Phillips, J., Patel, S.: Eyecontact: scleral coil eye tracking for virtual reality. In: Proceedings of the 2016 ACM International Symposium on Wearable Computers, pp. 184–191 (2016)
60. Shi, Y., Yang, P., Lei, R., Liu, Z., Dong, X., Tao, X., Chu, X., Wang, Z.L., Chen, X.: Eye tracking and eye expression decoding based on transparent, flexible and ultra-persistent electrostatic interface. Nat. Commun. **14**(1), 3315 (2023)
61. Landsmann, M., Augereau, O., Kise, K.: Classification of reading and not reading behavior based on eye movement analysis. In: Adjunct Proceedings of the 2019 ACM International Joint Conference on Pervasive and Ubiquitous Computing and Proceedings of the 2019 ACM International Symposium on Wearable Computers, pp. 109–112 (2019)
62. Augereau, O., Kise, K., Hoshika, K.: A proposal of a document image reading-life log based on document image retrieval and eyetracking. In: 2015 13th International Conference on Document Analysis and Recognition (ICDAR), pp. 246–250. IEEE (2015)
63. Augereau, O., Sanches, C.L., Kise, K., Kunze, K.: Wordometer systems for everyday life. Proc. ACM Interact. Mob. Wearable Ubiquit. Technol. **1**(4), 1–21 (2018)
64. Sanches, C.L., Augereau, O., Kise, K.: Using the eye gaze to predict document reading subjective understanding. In: 2017 14th iapr International Conference on Document Analysis and Recognition (icdar). vol. 8, pp. 28–31. IEEE (2017)
65. Sanches, C.L., Kise, K., Augereau, O.: Japanese reading objective understanding estimation by eye gaze analysis. In: Proceedings of the 2017 ACM International Joint Conference on Pervasive and Ubiquitous Computing and Proceedings of the 2017 ACM International Symposium on Wearable Computers, pp. 121–124 (2017)
66. Augereau, O., Fujiyoshi, H., Kise, K.: Towards an automated estimation of English skill via toeic score based on reading analysis. In: 2016 23rd International Conference on Pattern Recognition (ICPR), pp. 1285–1290. IEEE (2016)

67. Robert, H., Kise, K., Augereau, O.: Real-time wordometer demonstration using commercial eog glasses. In: Proceedings of the 2017 ACM International Joint Conference on Pervasive and Ubiquitous Computing and Proceedings of the 2017 ACM International Symposium on Wearable Computers, pp. 277–280 (2017)
68. Buscher, G., Dengel, A., van Elst, L.: Eye movements as implicit relevance feedback. In: CHI'08 Extended Abstracts on Human Factors in Computing Systems, pp. 2991–2996 (2008)
69. Nyström, M., Holmqvist, K.: An adaptive algorithm for fixation, saccade, and glissade detection in eye tracking data. Behav. Res. Methods **42**(1), 188–204 (2010)
70. Feng, G., Miller, K., Shu, H., Zhang, H.: Orthography and the development of reading processes: an eye-movement study of Chinese and English. Child Dev. **80**(3), 720–735 (2009). https://doi.org/10.1111/j.1467-8624.2009.01293.x, https://srcd.onlinelibrary.wiley.com/doi/abs/10.1111/j.1467-8624.2009.01293.x
71. Siegelman, N., Schroeder, S., Acarturk, C., Ahn, H.D., Alexeeva, S., Amenta, S., Bertram, R., Bonandrini, R., Brysbaert, M., Chernova, D., Fonseca, S., Dirix, N., Duyck, W., Fella, A., Frost, R., Gattei, C., Kalaitzi, A., Kwon, N., Lõo, K., Kuperman, V.: Expanding horizons of cross-linguistic research on reading: The Multilingual Eye-movement Corpus (MECO). Behav. Res. Methods **54**, 1–21 (2022). https://doi.org/10.3758/s13428-021-01772-6
72. Griffith, H., Lohr, D., Abdulin, E., Komogortsev, O.: Gazebase, a large-scale, multi-stimulus, longitudinal eye movement dataset. Sci. Data **8**(1), 184 (2021)
73. Yi, K., Guo, Y., Jiang, W., Wang, Z., Sun, L.: A dataset for exploring gaze behaviors in text summarization. In: Proceedings of the 11th ACM Multimedia Systems Conference, pp. 243–248 (2020)
74. Garain, U., Pandit, O., Augereau, O., Okoso, A., Kise, K.: Identification of reader specific difficult words by analyzing eye gaze and document content. In: 2017 14th IAPR International Conference on Document Analysis and Recognition (ICDAR), vol. 1, pp. 1346–1351. IEEE (2017)
75. Martínez-Gómez, P., Aizawa, A.: Recognition of understanding level and language skill using measurements of reading behavior. In: Proceedings of the 19th International Conference on Intelligent User Interfaces, pp. 95–104 (2014)
76. Yamada, K., Kise, K., Augereau, O.: Estimation of confidence based on eye gaze: an application to multiple-choice questions. In: Proceedings of the 2017 ACM International Joint Conference on Pervasive and Ubiquitous Computing and Proceedings of the 2017 ACM International Symposium on Wearable Computers, pp. 217–220 (2017)
77. Ahn, S., Kelton, C., Balasubramanian, A., Zelinsky, G.: Towards predicting reading comprehension from gaze behavior. In: ACM Symposium on Eye Tracking Research and Applications, pp. 1–5 (2020)
78. Piantadosi, S.T.: Zipf's word frequency law in natural language: a critical review and future directions. Psychon. Bull. Rev. **21**, 1112–1130 (2014)
79. Brishtel, I., Ishimaru, S., Augereau, O., Kise, K., Dengel, A.: Assessing cognitive workload on printed and electronic media using eye-tracker and EDA wristband. In: Companion Proceedings of the 23rd International Conference on Intelligent User Interfaces, pp. 1–2 (2018)
80. Eckstein, M.K., Guerra-Carrillo, B., Singley, A.T.M., Bunge, S.A.: Beyond eye gaze: what else can eyetracking reveal about cognition and cognitive development? Dev. Cogn. Neurosci. **25**, 69–91 (2017)
81. Upasani, S., Srinivasan, D., Zhu, Q., Du, J., Leonessa, A.: Eye-tracking in physical human-robot interaction: mental workload and performance prediction. Hum. Factors **66**(8), 2104–2119 (2024)
82. Augereau, O., Tag, B., Kise, K.: Mental state analysis on eyewear. In: Proceedings of the 2018 ACM International Joint Conference and 2018 International Symposium on Pervasive and Ubiquitous Computing and Wearable Computers, pp. 968–973 (2018)
83. Augereau, O., Brocheton, G., Neto, P.P.D.P.: An open platform for research about cognitive load in virtual reality. In: 2022 IEEE Conference on Virtual Reality and 3D User Interfaces Abstracts and Workshops (VRW), pp. 54–55. IEEE (2022)

84. Nourbakhsh, N., Wang, Y., Chen, F.: GSR and blink features for cognitive load classification. In: Human-Computer Interaction–INTERACT 2013: 14th IFIP TC 13 International Conference, Cape Town, South Africa, September 2–6, 2013, Proceedings, Part I 14, pp. 159–166. Springer (2013)
85. Pivec, M., Preis, A., Garcia-Barrios, V., Gütl, C., Müller, H., Trummer, C., Mödritscher, F.: Adaptive knowledge transfer in e-learning settings on the basis of eye tracking and dynamic background library. In: Proceedings of EDEN 2004 Annual Conference, pp. 295–301 (2004)
86. El Haddioui, I.: Eye tracking applications for e-learning purposes: an overview and perspectives. Cogn. Comput. Technol. Enhanced Learn. 151–174 (2019)
87. Rello, L., Ballesteros, M.: Detecting readers with dyslexia using machine learning with eye tracking measures. In: Proceedings of the 12th International Web for All Conference, pp. 1–8 (2015)
88. Lee, D.Y., Shin, Y., Park, R.W., Cho, S.M., Han, S., Yoon, C., Choo, J., Shim, J.M., Kim, K., Jeon, S.W., et al.: Use of eye tracking to improve the identification of attention-deficit/hyperactivity disorder in children. Sci. Rep. **13**(1), 14469 (2023)
89. Wan, G., Kong, X., Sun, B., Yu, S., Tu, Y., Park, J., Lang, C., Koh, M., Wei, Z., Feng, Z., et al.: Applying eye tracking to identify autism spectrum disorder in children. J. Autism Dev. Disord. **49**, 209–215 (2019)
90. Cruz, F., Coustaty, M., Augereau, O., Kise, K., Journet, N.: An interactive recommendation system for 2nd language vocabulary learning-vocabulometer 2.0. In: 2019 International Conference on Document Analysis and Recognition Workshops (ICDARW), vol. 3, pp. 28–32. IEEE (2019)
91. Jacquet, C., Augereau, O., Journet, N., Kise, K.: Vocabulometer, a web platform for ubiquitous language learning. In: Proceedings of the 2018 ACM International Joint Conference and 2018 International Symposium on Pervasive and Ubiquitous Computing and Wearable Computers, pp. 361–364 (2018)
92. Buscher, G., Dengel, A., Van Elst, L., Mittag, F.: Generating and using gaze-based document annotations. In: CHI'08 Extended Abstracts on Human Factors in Computing Systems, pp. 3045–3050 (2008)
93. Cheng, S., Sun, Z., Sun, L., Yee, K., Dey, A.K.: Gaze-based annotations for reading comprehension. In: Proceedings of the 33rd Annual ACM Conference on Human Factors in Computing Systems, pp. 1569–1572 (2015)
94. Jiang, B., Gu, M., Du, Y.: Recent advances in intelligent textbooks for better learning. Learn. Design. Future 247 (2023)
95. Ishimaru, S., Bukhari, S.S., Heisel, C., Kuhn, J., Dengel, A.: Towards an intelligent textbook: eye gaze based attention extraction on materials for learning and instruction in physics. In: Proceedings of the 2016 ACM International Joint Conference on Pervasive and Ubiquitous Computing: Adjunct, pp. 1041–1045 (2016)
96. Chaudhri, V.K., Cheng, B., Overtholtzer, A., Roschelle, J., Spaulding, A., Clark, P., Greaves, M., Gunning, D.: Inquire biology: a textbook that answers questions. AI Mag. **34**(3), 55–72 (2013)
97. Augereau, O., Kunze, K., Fujiyoshi, H., Kise, K.: Estimation of English skill with a mobile eye tracker. In: Proceedings of the 2016 ACM International Joint Conference on Pervasive and Ubiquitous Computing: Adjunct, pp. 1777–1781 (2016)
98. Bax, S.: The cognitive processing of candidates during reading tests: evidence from eye-tracking. Lang. Test. **30**(4), 441–465 (2013). https://doi.org/10.1177/0265532212473244, https://doi.org/10.1177/0265532212473244, publisher: SAGE Publications Ltd
99. Huettig, F., Rommers, J., Meyer, A.: Using the visual world paradigm to study language processing: A review and critical evaluation. Acta Psychol. **137**, 151–71 (2011). https://doi.org/10.1016/j.actpsy.2010.11.003
100. Kunze, K., Sanchez, S., Dingler, T., Augereau, O., Kise, K., Inami, M., Tsutomu, T.: The augmented narrative: toward estimating reader engagement. In: Proceedings of the 6th Augmented Human International Conference, pp. 163–164. Association for Computing Machinery, New York, NY, USA (2015). https://doi.org/10.1145/2735711.2735814, https://doi.org/10.1145/2735711.2735814

101. Tavakoli, P.: Pausing patterns: differences between L2 learners and native speakers. ELT J. **65**(1), 71–79 (2011). https://doi.org/10.1093/elt/ccq020, https://doi.org/10.1093/elt/ccq020
102. Godfroid, A., Hui, B.: Five common pitfalls in eye-tracking research. Second Lang. Res. **36**(3), 277–305 (2020). https://doi.org/10.1177/0267658320921218, https://doi.org/10.1177/0267658320921218
103. Takaike, T., Iwata, M., Kise, K.: Estimation of unknown words using speech and eye gaze when reading aloud comics. In: International Conference on Pattern Recognition, pp. 91–106. Springer (2022)
104. Takahashi, M., Kiyokawa, S.: Eye movement during silent and oral reading: How can we compensate the loss of multisensory process during silent reading? i-Perception **2**, 842–842 (2011). https://doi.org/10.1068/ic842
105. Vorstius, C., Radach, R., Lonigan, C.: Eye movements in developing readers: a comparison of silent and oral sentence reading. Vis. Cogn. **22**, 458–485 (2014). https://doi.org/10.1080/13506285.2014.881445
106. Rayner, K.: Eye movements in reading: models and data. J. Eye Mov. Res. **2**(5), 1 (2009)
107. Inhoff, A.W., Matthew Solomon, R.R., Seymour, B.A.: Temporal dynamics of the eye–voice span and eye movement control during oral reading. J. Cogn. Psychol. **23**(5), 543–558 (2011). https://doi.org/10.1080/20445911.2011.546782, https://doi.org/10.1080/20445911.2011.546782
108. Buswell, G.T.: An Experimental Study of the Eye-voice Span in Reading. No. 17, University of Chicago (1920)
109. Buswell, G.T.: The relationship between eye-perception and voice-response in reading. J. Educ. Psychol. **12**(4), 217 (1921)
110. El Baha, M., Augereau, O., Kobylyanskaya, S., Vasilescu, I., Devillers, L.: Eye got it: A system for automatic calculation of the eye-voice span. In: Uchida, S., Barney, E., Eglin, V. (eds.) Document Analysis Systems, pp. 713–725. Springer International Publishing, Cham (2022)
111. Ferro, M., Marzi, C., Nadalini, A., Taxitari, L., Lento, A., Pirrelli, V.: ReadLet: A Dataset for Oral, Visual and Tactile Text Reading Data of Early and Mature Readers. In: Calzolari, N., Kan, M.Y., Hoste, V., Lenci, A., Sakti, S., Xue, N. (eds.) Proceedings of the 2024 Joint International Conference on Computational Linguistics, Language Resources and Evaluation (LREC-COLING 2024), pp. 13595–13609. ELRA and ICCL, Torino, Italia (2024), https://aclanthology.org/2024.lrec-main.1188
112. Kobylyanskaya, S., Vasilescu, I., Devillers, L., Augereau, O.: Vers la compréhension des difficultés de lecture en L2 à travers des paramètres acoustiques et de mouvement des yeux. In: Environnements Informatiques pour l'Apprentissage Humain (EIAH). Brest, France (2023), https://hal.science/hal-04388887
113. Sabu, K., Rao, P.: Automatic prediction of confidence level from children's oral reading recordings. In: INTERSPEECH, pp. 3141–3145 (2020)
114. Zhang, T., Hasegawa-Johnson, M., Levinson, S.E.: Children's emotion recognition in an intelligent tutoring scenario. In: Proceedings of the Eighth European Conference Speech Communication and Technology (INTERSPEECH) (2004)
115. Pudil, P., Novovičová, J., Kittler, J.: Floating search methods in feature selection. Pattern Recogn. Lett. **15**(11), 1119–1125 (1994)
116. Ashok, M., Madan, R., Joha, A., Sivarajah, U.: Ethical framework for artificial intelligence and digital technologies. Int. J. Inf. Manage. **62**, 102433 (2022)
117. Chan, C.K.Y.: A comprehensive AI policy education framework for university teaching and learning. Int. J. Educ. Technol. High. Educ. **20**(1), 38 (2023)
118. Floridi, L., Cowls, J.: A unified framework of five principles for AI in society. Mach. Learn. City: Appl. Architect. Urban Des. 535–545 (2022)
119. Nguyen, A., Ngo, H.N., Hong, Y., Dang, B., Nguyen, B.P.T.: Ethical principles for artificial intelligence in education. Educ. Inf. Technol. **28**(4), 4221–4241 (2023)
120. Wynsberghe, A.: Sustainable AI: AI for sustainability and the sustainability of AI. AI Ethics **1**(3), 213–218 (2021)

121. Gretter, R., Matassoni, M., Allgaier, K., Tchistiakova, S., Falavigna, D.: Automatic assessment of spoken language proficiency of non-native children. In: ICASSP 2019–2019 IEEE International Conference on Acoustics, Speech and Signal Processing (ICASSP), pp. 7435–7439 (2019). https://doi.org/10.1109/ICASSP.2019.8683268, https://ieeexplore.ieee.org/abstract/document/8683268, ISSN: 2379-190X
122. Boidot, C., Augereau, O., De Loor, P., Lefort, R.: Benefits of using multiple post-hoc explanations for machine learning. In: 2023 International Conference on Machine Learning and Applications (ICMLA), pp. 794–799. IEEE (2023)
123. Lee, H., Lee, J.H.: The effects of AI-guided individualized language learning: a meta-analysis. Lang. Learn. Technol. **28**, 134–162 (2024)

Knowledge Transfer with AI

Ko Watanabe, Nicolas Großmann, Christoph Maerz, Shoya Ishimaru, and Andreas Dengel

Abstract Knowledge transfer is the transmission of mastered knowledge from one individual to another through communication. This intricate process depends on three critical facets of communication: the appearance and demeanor of the participants, verbal articulation, and nonverbal cues. Several projects worked on aim to analyze the full potential of quantifying and enhancing communication.

1 Introduction

In the concept of learning-lifecycle [86], *Perceive*, *Master*, and *Transfer* are important factors. *Perceive* is gaining knowledge from a textbook or lecture. *Master* is a process of perceiving knowledge usability by conducting exercises and experiments. *Transfer* transfers mastered knowledge to one another through a presentation or discussion. This section focuses mainly on *Knowledge Transfer*.

Understanding and accelerating knowledge transfer is essential in all kinds of fields. Allen et al. investigate that 11 million workplace meetings are held every day in the United States [2]. Employees spend an average of 6 hours in scheduled weekly

K. Watanabe (✉) · A. Dengel
DFKI GmbH (German Research Center for Artificial Intelligence), RPTU University Kaiserslautern-Landau, Kaiserslautern, Germany
e-mail: Ko.Watanabe@dfki.de
URL: https://dfki.de

A. Dengel
e-mail: Andreas.Dengel@dfki.de

N. Großmann · C. Maerz
DFKI GmbH (German Research Center for Artificial Intelligence), Kaiserslautern, Germany
e-mail: nicolas.grossmann@dfki.de

C. Maerz
e-mail: Christoph.Maerz@dfki.de

S. Ishimaru
Osaka Metropolitan University, Sakai, Japan
e-mail: ishimaru@omu.ac.jp

A. Dengel et al. (eds.), *The Future of Education with AI*,
https://doi.org/10.1007/978-981-95-1622-3_4

meetings, with supervisors spending 23 h [64]. Meetings are time-consuming for attendees and costly to the organization, ranging from 30 million to over 100 million US dollars annually [65]. Due to the importance of the field of study on knowledge transfer, the number of related publications is increasing every year [26]. Research on knowledge transfer is gaining attention and importance every year.

According to Shannon–Weaver model [71], *Knowledge Transfer* is defined as communication between the sender (transmitter) and the receiver using encoding and decoding knowledge. Previous studies work on the implementation of a sensor environment for estimation of learning difficulty [83, 99], and estimation of wakefulness while taking a video lecture [38]. Our study aims to quantify and accelerate the success of encoding and decoding knowledge.

1.1 Factor of Knowledge Transfer

To understand knowledge transfer, recognizing the activities and social-cognitive states in communication is essential. In communication, there are three key features, *Participants Appearance*, *Verbal Communication*, and *Nonverbal Communication* [18]. *Participant Appearance* represents features concerning the appearance of the participants in the communication. Schulte et al. found that in the communication scene, participant age and distribution have a significant positive relationship with forgiveness and the number of counteractive behaviors [68]. Due to the importance of participants' age for information transfer, Geng et al. have worked on age estimation from facial images using open-source datasets such as the FG-NET Aging Database [43] and the MORPH Database [61]. *Verbal communication* represents characteristics related to speech. Related research focuses on the analysis of conversational content [49], pronunciation [74, 100], speech volume [40], and voice pitch [48]. *Nonverbal communication* refers to behavior-related characteristics that do not include speech. The related study focuses on the analysis of posture [6, 67], smile [11, 102], eye contact [95, 101], and head motion [57, 98]. Previous studies work on social activity behavior analysis in communication. However, some factors of knowledge transfer, such as micro-behavioral analysis and engagement detection, are still being studied.

1.2 Estimation of Knowledge Transfer

Estimating the state of knowledge transfer is presented by Srivastava et al. [81]. The study works on the estimation of learning difficulty using contactless sensors. The study presents the use of the slider to collect a real-time understanding of the labeling. The contactless sensors are a Logitech webcam, a Tobii Pro X2-30 eye-tracker, and an Optris PI-400 thermal camera. After collecting data from 100 participants, the study found that the difficulty of the lecture depended on three factors: the pictorial representation of complex terms, the difference between the amount of verbal and visual information presented per slide, and the number of words spoken by the instructor per second [83]. Babaei et al. are then working on automatic tracking of attentional states using a webcam [4]. As a result, action units of the face, such as lips or eyelids, perform well in attention detection. Another work was done to discover the correlation between attention while watching videos and comprehension level [82]. Participants with higher prior knowledge made fewer eye movement transitions than those with lower prior knowledge. Prior knowledge estimation has been done by analyzing the web browsing logs [54]. Hence, the direction of web browsing analysis can perform well on knowledge transfer estimation. While the above studies deal with comprehension estimation, they focus on something other than the breakdown of comprehension into details of encoding and decoding in knowledge transfer.

1.3 Acceleration of Knowledge Transfer

Knowledge transfer is accelerated based on the state of knowledge transfer estimation results. Kuttal et al. work on human–human and human–agent comparison on pair programming [41]. The study discovered no significant difference in productivity, self-efficacy, code quality, and pair programming preferences when using an agent for pair programming. Test-driven programming can be done together with an agent. The acceleration of knowledge transfer happens when the agent can provide code skeletons and hints to lead their partner toward a solution. Haliburton et al. use wristband devices to give thermal feedback to the presenter to feedback audience engagement [27]. The work could enhance socio-emotional connectedness in virtual and hybrid meetings. As a result, the presenter and audience feel connectivity only if they are in the same atmosphere, which enhances the presenter's confidence in transferring knowledge. Some studies work on the acceleration of knowledge transfer. However, there still needs to be more work on enhancing communication.

2 Related Work

This thesis discovers an understanding of knowledge transfer. This chapter presents a literature survey about the background and related work.

2.1 Activity Recognition

Figure 1 shows the overview of publications investigating the importance and detection algorithms of key features in a meeting. The categories of important features can be separated into *Participants Appearance*, *Verbal Communication*, and *Nonverbal*

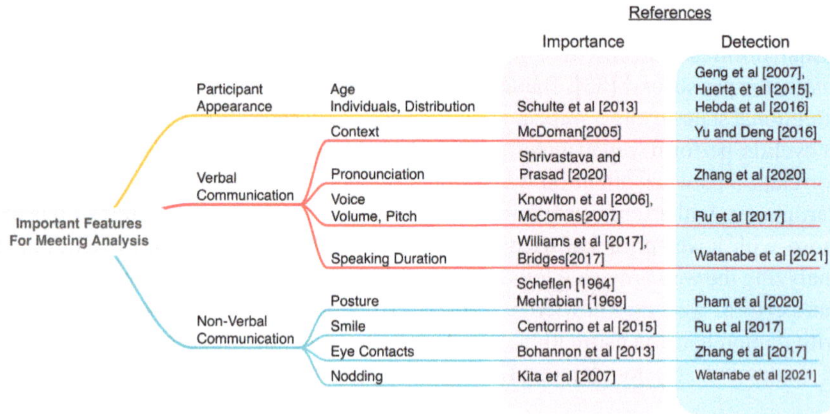

Fig. 1 A tree map summarizing important activities for meeting analysis and the position of our work. The importance shows references representing the significance of each feature. The detection shows references of researchers implementing the system in order to detect each features

Communication. Our target detection is not proposed in previous research studies. By showing the importance and progress of related works, we will highlight our contributions.

2.1.1 Appearance

Appearance represents features regarding the appearance of participants in meetings. Schulte et al. found that, in meetings, participants' individual age and distribution possess a significant positive relationship with forgiveness and the amount of counteractive behaviors [68]. Forgiveness has been defined as "a reduction in negative feelings, and a recovery of positive feelings toward an offender after the offense has taken place" [36]. Counteractive statements had a negative impact on team meeting outcomes such as meeting satisfaction and team productivity [37]. Hence, the age of the meeting participant is an important feature to be considered in the meetings. Geng et al. proposed method for age estimation based on facial aging patterns [25]. They used open-source database FG-NET Aging Database [22] and the MORPH Database [61] for the dataset. These datasets include the age and face images of people. From the facial image, they extracted features by using the Appearance Model [17]. Then, by using these features, they used SVM as the algorithm for estimating age. With respect to previous works, age detection or estimation from facial image or video has already been explored [28, 33].

2.1.2 Verbal Communication

Verbal Communication represents features regarding *speaking* that occur during meetings. McDorman et al. state that the context of what was discussed in the meetings is important [49]. Yu et al. have proposed a method of automatic speech recognition (ASR) technique for speech to text [97]. Shrivastava et al. have stated that unclear pronunciation produces unclear understanding for listeners [74]. Clear pronunciation results in high understanding of the context in meetings. In order to detect pronunciation errors, Zhang et al. have proposed a method of using deep learning technique based on advanced automatic pronunciation error detection (APED) algorithms [100]. Knowlton et al. have found that voice volume and pitch can enhance anxiety or provide comfort for listeners [40]. It has been also said that these factors also change the motivation of participants in terms of joining future meetings in some cases [48]. Therefore, voice volume and pitch are important.

Zhao et al. have proposed ROC Speak system, a platform that allows ubiquitous access to communication skills training. They collect voice information from the microphone in order to detect the volume and pitch of the speaker [102]. However, this system has a limitation in that the user can only be collected as a single person. In the meeting situation, sometimes the voice cannot be collected due to the privacy. In order to tackle the idea of collecting verbal information concerning privacy issues, we focused on participants' *speaking duration*. Many research studies pointed out the issue of *manterrupting* [9, 92]. Essentially, this paper suggests that men speak longer than women, or men cut off the topic when a woman is talking. In order to control the equality of turns, the collection of participants' speech duration is significant. We attempt to measure the duration of time by only using a camera as a sensor that does not include microphones.

Janin et al. introduced the ICSI Meeting Corpus, which collects meeting speech logs with microphones. They have used both head-mounted and table-top microphone [35]. Carletta et al. introduced the AMI Meeting Corpus, in which they used both cameras and microphones to collect meeting logs. They then created a transcript of meetings from the utterance data collected by microphones [10]. Riedhammer et al. then introduced automatic meeting summarization by using the transcript produced from ASR [62].

The advantage of verbal data analysis is the ability to collect detailed data of what was spoken in the meeting. However, the disadvantage of this approach is the privacy risk. Verbal data can be a risk during collection for a company or in the education field. It includes private or confidential information that should not be recorded. Hence, verbal data analysis will always face a privacy risk.

2.1.3 Nonverbal Communication

Nonverbal Communication is related to features related to actions and does not include verbal information. Posture is one of the important nonverbal information in the meetings [50, 67]. Pham et al. proposed 3D pose estimation from a single RGB camera. It can estimate body posture and activities by a camera [58]. Centorrino et al. have stated that a smile perceived as honest makes mutual trust and induces cooperation toward a person who sees the smile. With this in mind [11], Zhao et al. implemented the ROC Speak system in order to collect smiles automatically from the video [102]. Bohannon et al. have stated eye contact plays a role significant for human interactions [7]. Zhang et al. then proposed eye contact detection using a camera [101]. The method can both be used by ambient cameras and wearable glasses. Kita et al. have presented the significance of *nodding*. In this study, we focus on detecting *nodding* by a camera [39].

Ekman et al. stated that nonverbal information contains emotions and the feature of interaction between multiple people [18]. Effective use of nonverbal communication supports facilitating meetings and allows speakers to make attractive statements. Moreover, it is easier for listeners to understand the statement. Morency et al. used a robot to collect human head movements by camera while asking questions. They aim to collect participant's head nods and head shakes. The recognition rate was 73% for head nods and 83% for head shakes [52]. Yu et al. used optical motion capture in order to collect nonverbal behaviors during a meeting. This approach allowed collecting *nodding* recognition of 76.4% and head shaking recognition of 80.0% [98]. Ohnishi et al. used the inertial measurement unit (IMU) sensor to collect participant's head movements [57]. They achieved the recognition of 97.5% in utterance, 52.4% in *nodding*, and 53.6% for looking around actions. The advantage of the nonverbal data analysis is to lower the risk of privacy issues. It does not contain utterance information of each meeting. Moreover, it is an effective way of understanding emotions and the features of interaction between multiple people [18].

The disadvantages of previous research studies are the inconveniences and restrictions of the system settings. Connecting IMU sensors to the participants each time before a meeting is inconvenient. The preparation of a robot inflicts restrictions in terms of the location for holding the meeting. In order to create sustainable data collection or the sustainable use of the system, it must be simple, possess fewer devices and possess low restrictions of the use case environment.

2.2 Social Cognitive State Recognition

This section explains works on engagement recognition and gender consideration in social-cognitive state recognition.

2.2.1 Engagement Levels' Recognition

In this section, we will elaborate on the types of devices utilized for engagement analysis and their accuracy level in predicting engagement. Table 1 shows the position of our work compared to the previous studies. The table shows the device each

Table 1 Comparison of engagement estimation in human communications

Reference	Devices used	Participants	Labeling	Model	Results
Mohamad et al.	Webcam	20 students	Observer annotation	VGG-B	Binary classification 72.3% accuracy
Monkaresi et al.	Webcam	23 students	Self-report	Naive Bayes	Binary classification 75.8% accuracy
Hernandez et al.	Wristband	51 children	Observer annotation	SVM	Binary classification 81.0% accuracy
Di Lascio et al.	Wristband	24 students 9 teachers	Observer annotation	SVM	Binary classification 81.0% accuracy
DiSalvo et al.	Wristband	11 students	Observer annotation	SVM	Binary classification 81.0% accuracy
Sharma et al.	Webcam	15 students	Observer annotation	CNN	Binary classification 66.0% accuracy
Huynh et al.	Smartphone wristband depth camera	64 students	Self-report	RF	Ternary classification 77.0% accuracy
Watanabe et al.	Webcam	24 students	Role acting	MobileNetV2	Ternary classification 89.5% accuracy

research uses, the number of participants, how the annotation of engagement levels is conducted, the machine learning model, and the result of the prediction rate.

Hernandez et al. use Empatica E4 wristband to collect children and adults' engagement levels [30]. Using electrodermal activity (EDA) as an input and with SVM, it predicts the engagement level of around 81.0% accuracy. Di Lascio et al. use Empatica E4 wristband to collect participants' blood volume pulse, acceleration, peripheral skin temperature, and electrodermal activity while taking a lecture [14]. After the lecture, each participant was asked to answer a questionnaire to estimate their level of engagement. By using Support Vector Machine (SVM) model, they achieved 81.0% accuracy in binary classifying the engagement level of participants. DiSalvo et al. worked on predicting student engagement level during lecture [15]. Participants were asked to wear an E4 wristband to collect electrodermal activity (EDA) signals. The subjects collected are 11 students between 18 and 30 years of age. The annotation for the engagement is done according to the specific behaviors defined. Using the SVM model, they got the binary engagement level classification result of 81.0%. These are the references to works using wearable sensors for detecting engagement levels. An interesting finding for these wristband usage approaches was that the accuracy of engagement prediction all scored around 81.0% when using the Empatica E4 wristband.

Not only using wearable sensors but there are also research approaches to using a webcam. Mohamad et al. use a webcam to collect facial video and a convolutional neural network to binary classify users into engaged and disengaged [51]. The model contains two convolutional layers and two max-pooling layers with stride two and two fully connected layers, respectively. The last step of the CNN model includes a Softmax layer, followed by a cross-entropy loss, which consists of two neurons indicating engaged and disengaged classes. With this architecture, they achieved an accuracy of 72.3%. Monkaresi et al. use webcam for binary classify engagement levels. In the preprocessing, this work extracts facial action units [19] and heart rate [60] from the recorded video. Twenty-three undergraduate/postgraduate engineering students collect data from a public university in Australia. As a result, binary classification using Naive Bayes scored 75.8% accuracy. Huynh et al. worked on predicting engagement levels while playing smartphone game [34]. They collect smartphone touch actions, wristbands for photoplethysmography and electrodermal activity, and depth cameras for skeletal motion information. The ground truth of the engagement level is collected using Game Engagement Questionnaire (GEQ). They use Random Forest (RF) as a best-fit model for the classification model. As a result, they achieved a ternary classify engagement level of 85.0%. Sharma et al. presented a system based on neural networks to detect the engagement level of the students captured by a typical built-in webcam present on a laptop computer, and their proposed system was designed to work in real time [72]. They combined eye, head, and facial movements to produce a concentration index with three classes of engagement: "very engaged," "nominally engaged," and "not engaged at all." Facial features were extracted using the Haar cascade algorithm from the images captured by a webcam and then categorized by a convolution neural network (CNN). They tested the proposed system with 15 students in a typical e-learning experiment. They verified that the system could correctly distinguish between the three engagement classes with an accuracy of 66.0%. However, this study only focused on engagement level classification when watching e-learning video content. Hence, it did not cover the analysis of online meetings' behaviors.

Other than the studies above, some analyzed the correlation between engagement and collected sensor data. Babaei et al. classified low and high engagement levels using a webcam [4]. They annotated the level of engagement by using notifications to get labels from the participant. In this study, 15 participants' lab work data was collected. The camera device continuously records the participant's face while working. Using OpenFace to extract facial features, they found that the gaze angle and rotation in the vertical axis (pitch) significantly identify engagement levels. The study found that facial images can be good input data for predicting human engagement levels. Gao et al. worked on identifying the correlation between student engagement levels during lectures and the seating position [23]. They collected data from 23 students and discovered that students who sit close together are likelier to have similar learning engagement and tend to have high physiological synchrony.

2.3 Intervention and Applications

This section explains work on intervention and application for actuating social-cognitive states. We introduce the intervention of the meeting-encouraging system and the works on social-cognitive state augmentation.

2.3.1 Meeting Engagement Encouraging System

Encouraging participants' engagement in meetings has several works [47, 96]. Matsuyama et al. proposed a method using a facilitation robot to enhance engagement levels in offline meetings [46]. They set a condition for encouraging four participants, including the robot, in each set of experiments. The robot uses the mounted camera to discover the engagement status of the other three participants or how well they are harmonized with other participants. The study showed that instead of three participants having conversations, adding a robot as a fourth participant in the meeting was influential in encouraging all participants to join in the conversations. Aseniero et al. proposed the MeetCues system [3]. This system visualizes the emotions of attendees during online meetings. Participants click the like and clarify buttons to choose their status. The system then shows each participant's emotions, such as happiness, neutrality, and thinking. Each emotion is presented by emoji; hence, other users can recognize the participant's status from the interface. Gashi et al. targeted measuring physiological synchrony, which is the synchronization of the physiological states of multiple people [24]. The research shows that when synchrony happens between multiple people, the engagement level is high toward the content presented. Hence, they aim to implement a system for giving feedback on when synchrony happened in the lecture or conversation. It will support the teacher or presenter understand when and which slide interested the students or audience.

2.3.2 Social Cognitive State Augmentation System

Holstein et al. have proposed a method for the teachers to check the students' cognitive states as a dashboard [31]. In the dashboard, each student has an indicator display floating above the head. The work proposed visualizing multiple people's cognitive states combined as a dashboard. *Jumple* project aims to augment the virtual physical education experience [73]. The work supports visualized interactivity with remote participants. Niwa et al. state the importance of AI agents to augment human cognitive abilities [56]. Their approach is to implement a similar-looking AI avatar as a participant to investigate the trustworthiness level of agent statements. Lastly, Kyto et al. have proposed a method for visualizing public and personal information using digital profiles [42]. The work states that giving meta-information about a person communicating will support face-to-face communication smoothly. Concerning previous research, augmentation of the cognitive state positively supports change in behaviors and understanding humans.

3 Knowledge Transfer with Activity Recognition

Communicating with others is one of the most important activities for coming up with new ideas, making rational decisions, and transferring skills. Many knowledge workers spend a certain amount of their work time for meetings. For instance, it is estimated that 11 million meetings are held in the workplace every day in the United States [2]. An employee's average time spent on scheduled meetings per week is 6 hours, and supervisors spend 23 h [64]. The amount is increasing annually. So far we know that between the 1960s and 1980s, this has been doubled [64]. While there is no doubt about the importance of meetings, there is also another aspect in that they are time-consuming for the participants and make up large costs for organizations, ranging from USD 30 million to over USD 100 million per year [65].

Regarding these facts, researchers have been investigated how to increase the efficiency and quality of meetings [44, 45, 53, 59, 80]. After a survey of publications in social science and human–computer interaction, we found that appearances (characteristics such as age and role) [68], verbal information (e.g., spoken content/context and audio characteristics) [9, 40, 48, 49, 74, 92], and nonverbal information (e.g., body gesture and facial expressions) change the behaviors of meeting participants [7, 11, 39, 50, 67]. Compared to several existing approaches for detecting/analyzing information mentioned above, our aim is to design a system that does not utilize content-sensitive information that uses contactless devices, and that is reproducible.

Content-sensitiveness: The focus of the content-sensitiveness issue is mainly about the context relative to what was spoken in the meeting. If the transcript of the

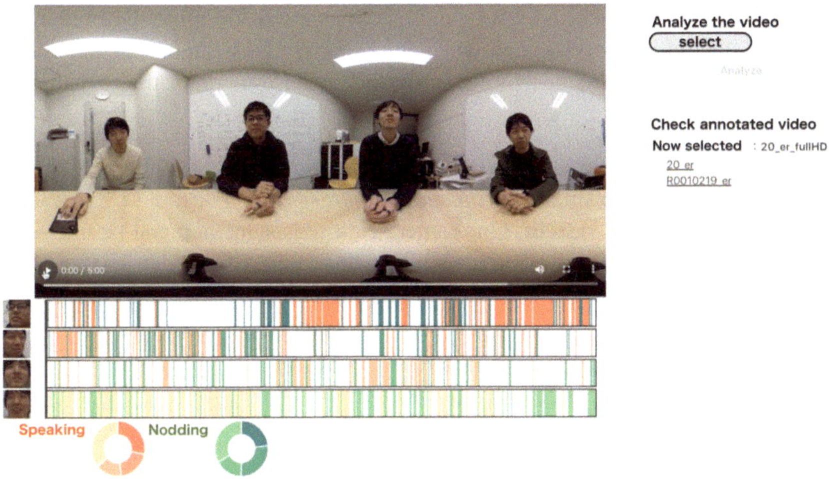

Fig. 2 Overview of a meeting review system. A user selects a video file, and the system classifies micro-behaviors in time series

meeting leaks outside, there are high risks for the company. We adopt an approach that extracts and stores only nonverbal data from the video stream during the meeting. Contactless: Use of contactless devices is also important for reducing time consumption of device setup. Systems must also be reproductive in order to be utilized at any location. According to these aims, we chose to collect nonverbal information for our main data. Instead of using bodily attached devices, we chose a camera as a sensor. Reproducible: The use of one device makes the system simple, which increases reproducibility. We came up with an idea of utilizing a 360 °C camera placed at the center of the discussion table that covers all participants.

Figure 2 shows an example application that uses our micro-behavior detection method. Visualizing the timing of *speaking* and *nodding* of each meeting participant enables them to reflect upon how they were actively involved in the discussion. For instance, in the first half of the meeting, the fourth participant from the top was actively *speaking* and the second participant was agreeing by *nodding*. In the second half of the meeting, the fourth participant was agreeing with the first participant's opinion. Therefore, our proposed work will be used for creating a system for automatic micro-behavior annotation. It will be important for both offline and online meeting analyses.

In this section, we discuss how a camera plays an important role as a smart sensor to recognize key micro-behaviors in a meeting. We propose a method that recognizes *speaking* and *nodding* from a video stream of face images and a Random Forest classifier. In order to evaluate the performance of the proposed method, we conducted data-recording experiments at two physical conditions. The first recording consists of 16 sets of 5-min meetings by 21 unique participants. The second recording includes 7 sets of 10-min meeting data with the help of 12 unique participants. Due to the COVID-19 pandemic, most of the meetings are held online. By creating an additional dataset, we investigated whether similar features can be calculated from the webcams connected to the PCs of each participant. In summary, the contributions are as follows:

C1 **Verify 360 °C camera**: A 360°C camera can recognize multiple participants' micro-behavior in a small size meeting.

C2 **Robustness of the system**: Our camera as a sensor method can be utilized to evaluate not only offline meetings but also online meetings. Also system can be used at any place, and the dataset can be mixed even if the collected place is different.

3.1 Methodology

The annotations of micro-behaviors are performed by using ELAN [77] shown in Fig. 3. ELAN is a GUI annotation tool for audio and video recordings. The users can choose to set any labels for the annotation. The participants are asked to annotate the time duration of each micro-behavior. Watanabe et al. focus on annotating *nodding* and *speaking* activities [91]. Chen et al. use the same dataset to also annotate *smile* activity [12]. Participants annotated right after each meeting sessions. The annotated data are extracted as a .csv file.

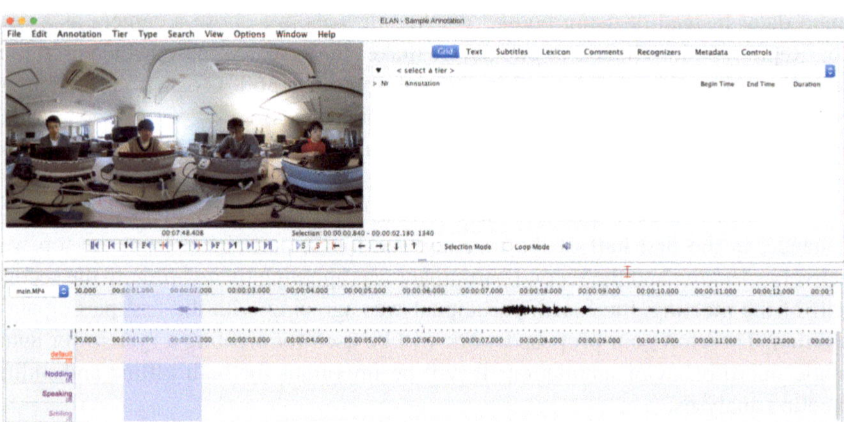

Fig. 3 Participants use ELAN to create annotations of micro-behaviors. Each annotation contains time duration. Annotations are performed right after each meeting sessions. After annotation, each participant exports data into a .csv file

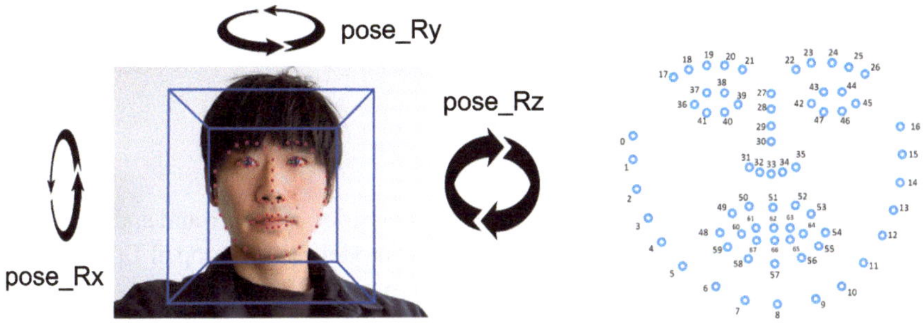

(a) Applied image (b) Landmarks

Fig. 4 Image after applying OpenFace and the 68 landmarks of the facial points

3.1.1 Extracting Head Rotations and Facial Points Using OpenFace

The study uses the open-source software OpenFace [5] to obtain features of the participant face. The landmarks of each facial points after applying OpenFace are shown in Fig. 4. OpenFace converts video data into several features: three head rotation data (*pose_Rx*, *pose_Ry*, and *pose_Rz*) and 68 facial points.

Nodding is the action of a human individual moving its own head in the vertical direction. Hence, we focus on using the rotation feature, *pose_Rx* component shown in Fig. 4. With the *pose_Rx*, we used the sliding window algorithm to extract features. We set a window frame of 32 frames and overlap at 50%.

Speaking is the action of an individual in moving their upper and lower lips. When a person speaks, the distance between the upper and lower lips becomes larger. In order to collect this feature, we used face point number 62 and 66, shown in Fig. 4. The distance between number 62 and 66 is the parameter. Then, we applied the sliding window algorithm. The window frame is set at 32 frames, and overlap is set at 50%.

3.1.2 Evaluation Protocol

By using the model, the tenfold random cross validation and leave-one-participant-out cross validation were applied. The tenfold random cross validation used a onefold random dataset as test data and the other ninefold random dataset as a training data. We used ten sets to perform cross validation. In the case of leave-one-participant-out cross validation, the test data includes one participant data and train data are used for all others. Since the amount of data relative to the labeled behaviors (*nodding* and *speaking*) is lesser than non-labeled behavior (*other*), we used down-sampling methods. The data for each are reduced to balance the actions of *nodding* or *speaking*. On the other hand, we also ran a prediction of online meeting micro-behavior analysis.

For online meetings, we classified *nodding* and *speaking*. The tenfold random split cross validation and leave-one-participant-out cross validation were applied.

3.1.3 Classification

For both offline and online meetings, the study classified *speaking* and *nodding* using deep learning models. For *speaking* detection the model works on top of TalkNet [85], and for *nodding* detection the model works on top of 6DRepNet [29].

3.2 Experimental Design

In order to evaluate the performance of the proposed approach, we prepared three meeting datasets. Note that our experiments do not include any EU citizens. Therefore, the General Data Protection Regulation (GDPR) does not apply to our recordings.

3.2.1 Offline Meeting Dataset A

Data were collected from 22 unique participants (18 males and 4 females) using multiple devices including 360 cameras (RICOH THETA V). Each recording was performed for 5 min. A total of 16 sets were collected. We removed the data of participants' gaze and the acceleration data of head movements, which are included in the original dataset. This dataset is publicly available [79].

3.2.2 Offline Meeting Dataset B

Data were collected from 12 unique participants (11 males and 1 female). Each recording was performed for 10 min. The combination of the entire dataset becomes 34 unique participants (29 males and 5 females). The total time collected is 150 min.

3.2.3 Online Meeting Dataset

For online meeting analysis, we collected data using Google Meet. Our main proposal is the offline meeting analysis, but we also performed online meeting analysis for discussions in future works. The data are collected from Kyushu University, Japan. Unique participants were six people in total, and each meeting is collected for 5 min. Seventeen sessions were collected. The total time collected amounts to 85 min.

3.3 Results

The study achieves to estimate *nodding* and *speaking* by the F1-score of 0.812 and 0.949 [12]. The model and application is publicly available.[1]

4 Knowledge Transfer with Engagement Detection

Engagement is another important factor in understanding successfulness of the knowledge transfer [21, 63, 69]. Due to the importance of engagement in learning effectiveness, several studies have examined ways to estimate student engagement during lectures [14]. Previous studies have used multiple sensors such as wristband [14] or seat sensor [23] to discover participants' engagement levels during offline lectures. However, due to the COVID-19 pandemic, offline meetings such as lectures, office meetings, job interviews, and musical events have expanded online [55]. Although participants see each other in an online meeting, they receive less information than in offline meetings [84]. For example, there is a limitation in computer screen size. Thus, only the upper body of a limited number of participants could be observed. Hence, the received nonverbal information, such as hand and body movements and gestures, is reduced. Furthermore, technical inputs such as a microphone, speaker, and computer screen are involved in verbal information. Limitations of these technical inputs sometimes lead to interruptions. For example, a faint voice may result in difficulties emphasizing speech. In the case of educational settings, such as e-learning, where many participants are involved in contrast to a few speakers, it is difficult for speakers or teachers to keep track of the participant's situations and technical and other difficulties. In such cases, an information gap between the speakers and listeners may encourage them to participate in other tasks.

This study [90] focused on participants' engagement levels in e-learning and educational settings. Students join online classes or meetings using desktop computers or laptops with webcam microphones. During these online sessions, students listen to the teacher or speaker and take notes on notebooks or devices. Our study aimed to quantify participants' meeting engagement levels. In particular, we focused on three points to make our quantification system more realistic. First, we only used a built-in camera on a personal computer instead of an advanced sensor. Second, we focused on identifying engagement levels close to real-life online meetings, where the participants perform natural actions such as speaking, taking notes, or readings. Third, we only used nonverbal information to safeguard privacy and avoid recording the context of information spoken during meetings. While considering three points, our contributions to this paper are as follows:

C1 **Best performed engagement level detection model**: Using a webcam as a sensor, we tertiarily classify high, middle, and low engagement levels with the

[1] https://github.com/humanophilic/MeetingPipe.

F1-score of 0.895. The accuracy was the best compared with previous work. We used the model of *MobileNetV2*, and the input data is only a facial image.

C2 **Implementation of the application**: We implement the engagement detection system called *EnGauge* using our own implemented deep learning model. The application shows the engagement level from 0 to 100 with the gauge-like interface. We also conducted a user study with the real-time system.

4.1 Deep Learning-Based Engagement Estimation

To preprocess the data, we utilized OpenCV, an open-source software library for performing machine vision tasks, to convert videos to images [8]. Specifically, we used a tool to convert videos to individual frame images with a frame rate of one frame per second. Images lacking clear faces were removed from the dataset, and we converted the remaining images to grayscale and applied image hashing to remove duplicates. We trained and evaluated four models for our classification task: VGG16, Xception, MobileNetV1, and MobileNetV2.

VGG16 [76]—In our study, we utilized the pre-trained VGG16 model [76] on the ImageNet dataset. For fine-tuning, a density of three and Softmax activation for the classifier were employed. Additionally, the top layer and the two layers above the model were fine-tuned.

Xception [13]—The model was trained on the ImageNet dataset. Next, global average pooling was incorporated, and a dense layer consisting of 512 units with ReLU activation was added. The classifier was activated using Softmax, and the top layer and blocks 13 and 14 of the model were fine-tuned.

MobileNetV1 [32]—The model was pre-trained on the ImageNet dataset, with pre-trained layers included for fine-tuning the size was reshaped to 1024. A single dense layer was utilized, and its weight was transferred to the final six layers. The activation function used was Softmax, and the last 23 layers were trainable.

MobileNetV2 [66]—The model, an updated version of MobileNetV1. For our implementation, we pre-trained it using the ImageNet dataset. The input layer modifies the image before passing it through two convolutional and fully connected layers. Finally, a Softmax layer with three neurons representing high, middle, and low classes was appended to the model.

4.2 Data Collection and Ground Truth Labeling

We used a built-in camera to record the video of each participant while conducting online meetings. We used the online group meeting platform Google Meet for the experiment. An example of the experimental setup is shown in Fig. 5. The frame rate was 30.00 frame per second, and the screen resolution was 1280 $\times$ 720 pixels. They removed the face mask and turned on the camera before the discussion. We captured

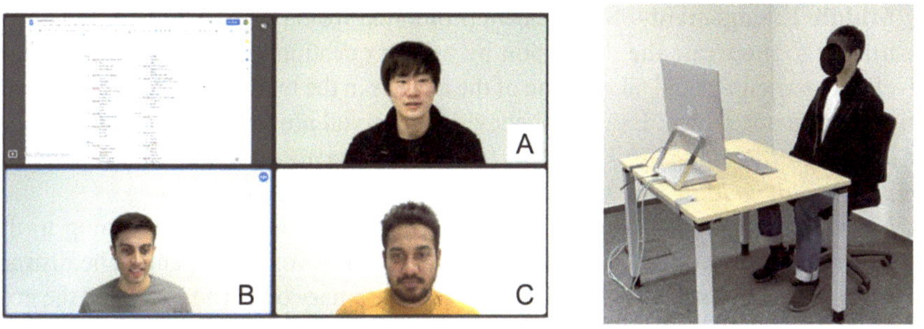

(a) Meeting video recording. (b) Experiment environment.

Fig. 5 Experimental setting with participants A, B, and C assigned to high, middle, and low engagement roles, respectively. User is in front of the computer with a webcam

the screen recording of each session but excluded voice information owing to privacy issues.

4.2.1 Participants

In this study, we recruit 24 participants (17 male and 7 female). Nationalities are South Asia, Southeast Asia, Eastern Europe, North Africa, and North America. Participants were between 22 and 36 years, and the average was 26. They were either university students or workers in Germany. Before the experiment, we obtained participants' general data protection regulation (GDPR) consent. The participants were allowed to opt out of the experiment at any time. At the end of the experiment, all participants who completed the experiment received an Amazon voucher of 10 euro.

4.2.2 Data Collection Procedure

In this study, we set up an experiment in which participants engage in online meetings and discussion-like sessions. The experiment was conducted in a secure and controlled manner. We designed an experiment with three participants per session to create a balanced dataset for engagement analysis. Each session lasted 5 min. In the experiment, each of the three participants was instructed to alternate between different engagement levels of behavior. The high, middle, and low engagement requirements are as follows:

High Engagement—Subjects are prohibited from doing distracting tasks and instructed to focus only on the discussion. The main task is to answer the question asked by the middle engagement-level role participant. Example behaviors observed are *answering question*, *listening to the questions*, *smiling*, *touching face*, *laughing*, *nodding*, *shaking head*, and *nodding and shaking heads*.

Middle Engagement—Subjects are prohibited from doing distracting tasks and instructed to moderate the discussion by asking questions to the high engagement level role participant and taking note of the answer in the text file document presented on the computer screen. Example behaviors observed are *asking questions*, *looking at a keyboard*, *typing on a keyboard*, *listen to the answer*, *reading notes*, *nodding*, *shaking head*, *nodding and shaking heads*, *touching face*, and *laughing*.

Low Engagement—Subjects work on a distraction task while listening to the conversations between high and middle engagement-level participants. The distraction task is to read a scientific article and write a summary of it. The paper and the note are on the same computer as the online video meeting. Example behaviors observed are *reading a paper*, *write a summary of a paper*, *ignore the conversation*, *looking at a keyboard*, *typing on a keyboard*, *touching face*, *stretching*, *head on hands*, *playing with hairs*, *yawing*, and *clean nose*.

The specific example behaviors for each engagement role are indicated, such as *asking questions*, *answering questions*, or *reading a paper*. Rather than using self-annotation [51], observer (additional annotator) annotation [51], survey [14], or using real-time notifications to get feedback from participant [4] to determine the level of engagement of participants, we came up with the idea of asking them to work in the role acting of each engagement level. This idea was adopted because of the following concerns. The questionnaire method could blur the definition of engagement levels due to individual differences in labeling, and the method of asking participants to provide real-time feedback on their engagement levels during the experiment would have distracted most participants from providing feedback and reduced their ability to concentrate, making uniform that data collection might not be possible. Therefore, the method used in this study was to have the participants participate in the meeting in the same role from the beginning to the end of the experiment. They repeated until two sets of the high, middle, and low engagement-level datasets were obtained from each participant. Hence, the experimental procedure consisted of six sessions discussing specific topics.

We prepared two topics for the meetings. The first one contained questions about the favors, such as "What is your favorite X?" where words, such as fast-food restaurant, movie, and sports, replaced "X." The second one contained questions about participants' current studies, such as "What do you think about your work or study?". Each group of participants was assigned an engagement role in a cyclic order. Thus, every participant was asked to perform the high, middle, and low engagement-level tasks twice. Hence, there was a total dataset of six sessions (30-min video) for each participant. It took roughly half a minute after the first recording session for participants to understand the assigned tasks clearly. Additionally, participants were joyful during the discussion in phase 1. Furthermore, we observed that a few participants were unhappy during the summary task because they needed more time to finish summarizing the paper within 5 min.

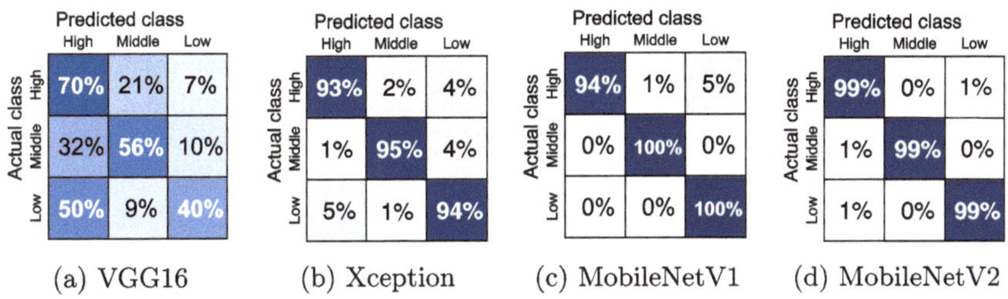

Fig. 6 Confusion matrix of deep learning-based engagement estimations

4.2.3 Deep Learning-Based Engagement Estimation

We present the results of the deep learning-based engagement estimation. When the experiment was conducted, it was found that the participants sometimes went outside the camera screen, making it impossible to track their faces. Therefore, all these images were removed as noise in this study. After removing the noise images, number of images with high, middle, and low engagement levels were 105,960, 149,004, and 105,088, respectively. Figure 6 shows the result of the confusion matrix for each transfer-learning model. The average F1-scores of VGG16, Xception, MobileNetV1, and MobileNetV2 were 0.549, 0.905, 0.917, and 0.923, respectively. As a result, MobileNetV2 achieved the highest classification rate in our case study.

4.2.4 Leave-One-Participant-Out Cross Validation of MobileNetV2

We apply the leave-one-participant-out approach to the best performed MobileNetV2 deep learning model. Figure 7 shows all participant results of the F1-score. The highest F1-score was 1.00 for five participants, and the lowest was 0.36. The mean F1-score of leave-one-participant-out cross validation was 0.895. Compared with the previous research [34], our model's ternary classification rate of engagement levels scored highest. Hence, the performance of the machine learning model is enough to be used for the primary model of the engagement-level classification application.

4.3 User Interface

The user interface of the application *Metacognition-EnGauge* [89] is presented in Fig. 8. The model predicts absolute-value percentages with regression of engagement levels from 0 to 100. The left side of the gauge represents low-level engagement. When the gauge bar goes to the right, it infers that the user's engagement level gets high. The gauge consists of three colors, blue, yellow, and red. These colors represent the classification level of low, middle, and high. The advantage of this user interface is that it triggers user motivation to use the system when participating in online meetings to increase the gauge, thus increasing engagement in a game-like manner. Users can benefit from understanding their engagement level using color and numeric percentage information.

We also make the visualization with heatmap using Grad-CAM [70] as explained in Fig. 8. The heatmap shows the important feature inside the input facial image. The red color represents a vital area feature for each engagement detection. On the other hand, the blue area represents an area of feature with a weak weight for detection. As shown in each image, the recognition model recognizes the area around a person's face as important information for classification. The mouth is more important than the eyes, especially in middle engagement-level detection.

4.3.1 User Study

We recruited 18 participants (4 females, 13 males, and 1 prefer not to say). Nationalities are 10 Japanese, 6 Indians, 1 German, and 1 Chilean. Participants were between 23 and 31 years old, and the mean age was 26 years old. They are either workers or university students in Japan and Germany. We obtained consent from all participants before the experiment. For participants in Germany, including general data protection regulation (GDPR). All participants were allowed to opt out of the experiment at anytime.

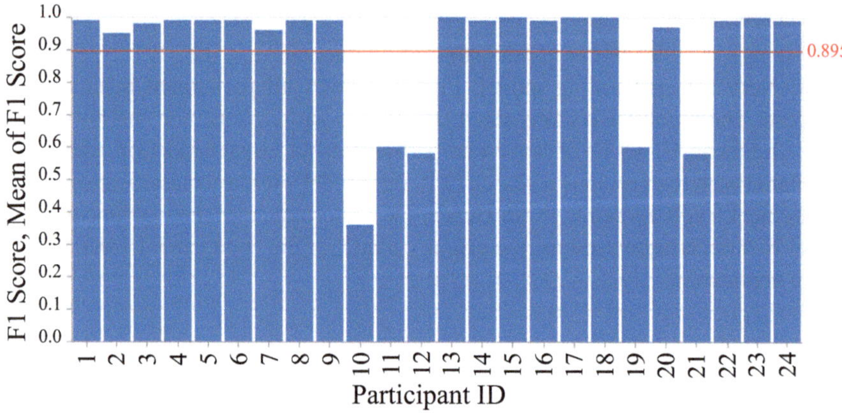

Fig. 7 F1-score of leave-one-participant-out cross validation for MobileNetV2

4.3.2 Experimental Design

In this study, we request participants to join from anywhere in remote conditions. In each experiment, three participants are asked to be in a group per session. In each session, we asked the group to discuss for 10 min. We asked participants to join under three different online meeting conditions: (C-1) Online meeting without intervention. (C-2) Online meeting with self-metacognition augmentation intervention. (C-3) Online meeting with group-metacognition augmentation intervention.

For the group discussion, we asked participants to work on *would you rather questions*. Example topics are as follows: (T-A) Would you rather live in a hot or cold country? (T-B) Would you rather choose to gain physical strength or brain intelligence augmentation? (T-C) Would you rather go to the future or the past?

4.4 Result

4.4.1 RQ1: Does Self-metacognition Augmentation of Engagement Levels Support the Participants' Engagement in the Meetings?

The answer to RQ1, Fig. 9 shows that self-metacognition augmentation performs an average engagement level during online meetings higher than without the interven-

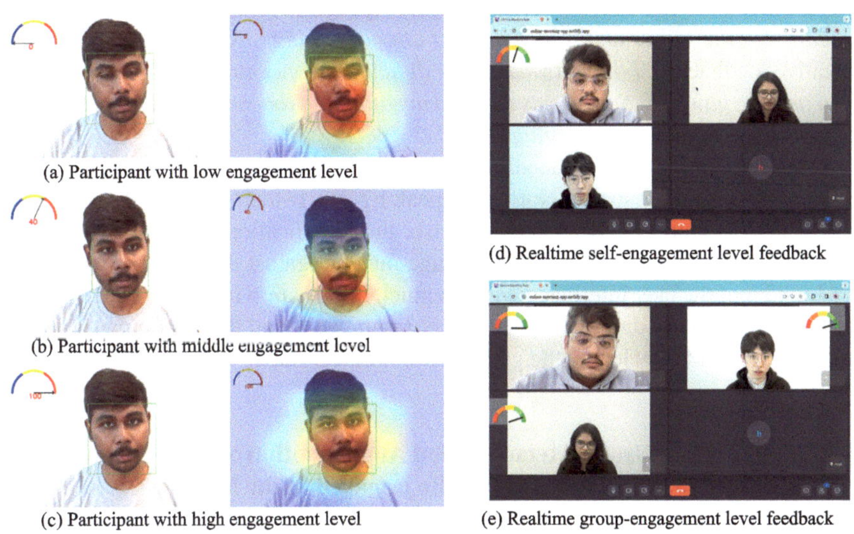

(a) Participant with low engagement level

(b) Participant with middle engagement level

(c) Participant with high engagement level

(d) Realtime self-engagement level feedback

(e) Realtime group-engagement level feedback

Fig. 8 User interface of the Metacognition-EnGauge application [89]. Engagement levels are displayed in the form of a gauge. As the gauge moves to the right, it indicates that the user is at a high level of engagement. The left image in each **a**–**c** shows a raw image, and the right image shows a heatmap after applying Grad-CAM [70]. **d**, **e** shows the real-time self-group engagement feedback interface while participants conduct online meetings

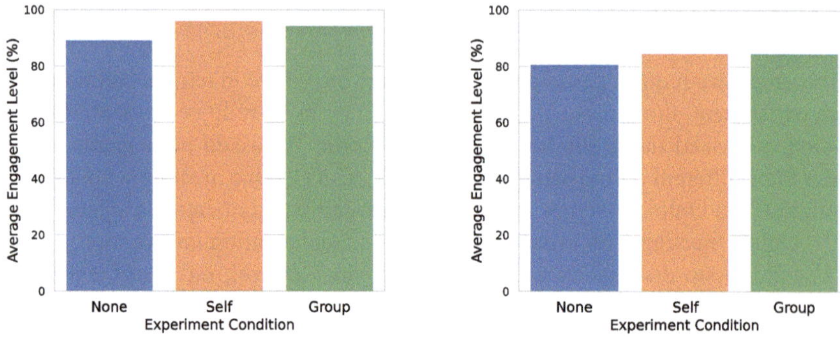

(a) Estimated by EnGauge deep-learning model.

(b) Calculate from Likert scale in post-survey (Q3).

Fig. 9 Comparison of average engagement level of participants in each different intervention conditions. Overall average engagement for all participants is highest for self-metacognition augmentation intervention. The participant preference is on group-metacognition augmentation intervention

tion. Deep-learning and subjective post-survey feedback were estimated to be higher than no intervention.

Looking at the post-survey, in Q7, participants mentioned some positive feedbacks. "*I tried hard to be more engaged.*" "*I felt that I responded more actively and could express my opinions appropriately while still listening to others' opinions.*" "*I was motivated to increase the gauge once the gauge went down.*" "*I tried to speak when I saw the gauge and realized that I am not talking.*" Also, we received some negative feedbacks. "*I think it was a little difficult to concentrate on both the discussion and the gauge.*" "*Sometimes I moved my attention too much to the gauge.*" "*No, since the gauge was not changing much.*"

Concerning the positive feedbacks, the intervention can change behavior to encourage people to speak. Not only speaking but listening behavior is actively changed by nudging active response. Also, the gamification perspective has been reported as motivated to increase the gauge meter. Against the negative feedbacks, we found that the user interface gives too much information for participants to focus on two things. Also, due to the experiment setup, we found that participants always tried actively to talk. Hence, the gauge did not move much.

4.4.2 RQ2: Does Group-Metacognition Augmentation of Engagement Levels Support Participant to Be Engaged in the Meetings?

The answer to RQ2, Fig. 9 shows that group-metacognition augmentation performs an average engagement level during online meetings higher than without the intervention. Deep-learning and subjective post-survey feedback were estimated to be higher than no intervention.

Looking at the post-survey, in Q7, participants mentioned some positive feedbacks. "*I checked other people's engagement carefully.*" "*I paid attention to the utterance rate of other people.*" "*I paid attention about who is most engaged at that time, and I tried to be engaged.*" "*When other people's gauge decrease, I tried to change the way to talk and describe.*" "*I am a person whom actively behave to show the others that I am highly engaged. With the system, I became more careful to keep the gauge higher.*" "*I carefully check when does the other people gets low engagement.*" Also, we received some negative feedbacks. "*No, because we were all engaged.*" "*No it was like regular conversation.*"

According to the positive feedback, group-metacognition augmentation performs significantly in behavior change. For example, participants carefully check whether they are speaking too much and other people less. Another thing mentioned is that participants actively tried to improve their ways of talking by looking at the other's engagement. However, some participants did not think the intervention was powerful since they had no change in behavior with the gauge.

4.4.3 RQ3: Do Participants Prefer None, Self, or Group-Metacognition Augmentation Intervention in the Online Meetings?

In the answer to RQ3, we found that most participants prefer group-metacognition augmentation. As a result, 11 participants voted for group-metacognition augmentation and 7 participants prefer self-metacognition augmentation as their preference.

Looking at the result of the quantitative feedback in Fig. 9, the average engagement is higher for the self-metacognition augmentation. The subjective feedback had the same average engagement for self and group. It means that subjective engagement can be improved using group-metacognition augmentation. However, self-metacognition augmentation should also be important according to the quantitative result.

Also, the participant gave feedback that "*I am a shy person, so it was easier for me to focus only on myself. I felt that open-minded people would prefer a system like condition 3 that allows them to understand what is happening around them.*" The comment supports our direction that the interface should be personalized according to the participant in the online meeting to augment or support their communication skills.

4.5 Conclusion

This study verified how to implement the engagement recognition model during communication and the effectiveness of real-time augmentation of self-and-group engagement-level understanding using *Metacogniton-EnGauge*. The study shows that self-and-group engagement level feedback by gauge interface improves engagements throughout the meetings. The average engagement through the meeting performed best for self-metacognition augmentation. According to the survey, we found that most participants prefer group-metacognition augmentation.

5 Knowledge Transfer with Avatars

In the twenty-first century, the convergence of technology and education has led to innovative methods for knowledge transfer. One such innovation is the use of avatars—digital representations of individuals or AI agents—in educational contexts. Avatars offer a unique interface that bridges the gap between humans and machines, providing interactive, personalized, and engaging learning experiences.

These digital entities can simulate real-life interactions, allowing learners to engage in scenarios that enhance understanding and retention of complex concepts. Moreover, avatars can adapt to individual learning styles, offering tailored feedback and support that traditional methods often lack. As a result, they not only foster a deeper connection between the learner and the material but also promote a sense of agency and motivation in the learning process. Additionally, the integration of avatars can facilitate collaborative learning environments, where students can work together in virtual spaces, sharing ideas and resources while receiving guidance from their digital counterparts.

This chapter delves into the role of avatars in knowledge transfer. We will explore how avatars enhance learning, their applications in various educational settings, the benefits and challenges they present, and their potential impact on the future of education. By examining current research and real-world examples, we aim to provide a comprehensive understanding accessible to both scientists and non-computer science readers.

5.1 Understanding Avatars in Knowledge Transfer

5.1.1 Definition of Avatars

An avatar can be defined as a digital representation or persona that serves to embody either a user or an AI agent operating within the expansive realm of a virtual environment, encapsulating the essence of the individual or entity it portrays.

These avatars can vary significantly in complexity and design, with some being as simplistic as basic 2D icons or images, while others can be elaborately crafted 3D models that closely imitate the appearance and behavioral characteristics of real human beings.

In the context of educational environments, avatars play a crucial role by acting as a dynamic medium through which learners engage and interact not only with the educational content but also with instructors and their fellow peers, thereby enriching the overall learning experience. This interaction fosters a sense of community and collaboration, essential elements for effective learning, as students can express themselves and share ideas in a more personalized manner [20].

5.1.2 Types of Avatars in Education

These avatars can be categorized into several types, including static avatars, animated avatars, and fully interactive avatars, each serving different purposes and enhancing the learning experience in unique ways. Static avatars often serve as simple representations of users, providing a basic visual identity without much movement or interaction, while animated avatars introduce a level of dynamism that can make interactions feel more engaging and livelier.

Fully interactive avatars take this a step further by allowing real-time communication and feedback, enabling students to engage in immersive learning experiences that mimic face-to-face interactions. These interactive avatars can also adapt to individual learning styles, offering personalized feedback and support that cater to each student's unique needs. This adaptability not only fosters a deeper understanding of the material but also encourages students to take an active role in their learning journey, ultimately leading to improved outcomes and greater retention of knowledge. Moreover, the integration of gamification elements within these platforms can further enhance motivation, as students are rewarded for their progress and achievements, creating a more enjoyable and effective learning environment [87].

5.1.3 Evolution of Avatars in Education

The concept of avatars in education has evolved significantly with advancements in technology: from simple static images to dynamic, interactive representations that can mimic human behavior and emotions. This evolution has enhanced the learning experience, making it more engaging and personalized for students. As a result, educators are increasingly integrating these sophisticated avatars into their curricula, fostering a more immersive and supportive learning environment.

In the initial stages, avatars were utilized within rudimentary educational games and simulations, delivering fundamental levels of interaction. As avatars continue to evolve, their integration into educational frameworks poses both opportunities and challenges that warrant further exploration. For instance, while interactive avatars can significantly enhance engagement and adaptability in learning environments, the reliance on technology may inadvertently lead to disparities among students who have varying levels of access to these resources. This digital divide could hinder the effectiveness of avatar-mediated education, especially in underserved communities where technological infrastructure is lacking [88]. The incorporation of artificial intelligence has facilitated avatars in the processing of intricate linguistic constructs, showcasing adaptive behaviors, and rendering personalized educational experiences. Virtual Reality (VR) and Augmented Reality (AR): Contemporary avatars function within immersive VR and AR ecosystems, thereby augmenting both realism and user engagement. These advancements have transformed the educational landscape, allowing for more dynamic interactions and tailored learning pathways that cater to individual student needs [94].

5.2 *The Role of Avatars in Facilitating Knowledge Transfer*

Avatars enhance personalization in learning by offering customized feedback and adapting to the unique learning styles of each student, thereby fostering a more effective educational environment. Interactive avatars can serve as subject matter experts, responding to student queries and providing additional information. These avatars utilize artificial intelligence to tailor responses based on a student's profile and learning goals, offering personalized support and tracking progress [78]. Avatars can adjust their teaching methods to suit visual, auditory, or kinesthetic learners. This adaptability not only improves comprehension but also encourages greater student participation and motivation, as learners feel more connected to the material presented.

5.2.1 Engagement and Motivation

Avatars increase engagement by making learning interactive and enjoyable by incorporating gamified elements and personalized feedback, which fosters a sense of achievement and encourages learners to actively participate in their educational journey [1].

- Interactive Dialogues: Learners are provided with the unique opportunity to engage in conversations with digital avatars, which significantly enhances and invigorates the overall learning experience by making it not only more interactive but also more engaging and dynamic.
- Gamification Elements: Avatars can introduce game-like features such as rewards, challenges, and progress tracking. These elements not only motivate learners but also create a competitive yet supportive environment that encourages continuous improvement and exploration of language skills.
- Emotional Connection: Human-like avatars can express emotions, helping learners feel more connected. This emotional connection fosters a sense of belonging, making learners more likely to persist in their studies and take risks in their language use. This connection can lead to increased confidence, as learners feel understood and supported in their journey, ultimately enhancing their ability to communicate effectively.

Example: In a comprehensive math tutoring application designed to enhance the learning experience, an animated avatar joyfully celebrates alongside the learner as they successfully solve a particularly challenging mathematical problem, thereby offering a form of positive reinforcement that encourages continued engagement and motivation in their studies.

5.2.2 Accessibility and Convenience

Avatars make education more accessible; they can be tailored to meet diverse learning needs, allowing students from various backgrounds and abilities to engage with content in a way that resonates with them. This personalization fosters an inclusive environment where every learner can thrive, breaking down barriers that may have previously hindered their educational progress [75].

- **24/7 Availability**: Learners can access avatar-guided learning at any time, accommodating different schedules. This flexibility ensures that students can pursue their studies at their own pace, leading to a more personalized and effective learning experience.
- **Remote Learning**: Avatars enable learning without geographical constraints, reaching students in remote or underserved areas. This opens up opportunities for collaboration and knowledge sharing across borders, enriching the educational landscape and fostering a global community of learners.
- **Multilingual Support**: Avatars can communicate in multiple languages, catering to a global audience. This inclusivity not only enhances understanding but also promotes cultural exchange, allowing learners to appreciate diverse perspectives and ideas.

Example: An innovative agricultural training program has been specifically designed to utilize advanced avatars that simulate real-life scenarios in order to effectively educate farmers residing in remote rural areas about the importance and implementation of sustainable farming practices, which are conveniently accessible through a variety of mobile devices that are commonly used in today's digital age.

5.3 Avatars as Personalized Learning Assistants

5.3.1 Monitoring Progress

Avatars track learner performance as they analyze data to identify strengths and weaknesses, offering tailored feedback that helps guide learners on their educational journey [93].

- **Assessment Tools**: They administer quizzes and assignments to evaluate understanding. They also provide insights into areas needing improvement, ensuring that each learner receives a customized experience that fosters growth and development.

- **Performance Analytics**: Avatars analyze data to identify trends, strengths, and areas needing improvement. They generate reports that can be shared with educators and parents, facilitating a collaborative approach to learning and ensuring that support is aligned with each learner's unique needs.
- **Adaptive Learning Paths**: Based on performance, avatars adjust the curriculum to optimize learning outcomes. They also suggest resources and strategies tailored to individual learning styles, enhancing engagement and motivation throughout the educational process.

Example: A science education application is designed in such a way that it includes an engaging avatar, which can recognize when a student is experiencing challenges or difficulties with various concepts related to biology and, as a result, it promptly adjusts its focus to deliver supplementary resources and targeted support specifically in that particular area of study.

5.3.2 Adapting Content

Avatars revolutionize content engagement by captivating learner interest; they assess personal progress and preferences, adjusting lessons to accommodate diverse skill levels and learning styles. They suggest topics or materials based on the learner's preferences. This personalized approach not only enhances motivation but also fosters a deeper understanding of the material, as learners feel more connected to the content being presented.

Avatars modify the complexity of content to match the learner's skill level. This dynamic adjustment ensures that learners are neither overwhelmed nor underchallenged, promoting a balanced and effective educational experience [16].

5.4 Examples of Real-World Usage of LLM-Based Avatars in Education

There are many real-world examples of using AI Avatars, but all of them are still in early stages but require further exploration and development to fully realize their potential. Some examples are as follows:

- Khanmigo, an AI-powered teaching assistant developed by Khan Academy, which uses text-based avatars to provide personalized tutoring and support to students, enhancing their learning experience through interactive and engaging methods.
- Berlitz offers language learning through immersive experiences with avatars that simulate real-life conversations, allowing learners to practice their skills in a dynamic environment.
- Basingstoke College of Technology integrated Avatars for their English for Speakers of Other Languages program, enabling students to engage in conversational

practice and receive instant feedback, which significantly boosts their confidence and proficiency.

These innovative applications highlight the versatility of avatars in education, paving the way for more interactive and personalized learning experiences across various subjects and age groups.

5.5 *Technical Feasibility Study at DFKI*

At DFKI we conducted a feasibility study to show that with today's technical possibilities it is possible to create a human-like real-time avatar with the use of different tools and platforms. The used tools where a web-based application which uses speech recognition (Whisper), a RAG system to process the user input based on a generative multi-user agent system which uses different tools as LLMs (ChatGPT, Mistral, Llama), and a Vector Database (ChromaDB) for the retrieval and generation. The answer was then sent to a real-time avatar (HeyGen) via a streaming API, allowing for seamless interaction and a more immersive user experience.

The RAG system contained information about the DFKI as text and images and showed the output parallel to the video avatar's output. The users could speak to the avatar in 40 different languages and the system answered in real time, adapting to their language preferences while maintaining context and relevance in the conversation (Fig. 10).

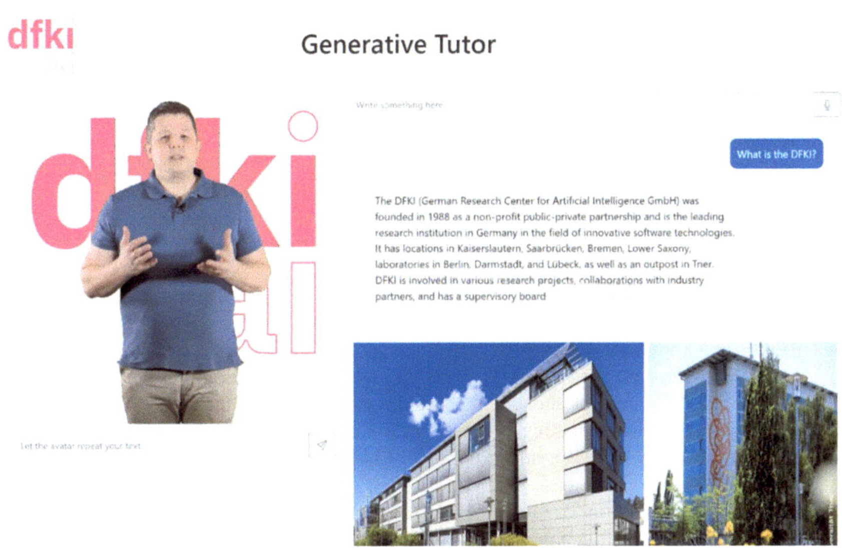

Fig. 10 DFKI avatar tour

With this study we showed that human real-time avatars are technically feasible but that there are still some challenges to overcome, like latency and synchronization issues, that can affect the fluidity of interactions. Further research is needed to enhance the responsiveness and accuracy of these avatars, ensuring they can effectively mimic human nuances in conversation because otherwise user doesn't feel comfortable communicating with the avatar (uncanny valley effect).

5.6 Conclusion

Avatars have emerged as transformative instruments in the landscape of knowledge transfer, revolutionizing the way educational experiences are delivered and experienced. These digital representations are not just faceless entities; they provide a personalized touch that enhances engagement, making learning not only more effective but also more enjoyable for users of all ages and backgrounds. By simulating real human interaction, avatars serve as a bridge between advanced technology and the essential elements of human connection, thereby enriching the educational process. Despite their promising capabilities, the integration of avatars in educational settings is not without its challenges. Concerns surrounding privacy, inherent biases in programming, and issues related to accessibility for individuals with disabilities must be addressed to ensure that these tools serve all learners equitably. However, the potential advantages of employing avatars in education are substantial, offering innovative ways to present information, facilitate discussions, and provide personalized feedback.

References

1. Abu Samah, L., Ismail, H.A., Hasan, M.K.: The effectiveness of gamification for students' engagement in technical and vocational education and training. Int. J. Adv. Comput. Sci. Appl. **13**(9), 172–179 (2022). https://doi.org/10.14569/ijacsa.2022.0130920
2. Allen, J.A., Rogelberg, S.G., Scott, J.C.: Mind your meetings: improve your organization's effectiveness one meeting at a time. Qual. Prog. **41**, 48–52 (2008)
3. Aseniero, B.A., Constantinides, M., Joglekar, S., Zhou, K., Quercia, D.: MeetCues: supporting online meetings experience. In: 2020 IEEE Visualization Conference (VIS), pp. 236–240. IEEE (2020).https://doi.org/10.1109/VIS47514.2020.00054
4. Babaei, E., Srivastava, N., Newn, J., Zhou, Q., Dingler, T., Velloso, E.: Faces of focus: a study on the facial cues of attentional states. In: Proceedings of the 2020 CHI Conference on Human Factors in Computing Systems, pp. 1–13. Association for Computing Machinery, New York, NY, USA (2020). https://doi.org/10.1145/3313831.3376566. https://doi.org/10.1145/3313831.3376566
5. Baltrušaitis, T., Robinson, P., Morency, L.P.: OpenFace: an open source facial behavior analysis toolkit. In: 2016 IEEE Winter Conference on Applications of Computer Vision (WACV), pp. 1–10. IEEE (2016). https://doi.org/10.1109/WACV.2016.7477553
6. Bello, H., Zhou, B., Suh, S., Lukowicz, P.: MoCapaci: Posture and gesture detection in loose garments using textile cables as capacitive antennas. In: Proceedings of the 2021 ACM Inter-

national Symposium on Wearable Computers, pp. 78–83. Association for Computing Machinery, New York, NY, USA (2021). https://doi.org/10.1145/3460421.3480418. https://doi.org/10.1145/3460421.3480418
7. Bohannon, L.S., Herbert, A.M., Pelz, J.B., Rantanen, E.M.: Eye contact and video-mediated communication: a review. Displays **34**(2), 177–185 (2013)
8. Bradski, G.: The opencv library. Dr. Dobb's J. Softw. Tools Prof. Program. **25**(11), 120–123 (2000)
9. Bridges, J.: Gendering metapragmatics in online discourse: "mansplaining man gonna mansplain...". Discourse, Context Med. **20**, 94–102 (2017)
10. Carletta, J., Ashby, S., Bourban, S., Flynn, M., Guillemot, M., Hain, T., Kadlec, J., Karaiskos, V., Kraaij, W., Kronenthal, M., Lathoud, G., Lincoln, M., Lisowska, A., McCowan, I., Post, W., Reidsma, D., Wellner, P.: The AMI meeting corpus: a pre-announcement. In: Machine Learning for Multimodal Interaction, pp. 26–39. Springer Berlin Heidelberg (2006). https://doi.org/10.1007/11677482_3
11. Centorrino, S., Djemai, E., Hopfensitz, A., Milinski, M., Seabright, P.: Honest signaling in trust interactions: smiles rated as genuine induce trust and signal higher earning opportunities. Evol. Hum. Behav. **36**(1), 8–16 (2015)
12. Chen, C., Arakawa, Y., Watanabe, K., Ishimaru, S.: Quantitative evaluation system for online meetings based on multimodal microbehavior analysis. Sens. Mater. **34**, 1–14 (2022)
13. Chollet, F.: Xception: Deep learning with depthwise separable convolutions. In: Proceedings of the IEEE Conference on Computer Vision and Pattern Recognition, pp. 1251–1258 (2017)
14. Di Lascio, E., Gashi, S., Santini, S.: Unobtrusive assessment of students' emotional engagement during lectures using electrodermal activity sensors. Proc. ACM Interact. Mob. Wearable Ubiquit. Technol. **2**(3), 103:1–103:21 (2018). https://doi.org/10.1145/3264913. https://doi.org/10.1145/3264913
15. DiSalvo, B., Bandaru, D., Wang, Q., Li, H., Plötz, T.: Reading the room: automated, momentary assessment of student engagement in the classroom: are we there yet? Proc. ACM Interact. Mob. Wearable Ubiquit. Technol. **6**(3), 112:1–112:26 (2022). https://doi.org/10.1145/3550328. https://doi.org/10.1145/3550328
16. Duckett, I.: Personalized Learning and Vocational Education and Training, pp. 391–396. Elsevier (2010). https://doi.org/10.1016/B978-0-08-044894-7.00789-2
17. Edwards, G.J., Lanitis, A., Taylor, C.J., Cootes, T.: Statistical models of face images—improving specificity. Image Vis. Comput. **16**, 203–211 (1998). https://api.semanticscholar.org/CorpusID:807316
18. Ekman, P., Friesen, W.V.: The repertoire of nonverbal behavior: categories, origins, usage, and coding. Semiotica **1**(1), 49–98 (1969). https://doi.org/10.1515/semi.1969.1.1.49. https://doi.org/10.1515/semi.1969.1.1.49
19. Ekman, P., Friesen, W.V.: Facial action coding system. Environ. Psychol. Nonverbal Behav. (1978)
20. Falloon, G.: Using avatars and virtual environments in learning: what do they have to offer? Br. J. Edu. Technol. **41**(1), 108–122 (2010). https://doi.org/10.1111/j.1467-8535.2009.00991.x
21. Freeman, S., Eddy, S.L., McDonough, M., Smith, M.K., Okoroafor, N., Jordt, H., Wenderoth, M.P.: Active learning increases student performance in science, engineering, and mathematics. Proc. Natl. Acad. Sci. **111**(23), 8410–8415 (2014)
22. Fu, Y., Hospedales, T.M., Xiang, T., Xiong, J., Gong, S., Wang, Y., Yao, Y.: Robust subjective visual property prediction from crowdsourced pairwise labels. IEEE Trans. Pattern Anal. Mach. Intell. (2016)
23. Gao, N., Rahaman, M.S., Shao, W., Ji, K., Salim, F.D.: Individual and group-wise classroom seating experience: effects on student engagement in different courses. Proc. ACM Interact. Mob. Wearable Ubiquit. Technol. **6**(3), 115:1–115:23 (2022). https://doi.org/10.1145/3550335. https://doi.org/10.1145/3550335
24. Gashi, S., Di Lascio, E., Santini, S.: Using unobtrusive wearable sensors to measure the physiological synchrony between presenters and audience members. Proc. ACM Interact. Mob. Wearable Ubiquit. Technol. **3**(1), 13:1–13:19 (2019). https://doi.org/10.1145/3314400. https://doi.org/10.1145/3314400

25. Geng, X., Zhou, Z.H., Smith-Miles, K.: Automatic age estimation based on facial aging patterns. IEEE Trans. Pattern Anal. Mach. Intell. **29**, 2234–2240 (2007). https://api.semanticscholar.org/CorpusID:8346560
26. Gu, Z., Meng, F., Farrukh, M.: Mapping the research on knowledge transfer: a scientometrics approach. IEEE Access **9**, 34647–34659 (2021)
27. Haliburton, L., Schött, S.Y., Hirsch, L., Welsch, R., Schmidt, A.: Feeling the temperature of the room: unobtrusive thermal display of engagement during group communication. Proc. ACM Interact. Mob. Wearable Ubiquit. Technol. **7**(1), 1–21 (2023). https://doi.org/10.1145/3580820. https://doi.org/10.1145/3580820
28. Hebda, B., Kryjak, T.: A compact deep convolutional neural network architecture for video based age and gender estimation. In: 2016 Federated Conference on Computer Science and Information Systems (FedCSIS), pp. 787–790. IEEE (2016)
29. Hempel, T., Abdelrahman, A.A., Al-Hamadi, A.: 6D rotation representation for unconstrained head pose estimation. In: 2022 IEEE International Conference on Image Processing (ICIP), pp. 2496–2500. IEEE (2022). https://doi.org/10.1109/ICIP46576.2022.9897219
30. Hernandez, J., Riobo, I., Rozga, A., Abowd, G.D., Picard, R.W.: Using electrodermal activity to recognize ease of engagement in children during social interactions. In: Proceedings of the 2014 ACM International Joint Conference on Pervasive and Ubiquitous Computing, pp. 307–317. Association for Computing Machinery, New York, NY, USA (2014). https://doi.org/10.1145/2632048.2636065. https://doi.org/10.1145/2632048.2636065
31. Holstein, K., Hong, G., Tegene, M., McLaren, B.M., Aleven, V.: The classroom as a dashboard: co-designing wearable cognitive augmentation for K-12 teachers. In: Proceedings of the 8th International Conference on Learning Analytics and Knowledge, pp. 79–88. Association for Computing Machinery, New York, NY, USA (2018). https://doi.org/10.1145/3170358.3170377, https://doi.org/10.1145/3170358.3170377
32. Howard, A.G., Zhu, M., Chen, B., Kalenichenko, D., Wang, W., Weyand, T., Andreetto, M., Adam, H.: Mobilenets: efficient convolutional neural networks for mobile vision applications (2017). arXiv preprint arXiv:1704.04861
33. Huerta, I., Fernández, C., Segura, C., Hernando, J., Prati, A.: A deep analysis on age estimation. Pattern Recognit. Lett. **68**, 239–249 (2015). https://doi.org/10.1016/j.patrec.2015.06.006. https://www.sciencedirect.com/science/article/pii/S0167865515001683
34. Huynh, S., Kim, S., Ko, J., Balan, R.K., Lee, Y.: EngageMon: multi-modal engagement sensing for mobile games. Proc. ACM Interact. Mob. Wearable Ubiquit. Technol. **2**(1), 13:1–13:27 (2018). https://doi.org/10.1145/3191745. https://doi.org/10.1145/3191745
35. Janin, A.L., Baron, D., Edwards, J., Ellis, D.P.W., Gelbart, D., Morgan, N., Peskin, B., Pfau, T., Shriberg, E., Stolcke, A., Wooters, C.: The ICSI meeting corpus. In: 2003 IEEE International Conference on Acoustics, Speech, and Signal Processing (ICASSP 2003), vol. 1, pp. I–I. IEEE (2003)
36. Karremans, J.C., Lange, P.A.M.: Forgiveness in personal relationships: its malleability and powerful consequences. Eur. Rev. Soc. Psychol. **19**(1), 202–241 (2008)
37. Kauffeld, S., Lehmann-Willenbrock, N.: Meetings matter: effects of team meetings on team and organizational success. Small Group Res. **43**(2), 130–158 (2012)
38. Kawamura, R., Shirai, S., Aizadeh, M., Takemura, N., Nagahara, H.: Estimation of wakefulness in video-based lectures based on multimodal data fusion. In: Adjunct Proceedings of the 2020 ACM International Joint Conference on Pervasive and Ubiquitous Computing and Proceedings of the 2020 ACM International Symposium on Wearable Computers, pp. 50–53. Association for Computing Machinery, New York, NY, USA (2020). https://doi.org/10.1145/3410530.3414386. https://doi.org/10.1145/3410530.3414386
39. Kita, S., Ide, S.: Nodding, Aizuchi, and final particles in Japanese conversation: how conversation reflects the ideology of communication and social relationships. J. Pragmat. **39**(7), 1242–1254 (2007)
40. Knowlton, G.E., Larkin, K.T.: The influence of voice volume, pitch, and speech rate on progressive relaxation training: application of methods from speech pathology and audiology. Appl. Psychophysiol. Biofeedback **31**, 173–185 (2006). https://api.semanticscholar.org/CorpusID:17505226

41. Kuttal, S.K., Ong, B., Kwasny, K., Robe, P.: Trade-offs for substituting a human with an agent in a pair programming context: the good, the bad, and the ugly. In: Proceedings of the 2021 CHI Conference on Human Factors in Computing Systems, pp. 1–20. Association for Computing Machinery, New York, NY, USA (2021). https://doi.org/10.1145/3411764.3445659. https://doi.org/10.1145/3411764.3445659
42. Kytö, M., Hirskyj-Douglas, I., McGookin, D.: From strangers to friends: augmenting face-to-face interactions with faceted digital self-presentations. In: Proceedings of the Augmented Humans International Conference 2021, pp. 192–203. Association for Computing Machinery, New York, NY, USA (2021). https://doi.org/10.1145/3458709.3458954. https://doi.org/10.1145/3458709.3458954
43. Lanitis, A.: Comparative evaluation of automatic age-progression methodologies. EURASIP J. Appl. Signal Process. (2008)
44. Lehmann-Willenbrock, N., Allen, J.A., Meinecke, A.L.: Observing culture: differences in U.S.-American and German team meeting behaviors. Group Process. Intergroup Relat. **17**(2), 252–271 (2014). https://doi.org/10.1177/1368430213497066
45. Lübstorf, S., Lehmann-Willenbrock, N.: Are meetings really just another stressor? the relevance of team meetings for individual well-being, vol. 20, pp. 47–69. Emerald Publishing Limited (2020). https://doi.org/10.1108/S1534-085620200000020003
46. Matsuyama, Y., Akiba, I., Fujie, S., Kobayashi, T.: Four-participant group conversation: a facilitation robot controlling engagement density as the fourth participant. Comput. Speech Lang. **33**(1), 1–24 (2015). https://doi.org/10.1016/j.csl.2014.12.001
47. Mauriello, L.M., Johnson, S.S., Prochaska, J.M.: Meeting patients where they are at: Using a stage approach to facilitate engagement, pp. 25–44. Springer International Publishing (2017). https://doi.org/10.1007/978-3-319-49206-3_3
48. McComas, K., Trumbo, C., Besley, J.: Public meetings about suspected cancer clusters: the impact of voice, interactional justice, and risk perception on attendees' attitudes in six communities. J. Health Commun. **12**, 527–549 (2007). https://doi.org/10.1080/10810730701508245
49. McDorman, T.: Implementing existing tools: turning words into actions–decision-making processes of regional fisheries management organisations (RFMO). Int. J. Mar. Coast. Law **20**(3), 423–457 (2005). https://doi.org/10.1163/157180805775098595. https://brill.com/view/journals/estu/20/3/article-p423_4.xml
50. Mehrabian, A.: Significance of posture and position in the communication of attitude and status relationships. Psychol. Bull. **71**(5), 359–372 (1969)
51. Mohamad, N.O., Dras, M., Hamey, L., Richards, D., Wan, S., Paris, C.: Automatic recognition of student engagement using deep learning and facial expression. In: Brefeld, U., Fromont, E., Hotho, A., Knobbe, A., Maathuis, M., Robardet, C. (eds.) Machine Learning and Knowledge Discovery in Databases, pp. 273–289. Springer International Publishing (2020)
52. Morency, L.P., Sidner, C., Lee, C., Darrell, T.: Head gestures for perceptual interfaces: the role of context in improving recognition. Artif. Intell. **171**(8–9), 568–585 (2007)
53. Mroz, J.E., Allen, J.A., Verhoeven, D.C., Shuffler, M.L.: Do we really need another meeting? the science of workplace meetings. Curr. Dir. Psychol. Sci. **27**, 484–491 (2018)
54. Nagano, K., Arakawa, Y., Yasumoto, K.: TrackThink: A tool for tracking a thought process on web search. In: Proceedings of the 2017 ACM International Joint Conference on Pervasive and Ubiquitous Computing and Proceedings of the 2017 ACM International Symposium on Wearable Computers, pp. 681–687. Association for Computing Machinery, New York, NY, USA (2017). https://doi.org/10.1145/3123024.3129267. https://doi.org/10.1145/3123024.3129267
55. Nichols, B.H., Caplow, S., Franzen, R.L., McClain, L.R., Pennisi, L., Tarlton, J.L.: Pandemic shift: meeting the challenges of moving post-secondary environmental education online. Environ. Educ. Res. **28**(1), 1–17 (2022). https://doi.org/10.1080/13504622.2021.2007220
56. Niwa, M., Masai, K., Yoshida, S., Sugimoto, M.: Investigating effects of facial self-similarity levels on the impression of virtual agents in serious/non-serious contexts. In: Proceedings of the Augmented Humans International Conference 2023, pp. 221–230. Association for Computing Machinery, New York, NY, USA (2023). https://doi.org/10.1145/3582700.3582721. https://doi.org/10.1145/3582700.3582721

57. Ohnishi, A., Murao, K., Terada, T., Tsukamoto, M.: A method for structuring meeting logs using wearable sensors. Internet of Things **5**, 140–152 (2019). https://doi.org/10.1016/j.iot.2019.01.005. https://www.sciencedirect.com/science/article/pii/S2542660518301677
58. Pham, H.H., Salmane, H., Khoudour, L., Crouzil, A., Velastin, S.A., Zegers, P.: A unified deep framework for joint 3D pose estimation and action recognition from a single RGB camera. Sensors **20**(7), 1825 (2020). https://doi.org/10.3390/s20071825. https://www.mdpi.com/1424-8220/20/7/1825
59. Poel, M., Poppe, R., Nijholt, A.: Meeting behavior detection in smart environments: nonverbal cues that help to obtain natural interaction. In: 2008 8th IEEE International Conference on Automatic Face & Gesture Recognition, pp. 1–6. IEEE (2008). https://doi.org/10.1109/AFGR.2008.4813432
60. Poh, M.Z., McDuff, D.J., Picard, R.W.: Non-contact, automated cardiac pulse measurements using video imaging and blind source separation. Opt. Express **18**(10), 10762–10774 (2010)
61. Ricanek, K., Tesafaye, T.: MORPH: A longitudinal image database of normal adult age-progression. In: 7th International Conference on Automatic Face and Gesture Recognition (FGR 2006), pp. 341–345. IEEE (2006). https://doi.org/10.1109/FGR.2006.78
62. Riedhammer, K., Favre, B., Hakkani-Tür, D.: Long story short–global unsupervised models for keyphrase based meeting summarization. Speech Commun. **52**(10), 801–815 (2010). https://doi.org/10.1016/j.specom.2010.06.002
63. Rocca, K.A.: Student participation in the college classroom: an extended multidisciplinary literature review. Commun. Educ. **59**(2), 185–213 (2010)
64. Rogelberg, S., Scott, C., Kello, J.E.: The science and fiction of meetings. MIT Sloan Manage. Rev. **48**, 18–21 (2007). https://api.semanticscholar.org/CorpusID:51796277
65. Romano, N.C., Nunamaker, J.F.: Meeting analysis: Findings from research and practice. In: Proceedings of the 34th Annual Hawaii International Conference on System Sciences, pp. 13–pp. IEEE (2001)
66. Sandler, M., Howard, A., Zhu, M., Zhmoginov, A., Chen, L.C.: Mobilenetv2: inverted residuals and linear bottlenecks. In: Proceedings of the IEEE Conference on Computer Vision and Pattern Recognition, pp. 4510–4520 (2018)
67. Scheflen, A.E.: The significance of posture in communication systems. Psychiatry **27**, 316–331 (1964). https://api.semanticscholar.org/CorpusID:31666916
68. Schulte, E., Lehmann-Willenbrock, N., Kauffeld, S.: Age, forgiveness, and meeting behavior: a multilevel study. J. Manag. Psychol. (2012). https://doi.org/10.1108/JMP-06-2013-0193
69. Seligman, M.E., Flourish, P.: A Visionary New Understanding of Happiness and Well-being, pp. 1–368. M. Selligman, Flourish pp (2012)
70. Selvaraju, R.R., Cogswell, M., Das, A., Vedantam, R., Parikh, D., Batra, D.: Grad-CAM: visual explanations from deep networks via gradient-based localization. In: Proceedings of the IEEE International Conference on Computer Vision (ICCV), pp. 618–626 (2017)
71. Shannon, C.E.: A mathematical theory of communication. Bell Syst. Tech. J. **27**(3), 379–423 (1948)
72. Sharma, P., Joshi, S., Gautam, S., Filipe, V., Reis, M.C.: Student engagement detection using emotion analysis, eye tracking and head movement with machine learning. arXiv preprint arXiv:1909.12913 (2019)
73. Shin, S., Cho, J., Kim, S.W.: Jumple: interactive contents for the virtual physical education classroom in the pandemic era. In: Proceedings of the Augmented Humans International Conference 2021, pp. 268–270. Association for Computing Machinery, New York, NY, USA (2021). https://doi.org/10.1145/3458709.3458964. https://doi.org/10.1145/3458709.3458964
74. Shrivastava, S., Prasad, V.: Techniques to communicate in virtual meetings amidst the new normal... a consideration. Wutan Huatan Jisuan Jishu **16**(6), 73–92 (2020)
75. Sillaots, M.: Using avatars for course management and immersion. In: De Gloria, A. (ed.) Games and Learning Alliance, pp. 163–173. Springer International Publishing, Cham (2015)
76. Simonyan, K., Zisserman, A.: Very deep convolutional networks for large-scale image recognition (2014). arXiv preprint arXiv:1409.1556

77. Sloetjes, H., Wittenburg, P.: Annotation by category: ELAN and ISO DCR. In: Proceedings of the Sixth International Conference on Language Resources and Evaluation (LREC 2008). European Language Resources Association (ELRA), Marrakech, Morocco (2008). http://www.lrec-conf.org/proceedings/lrec2008/pdf/208_paper.pdf
78. Solomon, P., Weinberg, B., McIntosh, A.M., Senderovich, I.: Educational teaching system and method utilizing interactive avatars with learning manager and authoring manager functions (2019). US Patent 10,249,207
79. Soneda, Y., Matsuda, Y., Arakawa, Y., Yasumoto, K.: M3B corpus: multi-modal meeting behavior corpus for group meeting assessment. In: Adjunct Proceedings of the 2019 ACM International Joint Conference on Pervasive and Ubiquitous Computing and Proceedings of the 2019 ACM International Symposium on Wearable Computers, pp. 825–834. Association for Computing Machinery, New York, NY, USA (2019). https://doi.org/10.1145/3341162.3345588, https://doi.org/10.1145/3341162.3345588
80. Sprain, L., Boromisza-Habashi, D.: Meetings: a cultural perspective. J. Multicult. Discourses **7**(2), 179–189 (2012). https://doi.org/10.1080/17447143.2012.685743
81. Srivastava, N.: Using contactless sensors to estimate learning difficulty in digital learning environments. In: Adjunct Proceedings of the 2019 ACM International Joint Conference on Pervasive and Ubiquitous Computing and Proceedings of the 2019 ACM International Symposium on Wearable Computers, pp. 399–403. Association for Computing Machinery, New York, NY, USA (2019). https://doi.org/10.1145/3341162.3349312. https://doi.org/10.1145/3341162.3349312
82. Srivastava, N., Nawaz, S., Newn, J., Lodge, J., Velloso, E., Erfani, M.S., Gasevic, D., Bailey, J.: Are you with me? measurement of learners' video-watching attention with eye tracking. In: LAK21: 11th International Learning Analytics and Knowledge Conference, pp. 88–98. Association for Computing Machinery, New York, NY, USA (2021). https://doi.org/10.1145/3448139.3448148. https://doi.org/10.1145/3448139.3448148
83. Srivastava, N., Velloso, E., Lodge, J.M., Erfani, S., Bailey, J.: Continuous evaluation of video lectures from real-time difficulty self-report. In: Proceedings of the 2019 CHI Conference on Human Factors in Computing Systems, pp. 1–12. Association for Computing Machinery, New York, NY, USA (2019). https://doi.org/10.1145/3290605.3300816. https://doi.org/10.1145/3290605.3300816
84. Surani, D., Hamidah, H.: Students perceptions in online class learning during the COVID-19 pandemic. Int. J. Adv. Sci. Educ. Relig. **3**(3), 83–95 (2020)
85. Tao, R., Pan, Z., Das, R.K., Qian, X., Shou, M.Z., Li, H.: Is someone speaking? exploring long-term temporal features for audio-visual active speaker detection. In: Proceedings of the 29th ACM International Conference on Multimedia, pp. 3927–3935. Association for Computing Machinery, New York, NY, USA (2021). https://doi.org/10.1145/3474085.3475587. https://doi.org/10.1145/3474085.3475587
86. Vargo, A., Iwata, M., Hutin, M., Kobylyanskaya, S., Vasilescu, I., Augereau, O., Watanabe, K., Ishimaru, S., Tag, B., Dingler, T., Kise, K., Devillers, L., Dengel, A.: Learning cyclotron: an ecosystem of knowledge circulation. In: Adjunct Proceedings of the 2022 ACM International Joint Conference on Pervasive and Ubiquitous Computing and the 2022 ACM International Symposium on Wearable Computers, pp. 308–312. Association for Computing Machinery, New York, NY, USA (2023). https://doi.org/10.1145/3544793.3560383. https://doi.org/10.1145/3544793.3560383
87. Visser, B., van der Putten, P., Zohrehvand, A.: The impacts of AI avatar appearance and disclosure on user motivation (2024). https://arxiv.org/abs/2407.21521
88. Wanless-Sobel, C.: Educational gaming avatars. In: Encyclopedia of Distance Learning, 2nd edn, pp. 746–753. IGI Global (2009)
89. Watanabe, K., Dengel, A., Ishimaru, S.: Metacognition-EnGauge: real-time augmentation of self-and-group engagement levels understanding by gauge interface in online meetings. In: Proceedings of the 2024 ACM International Symposium on ... (in review) (2024)
90. Watanabe, K., Sathyanarayana, T., Dengel, A., Ishimaru, S.: Engauge: engagement gauge of meeting participants estimated by facial expression and deep neural network. IEEE Access **11**, 52886–52898 (2023)

91. Watanabe, K., Soneda, Y., Matsuda, Y., Nakamura, Y., Arakawa, Y., Dengel, A., Ishimaru, S.: Discaas: micro behavior analysis on discussion by camera as a sensor. Sensors **21**(17), 5719 (2021)
92. Williams, J.: Women at work. In: Women vs Feminism, pp. 31–47. Emerald Publishing Limited (2017)
93. Wilton, L., Noel, T.: Avatars: usefulness in collaborative online learning environments. Collected Essays Learn. Teach. **4**, 115–120 (2011). https://doi.org/10.22329/CELT.V4I0.3282
94. Yang, H.: Explore how artificial intelligence and VR technology will change the development of future education. J. Phys: Conf. Ser. **1744**(4), 042146 (2021). https://doi.org/10.1088/1742-6596/1744/4/042146
95. Ye, Z., Li, Y., Fathi, A., Han, Y., Rozga, A., Abowd, G.D., Rehg, J.M.: Detecting eye contact using wearable eye-tracking glasses. In: Proceedings of the 2012 ACM Conference on Ubiquitous Computing. pp. 699–704. Association for Computing Machinery, New York, NY, USA (2012). https://doi.org/10.1145/2370216.2370368. https://doi.org/10.1145/2370216.2370368
96. Yoerger, M., Crowe, J., Allen, J.A.: Participate or else!: the effect of participation in decision-making in meetings on employee engagement. Consult. Psychol. J. Pract. Res. **67**(1), 65–80 (2015)
97. Yu, D., Deng, L.: Automatic Speech Recognition, vol. 1. Springer (2016)
98. Yu, Z., Yu, Z., Aoyama, H., Ozeki, M., Nakamura, Y.: Capture, recognition, and visualization of human semantic interactions in meetings. In: 2010 IEEE International Conference on Pervasive Computing and Communications (PerCom), pp. 107–115. IEEE (2010)
99. Zhai, Z., Chen, X., Zhao, Y., Zhao, L., Qian, J., Wu, J.: Smartcamera: realtime video stream-oriented action recognition platform in edge environment. In: Adjunct Proceedings of the 2021 ACM International Joint Conference on Pervasive and Ubiquitous Computing and Proceedings of the 2021 ACM International Symposium on Wearable Computers, pp. 88–89. Association for Computing Machinery, New York, NY, USA (2021). https://doi.org/10.1145/3460418.3479303. https://doi.org/10.1145/3460418.3479303
100. Zhang, L., Zhao, Z., Ma, C., Shan, L., Sun, H., Jiang, L., Deng, S., Gao, C.: End-to-end automatic pronunciation error detection based on improved hybrid CTC/attention architecture. Sensors **20**(7), 1809 (2020). https://doi.org/10.3390/s20071809. https://www.mdpi.com/1424-8220/20/7/1809
101. Zhang, X., Sugano, Y., Bulling, A.: Everyday eye contact detection using unsupervised gaze target discovery. In: Proceedings of the 30th Annual ACM Symposium on User Interface Software and Technology, pp. 193–203 (2017)
102. Zhao, R., Li, V., Barbosa, H., Ghoshal, G., Hoque, M.E.: Semi-automated 8 collaborative online training module for improving communication skills. Proc. ACM Interact. Mob. Wearable Ubiquit. Technol. **1**(2), 32:1–32:20 (2017). https://doi.org/10.1145/3090097, https://doi.org/10.1145/3090097

Skills Training in the Age of AI

Chris Blakely and Ralph L. Rose

Abstract This chapter looks at the shifting requirements for skills acquisitions of university students (especially focusing on undergraduate students) in the face of rapid AI innovation. The authors will examine the real-world costs to both educators and students as curricula adapt to changing needs in industry and academic research. Through this examination, the authors propose a dynamic policy and curriculum development framework (ADAPT-AI) for use by faculty and higher education administrators at the institutional, departmental, or classroom level to address the challenges and opportunities posed by the socio-technological advancements in AI across different sectors of society.

Keywords Artificial intelligence · Tertiary education · Policy · Curriculum development

1 Introduction

For many, attending and completing higher education—particularly undergraduate studies—is a social status marker, a pathway to personal enrichment and a means by which people seek to achieve greater knowledge and skills to gain a competitive advantage in the job market [44]. The practical and socio-cultural benefits of higher education are generally understood to be a return on investment for individual students and society as a whole. In an ideal example, students pay tuition and for various resources (textbooks, software, computers, etc.) and effectively go into debt to then, if all goes according to plan, graduate and enter the job market with a background that can help students stand out as more developed, adept individuals. Outside of labor market shortages, gluts, economic down-turns, and various other hazards that

C. Blakely (✉)
Kyoto College of Graduate Studies for Informatics, Kyoto, Japan
e-mail: c_blakely@kcg.edu

R. L. Rose
Faculty of Science and Engineering, Waseda University, Tokyo, Japan
e-mail: rose@waseda.jp

A. Dengel et al. (eds.), *The Future of Education with AI*,
https://doi.org/10.1007/978-981-95-1622-3_5

higher education institutions can do little to directly minimize, one significant area where tertiary institutions can intervene to positively help their students become more enriched and employable is through curriculum development.

Curricula developed by tertiary institutions and departments outline both a map of ideas, key concepts, and topics necessary for student awareness and literacy in a given domain and a list of techniques, exploration of ethical concepts and best practices, in addition to skills needed to apply knowledge ethically into real-world applications, innovations, and procedures according to established professional standards. While the degree to which a given domain is "theory-heavy" or "practice-heavy" will depend on the nature of that domain, we argue in a broad sense that the undergraduate higher education experience, which universities strive to provide, promises an even balance of theoretical investigation and practical experience. Moving beyond the university, technical schools and certification courses play an equally important role in developing future professionals who similarly hold expectations that their short-term investment in skills development will translate into greater access to new career options in the long run. From this perspective, the means to develop human intelligence can be considered a right because it is fundamental to human survival and existence.

Artificial intelligence (AI) is a culmination of research and design from several key scholars and programmers over the years to develop machine learning (ML) programs which, in recent years, are being released as new, generative technologies that can be used in hundreds of domains, industries, and procedures. While concerns about generative AI (gen-AI) replacing humans has its own precedent in the literature, the recent developments sparked by the initial release of ChatGPT in 2022 [71] have brought this topic into the public discourse once more and led to divided opinions on the role of AI in future society. Some argue a complementary position [27, 32, 85, 97, 100], whereby AI functions as a powerful tool steered by people in some AI–human collaboration scenario. Others argue an obsolescence position [5, 26, 52, 64], where AI tools progressively outpace human skill and knowledge at an exponential scale to render human input, feedback, or reflection unnecessary. In Fig. 1, we see how the collaborative and obsolescent positions reflect both the levels of socio-technical involvement of humans in AI systems but also if the resulting AI disruption improves or diminishes the experience of human work. There is additionally a newly growing literature on how higher education institutions can or should adapt to these looming future prospects with regard to AI literacy, education policy, academic ethics standards, and curriculum development.

In this chapter, we aim to review the history of AI and its uses in research and industry, higher education curriculum development and human skill development to synthesize a policy framework (referred to below as the "ADAPT-AI" framework) whereby educators and departments in higher education across the world can consistently write and implement policies on the use of AI for student education with a perspective on the most likely scenarios of a future AI world. We seek to achieve this adaptable framework by also investigating and addressing the real-world costs and considerations that will impact educators and their students' career futures and livelihoods.

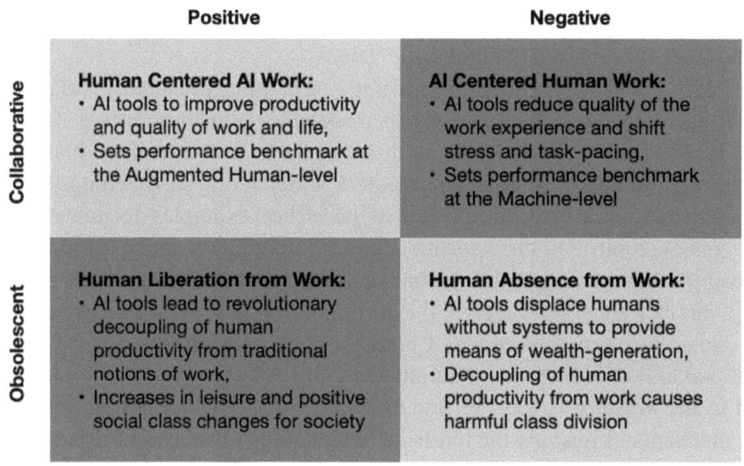

Fig. 1 Description of potential human–AI work relationships

1.1 The Rise of AI and Impact on the Job Market

AI is a broad collection of different technologies aimed at emulating various cognitive tasks such as perception, interpretation, and decision-making [20]. These technologies are an outgrowth of automation, optimizing repetitive tasks for greater productivity, but are capable of handling more discrete tasks involving pattern recognition. Generative AI (gen-AI) goes further by creating new content based on training data, pushing automated tools to accomplish tasks formerly considered too complex for machines [20, 45]. Contemporary gen-AI demonstrates a break with previous forms of automation and offers the potential to boost productivity with complex, non-routine tasks that require creativity, evaluation, analysis, and other tasks seen as uniquely humanistic.

With many discussions on AI, comparisons to the Luddite movement are made—some with a general fear of all AI automation and others with a more nuanced critique. The Luddite movement formed under the leadership of a legendary figure, known as "Ned Lud," and destroyed certain types of automated textile machinery in the early nineteenth century as a response to concerns of changing working conditions; specifically that high-skilled artisans would lose their vocations to unskilled laborers, such as women and children, and see their craft disappear [72]. O'Rourke et al. [72] note that the automation machinery in the era of the Luddite movement was biased in favor of unskilled labor, but that more contemporary automation technologies were skills-biased—requiring a degree of knowledge and ability to use such tools effectively. Many of the tools in our current discussion, gen-AI and large language models (LLMs), tend toward the creation of outputs that no longer require human skill, knowledge, or expertise in the generative process. This brings into question the future of human education and skills training in various careers and vocations that, just like the textile workers of the Luddite movement, were once considered skilled roles dependent on uniquely humanistic values.

Gen-AI is the most recent case of disruptive technology in history and is preceded by previous innovations that have reshaped societies—one may argue—for better or worse. It better serves our purpose in this chapter to first extend the historical perspective on automation in order to capture a wider scope surrounding the issue of automation and social disruption. Some of the earliest examples documented are various feedback-controlled mechanisms found throughout the late Classical and early medieval periods in Greek and Arabic societies, such as water clocks [36, 56] or random number generators used in the art of geomancy [80]. We likewise see musical automata developed in ancient China [22, 50], speaking further to a culturally diverse and universal interest for automated tools. As we approach the early modern period in the Western world, we find examples of steam engines and other water-driven mechanisms pushing the forefront of technology toward self-driven machines before the invention of the Jacquard loom. The feedback-control technologies developed prior to the Industrial Revolution in England did not seem to alter much of the socio-economic landscape in their areas compared to agricultural innovations or architectural and infrastructural achievements [66]. For example, innovations in agricultural tools or processes had broader impacts on social welfare, that is, greater capacity to feed people and survive crop failure, but this did not lead to a radical reshaping of social hierarchy, ownership of land or capital, or standard labor practices and training in skilled crafts. While recent literature on the divergence caused by the Industrial Revolution suggests pre-existing affluence had a role in priming the social and psychological acceptance of technological innovation in the context of early nineteenth-century England [12], we know these automated technologies were instrumental in reshaping the demand for skilled labor. This posed a threat to the job security of these skilled laborers and the future of their craft, further altering the standards and processes of specific industries as well as the norms of skill training in society.

The mid-twentieth century witnessed new voices and research on automation as early computer systems began to develop. We find this in the work of computer science pioneers, most notably Marvin Minsky [60], laying theoretical foundations and beginning to shape and steer the field toward realizing computer automation and machine learning. A general history of contemporary AI research and development can be described as a gradual shift of AI occurring in three booms with two intervening "winters" (cf., [20, 45, 54, 75, 99]). We begin the story with a niche subfield of computer science consisting mostly of academic specialists postulating the core principles of engineering AI systems; much of these initial ideas and developments rarely touched the lives of the general public or users outside of mentions in science fiction or other imaginative, fictional media. As the modern digital computer begins to take shape and space within several university research labs, the development of automated AI tools begin to appear as back-end support systems of industry, commerce, and research. These new technologies at the time provided useful functions to support various tasks in a wide array of fields, though still in a relatively hidden manner. These AI technologies were rarely used directly by public or computer/network users (i.e., the usage was more passive such as product recommendations, tailored advertising, or via search engines). Direct and pervasive use by the general public of gen-AI tools for completing work and leisure tasks has become more prevalent in the past few years; though such tool functions are limited to specific domains or require a bundle of different AI applications to complete more complex procedures.

Optimism and concerns for such new technologies existed then as much as now. We continue to share in this debate about if or when AI will render human intellectual input unnecessary. It is not just the threat of AI to creative and critical human intellectuality which should concern us, but also at a more practical level the threat of over-valuing efficiency at the expense of quality in production and the ease at which such efficiency can be invoked to justify downsizing, outsourcing, or obsolescence which has no proper plan to reorient or retrain human workers pushed out by new technologies. In more recent literature, there is a general consensus that the precise implications of AI on economies and societies around the world remain to be seen. However, nearly 40% of the global economy is expected to be impacted by AI, with 60% of jobs in more developed economies expected to bear the brunt of these changes while simultaneously reaping more of the anticipated benefits [20]. Researchers investigating these impacts on labor and economies note that these new LLMs and gen-AI technologies will mainly affect middle-skill level jobs [45, 94]. This means the polarizing of the labor skill pool to undercut middle-skill level jobs (i.e., jobs requiring training, involving many highly repetitive tasks such as coding) leaving either low-skill manual jobs or high-skilled professional jobs. Such a hollowing out of the human labor market would remove a means by which low-skilled laborers can learn new skills and improve their earning potential or social status, which would further exacerbate current inequalities in different nations.

It is also an important reminder to reflect on how initial impressions of AI implementation were first believed to have little or no impact on high-skill jobs; that is, jobs requiring significant training, education, or certification often involving a high degree of creativity and adaptability from task to task. In fact, some of the loudest critiques of AI have come from artists, engineers, and other professionals who at first believed their experience, creativity, or skill-sets could not be undermined by gen-AI. A broad range of tasks, not just simple routine tasks, can be automated or handled by these new AI tools. It is not just the disappearance of middle-skill jobs alone that marks this polarization, but also the erosion of low-skill and high-skill jobs adjacent to the middle-skilled roles under threat. We invoke again the Luddite movement's concerns with the degradation of their textile craft via automated machines built with the specific intent of erasing their valuable knowledge and skill-sets. Countries in the developed world, as well as developing economies seeking improved conditions and quality of life, have lauded information and communications technologies (ICTs) as solutions to social and infrastructural issues which require specific education and skills training to successfully implement and maintain these solutions. The need to train humans on these ICT skills and develop technological literacy is complicated by the performance of gen-AI.

However, this does not lead to an inevitable result if clear long-term strategy and policy-making are prioritized. We already find this polarization occurring to middle-skill level jobs: Autor [9] notes the polarization of jobs in the past few decades, whereby high-skill and low-skill jobs received significantly large wage gains. While Autor also claims further polarization is unlikely he also states that human capital investment must be at the heart of any long-term strategy to avoid replacement by AI automation, meaning that education and vocational-training institutions need to provide the skills and knowledge needed for anticipated future jobs, since training from the private sector is unlikely to occur. But what will middle-skill jobs of the future be like, if they continue to exist? How we choose to implement these gen-AI tools will dictate the shape of future job markets and skills in demand. This contrasts with views offered by Aoun [4], echoed by [19], where the vanguard call is Life-Long Learning; transforming institutional resource networks so each learner designs their own learning experience. This could facilitate some innovative results for human–AI collaboration but can just as easily lead to an exacerbation of skill-wage polarization. There are already concerns of AI veracity, the erosion of literacy and critical thinking skills and the abuse of AI tools for plagiarism and misconduct—it is important that AI tool-use can be taught in a learner-centered way without the loss of critical thinking skills or wider context and perspective on how these tools operate and how best to use them to collaborate.

There is also a more practical critique as reshaping higher education institutions at a global level comes with its own logistical complexities that go beyond partnership agreements: faculty layoffs via institutional mergers, cross-cultural or international curriculum development, necessary revisions to school charters or mission statements, inter alia. In a way, such a global-level networking of higher education institutions renders such institutions more in line with multi-national conglomerates, with the same headaches that accompany any other regional merger or market expansion. While many universities and colleges may have an eye toward a broad, holistic approach to education, which includes continued learning aimed at skills retraining, this is still not as extensive as the personal enrichment mission of Life-Long Learning. Such a goal for institutional transformation does not in itself offer a clear, effective counter-strategy to AI encroachment on human skill and intelligence. It is necessary to consider that the threat is not so much what the machines can or cannot do better, but rather that humans in positions of organizational and socio-economic status can choose to wipe out entire departments (perhaps economic sectors) via preference for mediocre AI performance. If the machines are competent enough, they are still cheaper and incur less liability than a human. It is more likely that human replacement by AI will occur through neglect or by prioritizing speed, efficiency, and quantity over reliability and quality.

The introduction and prominent use of gen-AI tools is not going to filter out to countries across the world like we saw with the early Internet or even social media—on the contrary, the access to these tools is capable of simultaneously impacting and distorting societies around the world with little concern for the level of technological infrastructure or digital literacy in a given society. For one class to hold access and utilize AI tools is enough to impact all classes within their societies and across the globe—the time to adjust and acclimatize to AI available to us currently exists because of concerns, restrictions, and cautioned investigation. In this time, we are witnessing massive shifts and changes to social views of human labor value, reassessing the scope of human cognitive input and creativity, with an increasing acceptance of convenience over content. AI tools can provide many benefits and have the potential to enrich human life and learning, but is this the underlying impetus for such tools currently in use or under development?

This ties back to arguments regarding the degree to which automation and AI can simulate or exceed human consciousness—itself a complicated issue with its own vigorous debate. While the scope of this paper does not include the broader discussion about consciousness (i.e., human consciousness, artificial general intelligence (AGI), and artificial super intelligence), we do want to note several key considerations: how many human tasks in different workplaces and positions require intense cognition, how much of the conscious human experience can be replicated by feedback control or synthetic modeling, how much of the social economy relies on the complexity of human existence to better serve customers, and what is the value of human education if or when the need for human skill and expertise expires?

From this point, we will speak on the history of education and skills training, with a focus on what human intellect is, and has been defined as, in previous generations and societies. In relation to this, we will also explore the idea of a social contract between higher education institutions and society. We will also include more contemporary ideas about Life-Long Learning and the promotion of social equity and individual vocational adaptability in high-tech, developed societies. Though the idea of Life-Long Learning necessarily exceeds the higher education institution in more traditional terms, notable responses to AI in higher education have included calls to overturn these traditional structures [4, 29, 62]. The objective of education and training was a mostly human-centered consideration in the past, but automation continually stresses and shifts our understanding of human capital and the value of knowledge.

1.2 History of Skills Training: Intellectual and Vocational

The type of skills in demand for different fields is not only widely varied, but the debate as to the prioritization of skills training over other elements in demand for different fields—such as in law, social work, medicine, and engineering to name a few—remains contested [29, 57, 106]. While the details of this debate are outside the scope of this chapter, we propose that elements such as moral or ethical purpose in a profession be seen as a type of soft skill for the purpose of this examination. Specifically, that there is a difference between the learner engaging with moral issues and forming their own position on the matter in contrast to prompting an LLM to feed students ready-made moral positions, irrespective of student introspection or sincerity.

Labor can be divided up not only by the complexity versus simplicity of tasks (i.e., non-repetitive versus repetitive) but also knowledge-heavy versus action-heavy tasks (i.e., analytical versus manual). We do not bring up these terms to prescribe value judgments about different types of labor, but rather to investigate how AI can—and, in some cases, already has begun to—displace human labor across different divisions of labor. For some commentators on the human–AI relationship, there was a perception that jobs which were action-heavy (i.e., manual labor) would be more threatened by AI advancements than jobs which were seen to involve more "humanistic" values and specifications—those involving such things as human creativity, leadership, expertise, and judgment. However, as we have seen in the past few years, AI is quickly putting various professional vocations and creative endeavors under threat of human obsolescence. In some ways, the picture we see taking shape implies that knowledge-heavy jobs are not exceptionally protected from AI and that, in fact, some manual tasks are more likely to require human involvement because they are more difficult for AI to replicate. Part of this, as has been pointed out by other scholars, stems from a lack of consideration for the range of complexity involved within tasks (non-repetitive versus repetitive) and further the lack of discussion regarding the nature of intelligence and consciousness and how these are connected to education and training with regard to career development and the creation of different levels and dimensions of human capital (i.e., labor).

The form and execution of educational and pedagogical systems reflects, in part, concepts and practices based in research findings about human physical and psychological development, especially mental cognition, memory, and communication [16]. In turn, curricula and educational objectives are often set and defined firmly on this conceptual foundation of the human mind and intelligence. According to Muller [65], classical interpretations of computation interpret human mental states as similar to computer functions, referred to as "machine functionalism." This view has come under criticism because while synapses do operate in a binary fashion, we can argue for greater complexity in human mental states by observing such features as follows:

- the Perception-Action Loop (i.e., do something, it changes its environment, that change feeds back into the perception);
- Predictive Processing Theory (i.e., the brain makes predictions first, then engages Perception-Action Loop to test that prediction);
- Embodied Cognition (i.e., our cognition is embedded in environments surrounded by other cognitive agents).

This is not to imply that all curricula or instructors base their pedagogical approaches and techniques on mechanical functionalism, but rather to start the inquiry about what knowledge or skill-sets surpass the boundaries of mechanical functionalism and the degree to which research and industries of various types employ or demand such rich, variegated human cognition. This distinction can be seen very often in the discussion between abstract/theoretical knowledge versus concrete/practical knowledge, or in the distinction between hard/technical skills versus soft skills.

Muller [65] also notes how humans throughout time and across the world have achieved goals by changing agents or changing environments; that is to say, the flexibility in goal achievement has been accomplished in the past by humans via culture (i.e., social and formal learning systems to make students knowledgeable and adept) or else by technological and infrastructural changes (i.e., roads, vehicles to drive on roads, AI systems, etc.). Contemporary higher education curricula incorporate, in many instances, both cultural and environmental changes to realize the goal of skill development and knowledge transmission among students.

Let us step back briefly and reflect on some concepts of learning and training in order to unpack and anticipate some of the issues and challenges new AI technologies pose to learners. If we refer back to Boettcher's work on the LeMKE framework [15, 16], which she describes as a four-component model to better understand the learner-centered environment and its dynamics, we can consider how these principles hold up with the intervention of AI technological systems in the learning process. A key aspect is the environment where the student learns and interacts with their mentor and the knowledge being imparted to them. This choice of environment (whether in-person or online, the balance of interactions between students and the mentor, etc.) is often deliberately selected as part of the course plan and shapes the experience of the knowledge interaction and its capture in the student's mind [16]. The environment in this case includes the tools and technologies available. We would argue that AI is a fundamentally different tool from previous tools used in the learning environment because of its tangential influence on the knowledge-interaction transference via the human–AI interface.

This means a number of concerns are raised and need to be investigated to better understand this interaction: uncertainty about the role of the mentor when learners can readily substitute or simulate mentors and peers via AI, uncertainty about the veracity of AI outputs given known tendencies to hallucinate, uncertainties and concerns about the retention of AI outputs in student memory, and the fear of AI technologies diminishing or erasing critical reflection and tacit knowledge in students. This raises the primary concern: When the majority of these core components of the learning environment are collapsed into each other via gen-AI, does the student actually retain any authentic, verifiable, or useful knowledge?

1.3 Education Social Contract and Life-Long Learning

The relationship of student to teacher, further enshrined in a relationship between the general public and educational institutions, stands as a cornerstone for cultural attitudes toward intellectualism, the valuation of learning over labor, and the integration of schooling into the lifecycle of families. We can effectively imagine an educational social contract—individuals limit or surrender current opportunities for work or leisure in the present with the aim of developing a standard of knowledge and skills provided by educational institutions which, in turn, provide rights of access, literacy, social mobility, and employability. While this educational social contract may not be explicit in every instance, a few historical examples can serve as precedence, such as the education of European nobility evolving into an appreciation for greater literacy and cultivation among the early modern middle classes [23] or the development of Confucian exam systems in East Asia to educate and promote literate classes into government positions [41].

While much of the ancient infrastructures have disappeared or transformed over time, there remains a continuity behind the social contract wherein occurs an exchange of a limited range of opportunities at present for a wider, more potent expansion of opportunities. This increased access to new opportunities previously unavailable is received or earned via enrollment and participation in the school system. This goes further into broader human rights arguments and proposals (cf., Universal Charter of Human Rights, Sustainable Development Goals, etc.) which argue for expanding literacy and schooling for all peoples—providing equitable access to education that includes a variety of minorities or disadvantaged individuals, both within a given society but also across all societies as a measure of development. There would not be such advocacy if education, in particular for our purposes higher education, was not considered a valuable or essential component to providing greater opportunities and, by extension, solving or addressing significant social ills and economic inefficiencies.

The role of higher education has been noted as a significant factor in increasing the quality of life in societies and noted as a public good, though as highlighted by [69] the mechanisms for funding higher education institutions stem from a shift away from *higher education as public good* toward a complex *private–public network* of government, companies, and academia. University curricula have changed in response to demands for entrepreneurism in the laboratory to bring new innovations to market faster or to prepare generations of students for new vocations according to anticipated industry and business trends. In the United States, for example, the Higher Education Act of 1965 sought to expand educational resources in American universities while also legislating programs and means of funding for post-secondary education via student scholarships and low-interest student loans to support an increasing university student population [95]. Many nations have developed similar laws in response to growing their own student populations in the higher education sector and to assist them, to some degree, in pursuit of public responsibility for the expansion and sustainability of higher education as a reflection of this educational social contract [101].

To return back to threats against employability by AI systems in the quest for short-term efficiency gains, we need to address the far-reaching implication wherein the value or purpose of human education is put into question at a fundamental level. Kochhar notes that, along with women and individuals of Asian descent, the higher paying jobs usually reserved for those with college education and stronger analytical skills are the most exposed to AI advancements [45]. The issue of employability after graduation from higher education institutions has in the past two decades been susceptible to global recession, a shrinking number of positions in several fields and the social push to train students on coding and other skills seen as vital to future tech careers. Preceding tech booms in the past three decades ignited interest in ICT careers as well as a belief in unquenchable growth and plentiful career opportunities. Many of these tech careers were seen as the new domain to direct efforts for retraining and changing curriculum standards.

However, the tech sector has been hit by layoffs in recent years and there has been a general shrinkage of the number of positions that need to be filled in this domain now with the rise of gen-AI tools like ChatGPT. This poses two concerns with regard to skills development in students and others exposed to AI: (1) With several skills formerly reliant on the human execution of creative or analytical tasks now likely being ported over to cost-cutting AI tools that increase productivity, will knowledge and literacy of these skills remain necessary for higher education curricula, and (2) with this shift in demand for skills and knowledge, will the demand for higher education shrink and do societies face the threat of greater inequality via decreases in educational access?

Through the latter half of the twentieth century [95, 101], several societies have legislated laws and programs to increase the number of people eligible to attend and graduate from tertiary education institutions, with a tacit goal of these individuals becoming enriched in order to access careers previously unavailable; develop skills and knowledge to further innovation and productivity; and address social problems such as inequality, poverty, and brain-drain. The human–AI collaborative viewpoint posits some continuation of this version of skills training, but now with integrated AI skills included to augment future researchers and workers. This scenario is not an eventuality we can await with any degree of ease or anticipation. It will require a concerted and thorough effort to address the potential threats, abuses, and perverse effects we expect to encounter with the expansion of AI tools into our lives. This includes consideration and strategic preparation for how organizations and vested interests could potentially exploit such threats, abuses, or perverse effects to the detriment of the educational social contract of greater access, literacy, social mobility, and employability. With this consideration in mind, it is necessary then to examine what AI tools have been developed and applied to different vocations and industries. In doing so, we hope to explore the various industry trends taking place and give a clearer context for how to pursue a policy framework that enables and protects a positive human–AI collaborative approach as a gold standard.

1.4 Summary

The following is a summary of the above section, providing three key takeaways informing the framework of this chapter:

- Despite continuing debate about the social and economic impacts of AI, the nature of the human–AI relationship can manifest in four types depending on the measure of performative benchmarks and the extent of human input and supervision.
- Socio-technical values of human capital, knowledge production, and intellectuality are not inherent to how new tools and technologies are designed or implemented, as seen both in the history of automated technologies and the history of education theory.

- The historical division between skilled and unskilled labor has often been bridged by new automation technologies that render specific skill-sets obsolete, simultaneously both liberating and undermining. However, not all technological innovations follow this trajectory as it is also possible that new technologies can require the creation of new trades, standards, and knowledge. When considering the future of skills training in the AI age, it is important to assess whether AI technologies collectively require more skill or less skill in the hands of users.

2 Applications of AI

Despite numerous uncertainties outlined above about the full consequences of the introduction of gen-AI into the workforce, it is clear that industries will forge ahead with a wider implementation of gen-AI at various levels of the workforce. For many issues or abuses resulting from AI, the solution is often described as implementing different AI tools—for example, the use of facial recognition algorithms to spot AI-generated deep fakes [28]. In effect, whether new AI tools are accepted or rejected, there is a need for a greater awareness of AI potential, literacy in identifying AI results, and skills in using AI tools which can either verify or process data. Fighting AI with AI seems to be an inevitable scenario, posing a challenge to any wholesale, reactionary push against the influence and use of gen-AI. This accentuates the critical importance of giving the use and expansion of AI technologies' sober consideration. In order to understand the best approach in the development and implementation of educational policies to address AI usage and the future of human education and skill training, it is critical that a picture of a realistic, AI-impacted world can be described. This allows for a more accurate understanding of how AI technologies will augment or erode human labor activities, knowledge production, literacy, creative production, and problem-solving. We examine the current and future applications of AI in three different areas: the industrial sector, academic research and analysis, and vocational and certified services. Through a review of several examples of gen-AI applications currently in use or in development, we can gain a more holistic view of the demand, opportunities, and risks resulting from AI. Further, we try to interpolate what the demand for an educated human labor force could look like with various future AI systems in place.

2.1 Industrial AI Applications

New applications of gen-AI in various industries have begun to populate headlines and garner attention from the wider public since the initial release of ChatGPT and other tools in 2022. Though there is still uncertainty as to how higher education institutions should form policies and curricula in response to these changes, we are witnessing the adoption of gen-AI tools in different industries and work practices. From this, we can gain a preview of some of the shifts occurring with regard to AI-augmented work and best practices. To this end, a distinction has been observed regarding two classes of AI-facing professions: those which require skills critical to the training and development of AI programs and those who augment and use AI tools but do not have a critical role in the training or development of these tools [35]. Green et al. describe a distinction between managers and engineers intimately involved in the training and maintenance of the AI system from the very beginning versus a larger percentage of workers merely exposed to AI tools in their daily routines [35]. Hazan et al. note an increased demand for high-skilled workers, particularly in STEM-related and healthcare areas, and the importance of AI development skills as a key ingredient along with the need for social and emotional soft skills to create, maintain, and improve these tools to realize productivity growth [37].

The adept usage of gen-AI and its successful integration into industry operations is not just a matter of technological prowess but also borne out of knowledge and experience with a variety of soft skills. Kochhar [45] finds that jobs which receive more exposure to AI will have a greater need for analytical skills, namely, critical thinking, writing, knowledge of science and math, while mechanical skills will have less importance. There is a notable increase in demand for such soft or human skills like critical thinking and emotional intelligence to complement the rise of AI tool-use [24]. This points out several key considerations: (1) hard skills and literacy with automation tools, data science and engineering principles will become more integral and critical for more fields that incorporate AI into their operations and projects; (2) at the same time, exclusive specialization with hard technology skills, especially in STEM-related fields, will no longer suffice as programmers, engineers, and other technical positions will require greater skill with emotional intelligence, socialization, and literacy with concepts or knowledge traditionally associated with the humanities and management studies; (3) while there may be a decrease in the number of high-skill positions as a result of the efficiency and productivity gains of AI tools, this also comes with a greater breakdown of the separation of technical sciences versus humanities or hard versus soft skills as the balance and integration of both becomes crucial to successful AI design, output verification, and result generation.

The exponential rate at which AI tools have evolved and adapted to improve task execution, analysis, and problem-solving makes it difficult for researchers investigating future implications and needs. However, this is a good opportunity to examine the case of the prompt engineer. The nature of AI output generation, by means of typed prompts, has led to the proposed job position of the prompt engineer [98]. The idea stems from observations and concerns about the tendency of AI tools to fabricate or hallucinate information, or else produce poor results requiring additional human guidance or correction. This holds some weight as even now AI tools still have the potential for hallucinations or data fabrication [6, 109], but AI tools have also been trained to review and learn to improve their outputs and thereby require less human oversight [86]. Of course, it has been discovered that AI programs trained exclusively on AI-generated content breakdown and suffer a severe reduction in the quality of their outputs [33, 107]—yet we cannot rest assured that AI will continue to suffer this data poisoning issue as the technology continues to evolve under the direction of current AI engineers and firms. It is not unreasonable, then, to anticipate future AI tools designed and fine-tuned to continually minimize the need for human correction and bias checks. As this erosion of human corrective action with AI occurs, a possible consequence is a shrinkage in demand for prompt engineers. This example demonstrates how initial prospects for future domain and career development are inherently unstable when considering how AI can be used, whether or not human prompting or corrective action remains a critical factor and whether such changes will have a long enough future to matter to students by the time they graduate from their program. Just as AI tools are envisioned at one moment as opening up new opportunities for pioneering career options, they just as quickly evolve and undermine the value of human skill and knowledge.

Many of the current AI tools at the time of this publication would fall under the label of weak AI. As an example, let us consider the skills and experience required to fill a web programmer position. Under such circumstances, knowledge in multiple programming languages, such as Python, R for data science, JavaScript, HTML for web applications, along with knowledge of legacy languages, like C or Java, will for the time being continue to play an important role in different industries and businesses. The transition and adoption of AI into these domains means that significant aspects of the coding and repetitive testing and debugging tasks can be farmed out to AI tools. For a web programmer, such technical skills and literacy in these languages would be requirements for a given position in a company. In addition, the hypothetical job posting for this web programmer position would also be seeking individuals with demonstrable experience and practical knowledge of industry-specific details (i.e., products, market conditions and the business environment, customer demographics or trends, relevant regulations or certifications/qualifications for the position, competitors, etc.) that would be vital to tackling the tasks of the position and show familiarity and interest in the position, the company, or domain.

When considering the perspective of a job candidate preparing for their application to this position, we may start to question which of these skills and knowledge areas could currently be transferred to AI and what level of input, corrective analysis, or degree of control the candidate would need to demonstrate. It could be argued that much of the coding can be done by an AI, and then the resulting code would be tested and refined by the job candidate. However, it is not only in the industrial sector where the increased role of AI will unfold in a complex way. The efficiency and productivity gains derived from such AI applications can also be used in service of academic knowledge production and research. Though these gains also incur changes and issues which could alter the nature of research.

2.2 Research and Development with AI

AI applications to augment research and streamline development offer several possibilities to increase productivity, though their use also puts into question concepts of data accuracy, critical and analytical reflection, the integrity of experiment design and approaches toward research design. Coupled with these concerns is a need to evaluate and plot a course for higher education institutions with regard to how academic integrity policies, course work assignments, and verification of student achievements are handled and processed given the push of AI-generated contents [39]. There are several examples of gen-AI being abused or used in novel ways which can produce odd or problematic results. This includes cases of surreal pictures and visuals created by AI appearing in published works [47], instances of fake sources or data fabrication [25, 79] and AI plagiarism or wholesale AI generation of work without any student involvement or reflection beyond the initial prompt.

However, the use of AI translators plays an extremely helpful role in providing access to resources outside one's native tongue, as well as serving as a communication support tool for English as a second language (ESL) student in various technical fields of research. The creation of AI images, fraught with its own complex issues of training-via-copyrighted works, hallucinatory style, or brute substitution of human illustrators and graphic designers, can produce some good work in the hands of a knowledgeable and responsible user. AI tools can help to crunch extremely large datasets and speed up analysis for various experiments or tests [18]. Even the research publication process is re-envisioned by Montgomery to replace human peer review, deemed outdated and inefficient, with AI systems of scientific validation [62]. Moving further to consider the use of AI for education, AI tools are currently in development or in use to engage individual students in two-way discussion on a given topic, easily produce course rubrics for grading and create AI-generated transcriptions of lessons, meetings, or presentations.

There is a persistent question of which skills will become de-emphasized or outmoded with the incursion of AI into academic research. We see similar trends with elements of coding, proposal-writing, and experiment design easily handed over to AI to relieve researchers from repetitive tasks. While a variety of basic computational skills may be done with AI, similar to how we can imagine calculators and spreadsheet software replacing formerly analog tools or human computation, there are additional considerations to be included: note-taking and record-keeping skills to document the version history of different studies or experiments, accuracy and bias checks to verify AI output and prevent or correct hallucinated data or sources and a consistent global practice on acknowledging AI tool-use. The latter has seen some success in recent years with many academic programs asking students and faculty to treat responsible AI usage in a manner similar to citations.

2.3 *Vocational Services and AI*

The impact of new technologies and systems also entails the need to retrain the current workforce to learn such new technology in order to continue their employment or else gain new employment under a different career. There is already literature on the use of AI tools for training, career guidance, and vocational rehabilitation [7, 82, 104].

However, others have documented or raised issues regarding the implementation of AI tools for vocational rehabilitation in the workplace [13] or the uneven impact of AI tools on technical and vocational workers in different countries [88]. While a traditional model of higher education may not see vocational training as a significant component of the institutional mission, nonetheless it is important to consider if higher education does, in fact, expand its mission in response to the socio-economic impact of AI systems around the world. In this regard, the Life-Long Learning mission described by Aoun as a response to AI in higher education [4] or the inflow of vocational workers into higher education programs for retraining is a matter that universities need to prepare for. The impact of AI on human skill training and work, as mentioned earlier, may foster the need to learn new skills to effectively use AI or it may breakdown the skill prerequisites of various domains and positions to open these roles up to unskilled laborers.

2.4 The Shape of the Future Job Market

Considering the opportunities and risks brought forth by the implementation of AI tools in different industries, academic research projects, and vocational training, the direction and objectives of higher education curriculum and policy responses to AI can be more clearly defined. Productivity increases resulting from AI, or instances of human–AI collaboration, can provide greater efficiency in task execution and potentially serve as an information verifier or workhorse tackling difficult or repetitive tasks, thereby freeing human workers to focus on other tasks.

However, this is not to suggest that AI-adoption will result in wholesale improvements. Acemoglu estimates in most cases that AI will not lead to significant wage increases for most workers or reduced inequality in the US [2]. The impacts of AI on the global job market will be uneven and impact regions differently—Acemoglu in the same study finds that the gap between capital and labor will increase more as a result of AI systems [2]. Thakkar notes the perceptions of vocational workers in India who do not see AI tools as anything more than a straight-forward machine but, when informed of what AI actually does and is capable of, their perceptions shift toward anxiety over their roles and job futures [88]. The perception of these AI tools entering into industry and daily operations carries mixed results in other countries, though many of these results highlight the importance of awareness about the power, agility, and limitations of AI in practice [45].

Advocating greater awareness of the actual capabilities of AI remains a critical component, not only for AI literacy as a key educational objective but because a solid grounding on what is feasible versus what is aspirational with new AI technologies can guide students, faculty, and higher education policy-makers to better assess the constant stream of updates and navigate the exponential rate of change.

The future of the job market in the age of AI centers around the demand and willingness to invest in human capital in the face of new tools and, more importantly, how organizations, companies, and the public interpret the benefits and costs of human capital versus AI capital. Value can be added to human–AI collaboration with "new good tasks" created by AI systems, however there are significant social and welfare harms that can come from AI-created "new bad tasks" such as deepfakes, misinformation, and the like [2]. In addition, lingering issues of trust with AI results, porting key management or operational tasks to "algorithmic management" processes, as well as the continued uncertainty over explainability in AI and trust in generated results [34, 53, 96].

Nonetheless, Acemoglu [2] argues that gains are still to be had from gen-AI which benefit society overall if LLMs and other gen-AI tools switch their focus to generating reliable expert information rather than human-like conversation. Much of the historical focus for AI development has been on language and psychology; for example, Minksy's Framework for Representing Knowledge [61]. This would mean current and future AI research and development would need to shift focus toward data veracity and value construction, a move that could both render human oversight/collaboration unnecessary and create AI tools that could be more productive and useful to humans. As of October 2024, ChatGPT announced the launch of SimpleQA—a benchmark aimed at helping ChatGPT better avoid hallucination and evaluate the factuality of basic fact-seeking questions [102]. The continued advancement of AI toward AGI (that is, weak AI becoming strong AI) continually pushes the direction of future systems to operate without human intervention. Whether this forms a specialized occupational class of AI workers, renders current hard skill tech-positions into unskilled labor roles, or some other future scenario remains to be seen. Serious consideration needs to be given to the possibility that all skill-sets and forms of human knowledge are endangered without concentrated efforts to promote human capital investment via academic and private industry coordination.

2.5 Summary

The main points of the above section are summarized here to highlight important factors and considerations with regard to the future vocational landscape.

- Across different industries and academic domains, AI tools and systems are in development or currently in use to streamline operational procedures, reduce repetitive tasks and perceived inefficiencies—however, the scope of changes resulting from new AI tools puts forward radical changes to verification and validation processes that aim to remove the human element from the work.
- The changes brought about by AI tools emphasize a new demand for laborers in various fields to develop skills in socialization, emotional intelligence, and trust-building to complement mechanical AI processes. While the demand for technical skills will likely persist, the advancements in AI technologies to create artificial general intelligence and then Artificial Super Intelligence strive to reduce or dispense with human collaboration.

3 Role and Purpose of Education/Training in the Age of AI

Given the broad needs of AI-related skills in industry as outlined above and the social expectation that tertiary institutions will provide the education and training necessary to foster these skills in entrants to tomorrow's workforce. Institutions need to accept this role and develop a clear understanding of exactly what they need to provide to students as well as how to go about providing it. This section overviews factors that influence this curriculum (re)development process to the extent that reports on such efforts exist. At this point it is worth noting that, in fact, formalized study of these factors in the context of AI skills development is scarce: In some respects, much can be found in terms of national policy statements, or in very specific domains, but given the short time frame during which AI has come of age in the workplace, the literature is shallow, consisting more of case studies and qualitative reports rather than systematic, extensive, or longitudinal quantitative investigations. This section is organized around understanding these factors and their influences at three levels: national governments, educational institutions, and industry.

3.1 National Policy on AI Skills Training

Several countries throughout the world have now published policy statements specifically on or including statements about the development of AI skills within their educational systems (see [94] for a broad but not comprehensive list). Interestingly, this includes not only developed nations but many developing nations as well (though we could not find any policy statements from under-developed nations). According to OECD data [70], there are 63 policy initiatives worldwide from 19 different countries which address AI skills in education. While this data is likely not comprehensive and many more countries have policy initiatives, it is surprising that less than half (24) of these initiatives explicitly address the specific workforce AI skill-needs of graduates (i.e., "programs for the development of job-related skills"). These policy statements range in their specificity from broad statements such as "Train the next generation of industry ready AI Graduates" to specific, practical initiatives such as Australia's Cadetship program for STEM undergraduates and establishing the Center for Augmented Reasoning at the University of Adelaide [8].

3.1.1 Japan

Another developed country with an explicit policy statement on AI skills training and education is Japan. In its *Artificial Intelligence Technology Strategy* [3], it lays out its vision for the development of AI across industry, government, and society. The majority of the statement focuses on infrastructure and technology development via hoped-for initiatives. Early in the document appears an explicit admission of the need for AI skills training.

> [T]here is a shortage of AI technology researchers as well as engineers and data scientists (AI personnel) who handle AI technology. In addition, development of vocational abilities of laborers in association with reform of the industrial structure may be required. Based on such a background, it is necessary to move forward with measures for fostering researchers and AI personnel immediately. (p. 2)

They define the overall initiative in three phases and assert that the need for AI skills training begins in Phase 1. They foresee training toward three capabilities of skilled AI workers.

- Solving the problems of AI technology: These workers are pioneering experts in AI technology development.
- Realization of AI technology: These workers bring theoretical and visionary ideas to practical reality with strong knowledge of computer science and programming skills.
- Utilization of AI technology: These workers have specific domain knowledge on how to use AI technology in various service and manufacturing applications. (Attachment 3, p. 3).

It is evidently clear that nations see the need for enhancements and developments to AI skills training as primal in its efforts to adapt to the rapid growth of AI technology. That is, they clearly recognize the necessity of present training for future needs of an AI-skilled workforce, even if rapid and perhaps unexpected changes in AI technology mean that the precise future needs cannot yet be determined.

3.1.2 India

The Government of India—a developing country—opens its policy statement [68] with a recognition of the transformative—even "disrupt[ive]" (p. 5)—nature of AI technological development in society. They immediately highlight several impediments to the creation of a future society with a harmonious relationship to AI, the first of which is the "[l]ack of broad based expertise in research and application of AI" (p. 7). The policy statement (like most other national policy statements) spells out clearly a number of expected consequences in the labor force with respect to AI skill-needs while relating this to proposed changes and developments in education. However, a unique feature of the Indian statement is its attempt to brand its particular policy recommendations in order to foster greater awareness, acceptance, and even pride in the various initiatives. The catchphrase, *#AIforAll*, is intended to express the desire to ensure that the disruptive transformation of AI technology in society is for the greater good.

3.1.3 Brazil

The government of Brazil—also a developing country—provides an innovative view of its AI policy [59] by distinguishing two separate axes of the influence of AI technology in society. "Education" and "Workforce and training" (along with such areas as research and development, applications, and security) are oriented on a "vertical" axis while a "transverse" axis consists of "Legislation, regulation, and ethical use," "AI governance," and "international aspects" (p. 4). This view highlights the fact that AI skills training cannot be taken as a modular or encapsulated effort, but is influenced by and beholden to a variety of influences across society. Thus, the policy incorporates statements on AI skills training to take into account personal data protection rights, to update their Common National Curriculum Base (BNCC) to oversee developments, and to promote interactions between institutions and private industry which may lead to greater international cooperation.

3.2 Educational Institution Efforts to Enhance AI Skills Training

In this section, we arrive at what may be seen as the crux of the present work—the effort by institutions to develop or enhance AI skills training to better prepare graduates to enter an AI-needs-based workforce. As we will outline herein, the various factors involved in this process put institutions into somewhat of a unique position. While there is an extensive literature in the domain of education on curriculum development and various useful frameworks that institutions and practitioners may refer to, the relative newness of AI technology and the sudden and pervasive influence it has had on the workplace means that there is very little literature that specifically deals with the present case (cf., [51, 84]). For instance, one approach to educating students to work with AI in the future workplace is to see AI tools as collaborators. As such, literature on collaboration in education may become relevant. However, that literature has the underlying assumption that collaborators are sentient, independent, and responsible agents—an assumption that does not hold with AI agents. Alternatively, literature on computer-assisted learning does not typically assume the human-like behavior of the tools used in such investigations—making the literature an imperfect precedent for AI skills training. As such, this section outlines various efforts and the factors involved while also trying to characterize the uncertainty of these factors.

3.2.1 Stakeholders

We begin with identifying the various stakeholders in curriculum development at the tertiary level. This obviously includes the students as learners and potential workers but also the faculty and institutional staff as managers, overseers, and implementers of the curriculum. However, further stakeholders can be identified: industries that will eventually employ graduates of these curricula, the greater community that will depend on these workers in the future as they take advantage of industry services and products, and the government which will take an advisory or regulatory role over implementations of these educational systems. In a sense, it is hard not to see *everyone* as having some stake in AI skills training at the tertiary level (hence the suitability of the Indian Government's *#AIforAll* catchphrase).

Students are the most direct beneficiaries of AI skills training as it ostensibly prepares them for their roles in a future workforce, though perhaps ensuring their training is sufficient and that students themselves recognize that their training is sufficient may be a greater challenge than it seems in the age of AI. Abdelwahab, Rauf, and Chen [1], for instance, surveyed final-year and recent graduate students of business schools in the Netherlands and observed that many show a cursory knowledge of AI but are unclear whether their education has provided them with the skills needed for a future work environment using AI systems (see also [63, 76]). This would suggest that not only do students need the skills to use AI effectively in the workplace, they further need a meta-awareness of what constitutes these skills and how and whether one attains them: in short, "AI literacy"—a construct about which a consensus has not yet been reached in the literature (to be discussed further below).

Faculty members and administrative staff in tertiary institutions serve as the face of AI skills training. This means the responsibility for implementing AI skills training curricula falls most directly on them at the institutional, departmental, and even the classroom level. For those who are in certain fields such as computer science, for example, incorporating such training into their everyday teaching may be a much easier task given their own expertise in AI skills. However, many faculty and staff may find that they themselves first need AI skills training for use in their own work (research, teaching, and administration) before they are sufficiently confident at training students in the effective and ethical use of AI in work. In fact, some faculty and staff might actually be opposed to these efforts, believing, for example, that AI skills and tools might actually be detrimental to the performance of certain jobs (e.g., highly creative work or high-stakes work). Here is one place where the literature is lacking and insights into faculty and staff's attitudes to AI skills and training for the workplace is greatly needed (cf., [1, 98]).

Industry is clearly affected by AI skills training, although the effect is not necessarily constructive. Certainly, where industry has a voice in the training process and where the training actually matches the specific needs of various positions in the workforce, industry benefits in that they do not need to engage in on-the-job training for newly hired workers out of the tertiary system. Yet, a poorly designed curriculum or one that is severely out of date (as the rapid change of AI technology makes ever more possible) could lead to graduates that enter industry unprepared for the jobs, perhaps even necessitating complete retraining—a redundant cost given that new hires had already been "trained" earlier as students. The pace of AI innovations outstrips the speed at which many programs can successfully educate ready and capable future workers. Clearly, close cooperation—if not partnership—with industry should be an essential part of the curriculum development process and its ongoing implementation (cf., [48, 78, 84, 87]; to be discussed further below).

Finally, the community served by higher educational institutions as well as government has roles to play in AI skills training, while also benefiting from a more AI technology-enhanced workforce.

3.2.2 Curriculum Design

Designing an effective curriculum fundamentally involves (1) knowing who the key stakeholders are, (2) what content or skills are to be mastered by the learners, and (3) methods for teaching this content and skill as well as for assessing learners' mastery of the skill (cf., [11, 51, 83]). In the context of AI skills training, each of these aspects faces a number of challenges and barriers. Since the previous section has already discussed the stakeholders, the present section will focus on (2) and (3) and then summarize two implementation cases for illustrative purposes.

As discussed above, learners will need a mastery of two conceptually different things. First, they will need training in the practical skills of using the various AI technological tools and how these tools may be used effectively and ethically in various jobs to meet industry needs, societal expectations, and regulatory structures. This means that any AI skills training curriculum will need reference to—if not direct cooperation or partnership with—industry and government. It is not surprising then that many national policy statements emphasize a "strong industry-academia-government collaboration" (Japan's AI policy statement [3], Appendix 3, p. 1) to effect this goal.

Second, learners will need what has been referred to in the literature as "AI literacy" (cf., [21, 38, 46, 49, 67]). Following an understanding of classical literacies, AI literacy may be broadly defined as the ability to know and understand, use and apply, evaluate and create, and ethically engage with AI technologies (cf., Bloom's taxonomy: [14, 67]). At a minimum, AI skills training could simply consist of the use-and-apply modality and perhaps in certain jobs that is sufficient. However, many jobs requiring AI skills will no doubt require more of workers, incorporating the other three aspects of AI literacy: know and understand, evaluate and create, and broader knowledge of ethical practice. That said, there is no consensus yet on what precisely constitutes this literacy in detail. Views differ as to whether literacy constitutes specific knowledge of AI or rather the readiness to learn AI as well as how computational thinking and problem-solving interacts and supports the learner's use of AI technologies.

While there are several examples of efforts to nail down AI literacy (see below case summaries), the lack of a consensus makes it more difficult to establish methods of teaching and assessment. Given this and the short time frame in which the need for AI skills training has been recognized, the literature on effective methodologies is relatively shallow (cf., [31, 58]). Walter [98] details the need for training in prompt engineering with an extensive description of the needs for learners as well as the accompanying facets of AI literacy that support development of the skill.

However, the novelty of the situation means that methodological validation remains as future work. Empirical work on AI skills training done by Wen, Lin, Liu, and Su [103] looks at a teaching methodology aiming to raise the learner's view of AI tools as cooperative co-creators and measures student development via survey methods. Their work confirms their hypothesis that greater understanding of AI tools leads to greater engagement with the tools as co-creators. They acknowledge, however, that an experimental design would be necessary to confirm their findings. These early works (among others) clearly lead the way in testing the validity of AI skills training methodology, but, indeed, controlled systematic and longitudinal investigations are warranted to advance understanding of effective methodologies.

Tied together to methodologies in any curriculum is assessment and here also the literature is relatively shallow. In a survey analysis, Lintner [49] looks at evaluations of 16 different AI literacy scales and their suitability as assessment tools. While the scales can be identified as having internal consistency, all are in need of further validation with respect to other factors such as construct validity and cross-cultural validity. Furthermore, only three of the scales investigated are performance-based measures while the other 13 are based on self-reporting.

3.2.3 Sample Case: University of Florida

The University of Florida (USA) has initiated a top-down approach in which AI skill-use and training is implemented across the entire university curriculum, ultimately extending into all schools, departments, and classrooms [84]. The initiative, with significant financial backing, includes the hiring of over 100 new faculty dispersed widely across the university and the establishment of a coordinating center for AI educational efforts with the university. A clearly defined view of AI literacy (similar to the four-part view described above, adding a fifth aspect as "enabling AI") underlies the efforts and leads to clearly defined targets for student development. The center also coordinates faculty pairings between novice and expert AI faculty as well as industry partners who provide class training, internships, and other support.

3.2.4 Sample Case: Radiology Training Programs

Smaller scale programs may target specific vocations. One of the leading examples of this is training for radiologists [48, 78, 87]. Led by radiology professional organizations and societies, radiology students and trainees may take self-paced online courses via well-known web services such as Coursera and Fast.ai which train them on how to use AI in radiology work, with the possibility of certification. One admitted challenge with this training method is the availability of suitable mentor support for learners.

3.3 Summary

The following is a summary of the above section, attempting to synthesize the various explicit or implicit factors addressed in this section that underlie the importance and ultimate effectiveness of AI skills.

- Stakeholders: While students and faculty are at the very center of AI skills training, several other stakeholders with somewhat less central but still important roles can be identified: industry, administration and broader academia, government, and the community.
- Content: What is to be taught to learners can be seen in two parts—knowledge and skills.
- Pedagogy: Methods of instruction as well as methods of assessment are central to the process of AI skills training.

4 Future of Skills Training

The present situation in the workplace and the concomitant needs for AI skills training as well as the institutional infrastructure to train students in these needs is still in flux as indicated above. Nevertheless, we believe it is not too early to anticipate upcoming changes or areas of likely but unknown changes—some of which may be quite substantial—that will influence ongoing efforts to develop suitable curricula that address the main goal of preparing students for the AI-enabled workplace. This section reviews some suggested—but not necessarily comprehensive—areas where relevant changes may occur.

4.1 Developments in the Workplace

The rapid advances of AI technology mean continued disruption of the workplace for the foreseeable future [31, 81]. As such, it is not inconceivable that some of the AI skills that students now are being trained to use may already be antiquated by the time they reach the workplace just a few years later. One example of this is the anticipated onset of AGI—generative AI agents that are also capable of reasoning in the way that humans do. At present, given the lack of general reasoning capability of AI technologies, it is not hard to envision a role for workers in filling that role as humans collaborate with AI technologies. However, AGI may erase (or at least fundamentally change) that role for human workers, leading to as-yet unknown roles for human workers once AGI is widely available. As such, in curriculum design, ongoing close consultation with industry is needed (cf., [94]) as well as flexibility in curricula so that rapid changes may be made to accommodate rapid AI technological advances [31, 81]. In anticipation of this, some institutions are taking a proactive approach in areas such as health education [55] and engineering [10], laying the groundwork for the introduction of AGI into the execution of the curriculum itself through teaching methods, assessment, and instructor support as AGI becomes more sophisticated. This then brings learners into contact with AGI and leads to an easier introduction of it into the curricular learning goals. This approach is also in line with advice in the literature to lead by example [51, 87]: Rather than merely teach AI tools, institutions are advised to implement them into the curriculum as well as institutional administration.

4.2 Developments in Education

As noted above, empirical studies of teaching and assessment methods remain rather limited [31, 58]. However, this will surely change as the near universally recognized need for AI skill development drives more and more pedagogical studies and education researchers to explore and examine teaching and assessment. This will then lead to changes in our understanding of effective pedagogy for AI skills development, necessitating adjustments in curriculum design. Hence, it would seem impractical for curriculum developers to invest too much in specific (let alone expensive) methodologies or assessment tools which are as-yet unproven. Even where committing to certain methodologies or assessment tools is necessary to launch a program, maintaining a flexible [31, 81] design that allows change would be prudent.

4.3 Developments in Society, Government, Law, and Ethics

Changes in technology will naturally lead to responsive or possibly even proactive changes in government agencies and regulatory bodies that oversee educational institutions over time. This could lead to curriculum changes at the primary and secondary educational levels that output students who are far better prepared for AI skills training at the tertiary level. These students may arrive at university and vocational schools with skills that already surpass the goals of the curriculum, fundamentally changing, or maybe even negating some of the educational needs that presently seem apparent. Perhaps another way to think of this trend is that the current digital generation may yield to a future "AI generation" [42]. As AI technology becomes more pervasive in society, we may find that the children who grow as digital natives—often referred to collectively as the digital generation—give way to a new sort of youth who might be called "AI natives" [73]—those who have grown up surrounded by and perhaps even partially nurtured by AI technology and robotic agents. Clearly, this will necessitate a different curricular approach.

Questions of digital rights with respect to copyright law are currently making their way through various courts and law-making bodies are responding accordingly, leading to changes that may affect AI skills training (cf., [77]). But another legal issue that is somewhat behind this is that of liability. For instance, if a civil engineer is using AI to develop a bridge that collapses, where does the liability fall: on the engineer or on AI? Can AI agents—or perhaps the companies that produce or provide them—be held responsible for their mistakes? These are important questions that have yet to work their way through courts and legislative bodies (cf., [17, 43, 108]), with resulting regulatory structures that could also have significant consequences for AI skills training at the tertiary level.

The rapid change in AI technology also tends to outpace consideration of consequences for workers' knowledge of the ethical use of these tools. A full discussion of the ethics of AI is beyond the scope of the present work, but we note that there is a lengthy literature on it and consensus seems to have formed around five basic principles (cf., [30, 40, 92, 93]), which we cast here in the context of AI use by workers in industry.

- *Beneficence*—AI should be used in a manner that benefits workers and the clients or customers they serve.
- *Non-maleficence*—The use of AI should not lead to harm of the workers or others, especially maintaining security and privacy.
- *Autonomy*—Workers should be afforded freedom and independence in their use of employer-specified AI tools.
- *Justice*—AI tools should treat the workers fairly and help the workers to do their work fairly toward others.
- *Explicability*—The AI tools output and products should be intelligible and accountable to the workers who use them.

Of course, the ethical use of AI tools extends to university workers as well: faculty and administrators who will serve as examples within the academic community. They, too, will need to be sensitive to various developments in the ethics of AI as part of their overall digital literacy.

4.4 Summary

Following is a short summary of this section, identifying two central tenets that may be distilled.

- Review and revise: Given rapid changes in AI technology leading to consequential changes in industry needs, regulatory structure, community attitudes, and ongoing pedagogical research, there is a need for AI skills training structures to be under regular review with flexibility for curricular revision.
- Exercise good role modeling: Institutions that implement AI skills training curricula should also implement AI technology throughout their institutional structure and reinforce the necessity of both administration and faculty to "practice what they preach."

5 Education Policy Framework for AI Literacy: "ADAPT-AI Framework"

In this section, we attempt to weave together the various threads that we have discussed previously in this chapter to suggest a framework for developing institutional policy—and ultimately curriculum—for AI skills training. We will call this framework the "ADAPT-AI" (Adaptive Development and Assessment of Professional Training in AI). Like most well-known curriculum development frameworks (cf., [90, 91, 105] inter alia), we understand this development process to remain ongoing: That is, once created and implemented, the policy and curriculum remains under continuous review in a dynamic process, even if actual subsequent revisions and implementations occur only at institutionally convenient junctures such as academic terms or academic years. We start describing ADAPT-AI with an understanding of the curriculum itself, then move on to describe the extended context in which it resides, and finish with suggesting an understanding of the dynamic process of policy and curriculum development.

The practical implementation of tertiary education curriculum policy involves three immediate players: faculty, students, and administration. The policy itself constitutes a contract between the faculty and the students that seeks to guarantee that faculty will engage in educational activities for and with students that leads to the development of specified knowledge and skills in these students. Administration serves a supporting role to oversee and facilitate this learning process (see Fig. 2 for a visual representation of these relationships). This description therefore necessitates decisions about content (see Sect. 3.2.2): the specific knowledge and skills to be developed. For present purposes, we distinguish between knowledge—a mental understanding of what AI is, what its capabilities and limitations are, and what constitutes ethical and responsible use of AI technologies as well as why (in sum,

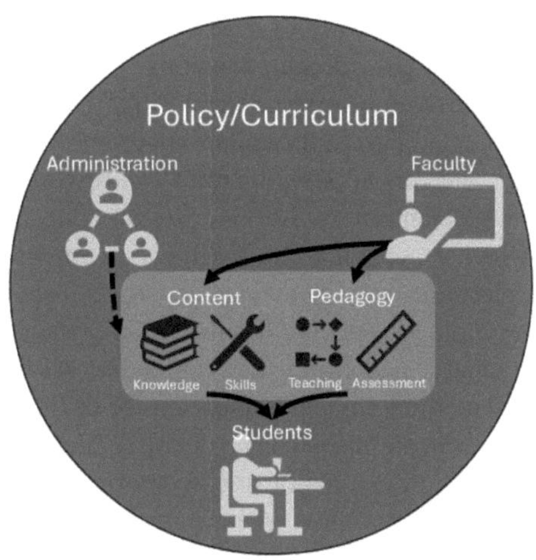

Fig. 2 Key elements of a policy/curriculum implementation in ADAPT-AI

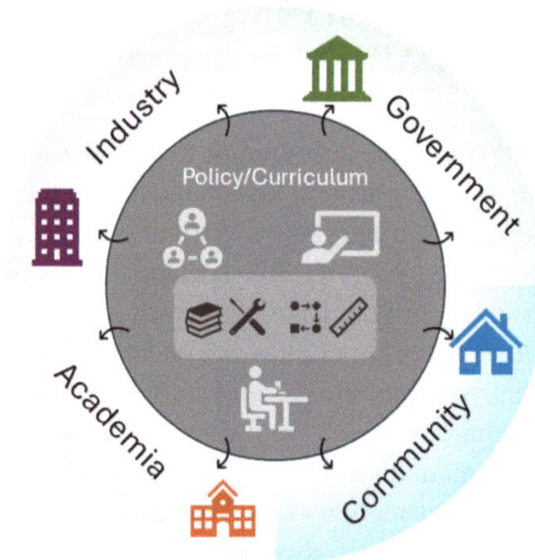

Fig. 3 Curriculum in practice: interaction with context in ADAPT-AI

what has been referred to above as "AI literacy")—and skills—the actual proven capability to use AI technologies to accomplish specified tasks. The extent of the knowledge and the exact set of skills to be taught will, of course, depend on the specific scope of the institution or program for which the policy is being developed. Alongside content is the necessity to decide pedagogy: instructional methodologies and assessment procedures—how the knowledge and skills will be taught and how the students' mastery of them will be assessed. This leads then to the last key element of the central part of our framework: ensuring that faculty have suitable AI literacy and skills themselves in order to train students as well as ensuring that administration has the concomitant AI technology-related resources to support faculty and student pedagogical interactions.

Our representation of the curriculum is not intended to be insular. The ADAPT-AI framework accounts for the fact that this curriculum takes place within a larger context consisting of massively overlapping and interactive entities that make up industry, government, academia, and the community (see Sect. 3.2.1). Elements of the curriculum may connect directly outward (see Fig. 3) to various entities in this context as part of the pedagogy through such things as internships, professional testing and certification, institutional research on skills training, and volunteer service in the community. But our present concern is the development of the curriculum in which we see the flow of influence turning inward as the status of this context helps to determine both content and pedagogy (see Fig. 4). As alluded to in Sect. 3.2.2, industry indicates specific desired skills in their workforce, government helps to establish standards and ethics that help define AI literacy, academia establishes a theoretical and methodological foundation for skills training and assessment, while the community indicates its need and desire for these skills as consumers and laborers. Thus, the context plays a major role in determining the curricular structure and examining the status of the context is a necessary step in developing any AI skills training policy and curriculum. Even if its ultimate implementation is largely contained within the aca-

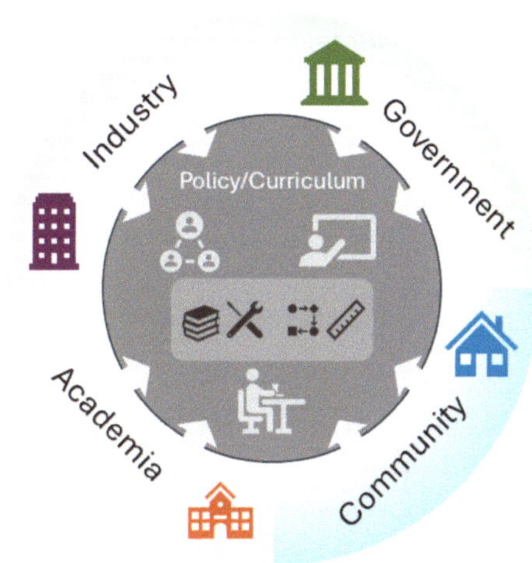

Fig. 4 Curriculum in development: context informs curriculum design in ADAPT-AI

demic walls of the institution, this context aims to promote informed and proactive curriculum development given the dramatic rate of change in AI innovation.

Finally, as noted above, although the curriculum development process in ADAPT-AI may result in a curriculum that is implemented statically, say, to suit academic terms or academic years, the development process continues dynamically to respond to various changes, leading to newer versions of the curriculum that may be implemented at the next convenient juncture (see Fig. 5). These changes are expected to come from various places already discussed in Sect. 4 and other places in this chapter: advances in AI technology will lead to differing skill training needs, industry, and government policy and law may lead to more refined understandings of AI literacy, especially ethics, and these changes may lead to changes in community attitudes toward AI technology and skills training, and educational research may lead to deeper understanding of effective pedagogy for skills training. In Fig. 5, this process is visualized as a spiral staircase with the central column representing the developmental process which is gradually built up until a full policy/curriculum is finalized and initiated. The stairs form conduits by which the context—represented as the stairwell—feed into the developmental process. After implementation of a policy/curriculum, development continues via review and revision with continued reference to the context until a new version is solidified and implemented.

With the ADAPT-AI framework in mind, we offer a few practical suggestions to those tasked with developing or adapting curricula for teaching AI skills:

- Consult with various stakeholders in the context (i.e., Academia, Government, Industry, the Community). What skills do workers need? What level of literacy is required?
- Consider the scope of the policy and curriculum. Is it necessary to make it institution-wide? Or could it be dealt with at a program or department level?

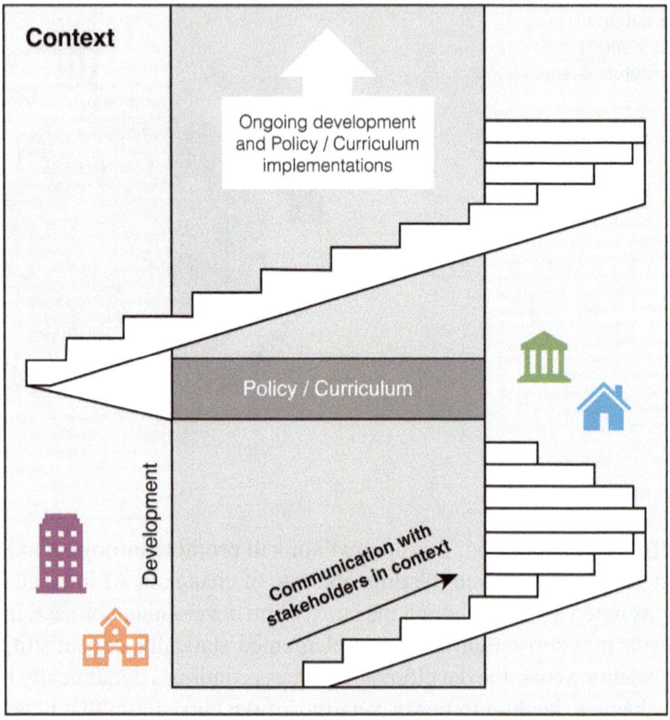

Fig. 5 Policy/curriculum development and implementation in the context of ADAPT-AI

- Consider centralization (cf., [84]) of such things as information, faculty training, and assistive resources for students. How may it best serve the interests of the stakeholders without becoming a bureaucratic burden?
- Anticipate changes. How will changes in the context be monitored so that new implementations may be made in a timely manner?
- Monitor and review each implementation. What structure will be in place to monitor and review the success of each implementation? Where will responsibility for (ideally independent) oversight reside?

6 Conclusion

The future of skills training in the age of AI provides an opportunity for the examination and, perhaps, re-evaluation of tertiary education values and practices. The exponential speed and game-changing wildcards that come up in AI research and development may not persist into the future, but there is also no security in assuming that it will stop or slow down anytime soon. The productivity gains and cost-saving aspects of AI tools will allow organizations to stay afloat and grow, in the process leading society to new industrial practices, new job positions and a new look at how knowledge and skills are transmitted to both students and workers of the AI age. This is not to gloss over and forget that the potential for obsolescence of current practices, positions or values with regard to skills training may occur. Much of the future of AI is murky at present, given the quick speed of new developments and research findings as well as the ongoing public discussion about the harms or benefits of AI in human professional and academic work. Yet there is an important point we wish to remind the reader: the charge into how these new AI tools can be used to augment or diminish human knowledge creation, skills training and the quality of work can be shaped by the interaction and cooperation of academia, industry, government, and the community as per the ADAPT-AI framework. This provides a significant opportunity to demonstrate and teach the value and necessity of human–AI collaborative approaches, laying a foundation whereby future AI engineering developments can keep the human worker in the process and quite possibly make the process more enriching.

In our investigation of skills training in higher education institutions and the role of policy and curriculum development to adapt and steer learning toward successful knowledge production, we detailed a social contract for education and vocational advancement which is now in danger of losing its historical mandate. It must be noted that technological innovation and changes in socio-technical practices have been addressed in prior literature on the educational social contract. Toukan and Tawil [89] emphasize the need for renewed trust in the values, leadership, and the potential of higher education institutions to cast off *status quo* solutions to reinvigorate their mission. While the interactive cooperation between academic, government, industry, and community stakeholders is necessary for quick adaptation in the face of rapid change in the age of AI, this cooperation needs to be centered on an appreciation that long-term human capital development is a public good which each stakeholder can share and participate in. As noted by Patil [74], the involvement of industry (private technology companies in this article) brings its own risks as private businesses operate and function in a manner that is opposed to the operations and goals of academia. It needs to be appreciated that private–public partnerships come with the risk of educational governance being diluted as a result of conflicting needs and interests. However, the future shape of the AI workplace does build some common ground for concern among all stakeholders. We need to keep in mind that any of these stakeholders in the context of the ADAPT-AI framework can advocate conflicting initiatives based on different views of the importance or necessity of human skills versus the potential benefits or risks of human obsolescence via skill erosion. The risk of conflicting values and goals among stakeholders applies to all policy frameworks, and as a result there is a consistent need to establish appropriate checks and balances tailored to the specific context of a program—again, this framework may be implemented at the institutional, departmental, or classroom level. With that said, we believe the ADAPT-AI framework provides a more resilient approach to the looming risks and concerns with gen-AI and its threat to human knowledge and skills training with an adjustable and continually adaptable scope.

With this in mind, future work on this topic should include controlled systematic and longitudinal studies on effective AI skills training methodology, conflict management techniques, and principles to foster alignment among the diverse stakeholders affected by AI skills training as well as experimental investigations into the design and impact of human interaction with AI tools. Though the status and new features of AI tools seems to be in constant flux, focusing on these areas would better help to understand how and if AI tools are trusted and perform as people and organizations expect. Additionally, forming methodologies and assessment practices to verify AI skills and knowledge at the tertiary education level requires a clearer perspective on human relationships with AI and how these relationships are used to create, research, analyze, and produce outputs of various professional and academic domains.

Much of the uncertainty of the future of skills training is not just a matter of frequent updates and developments in AI technology—the abuse of AI tools remains a prominent concern and an obvious area that can motivate and define AI educational curricula. Though there is the equally daunting uncertainty that the foundations of an educational social contract—or even more simply an individual interest in a subject—will be undermined by a shrinking scale of human investment in time and effort. Some individuals may be willing to engage in the cost expenditures of higher education, financial or otherwise, but how many people will pursue higher education when the terms of investment are volatile? The investment risk may lionize values of detachment or intrinsic motivation but that is not every student: the transformation of institutional structures will be a long-term logistical project but developing adaptive policy and curricula is feasible and more potent for our current situation. At present, with weak AI tools, a human–AI collaborative vision with augmented humans performing tasks may be the standard for the near future though the next disruption of strong AI is coming. In contemplating the human future in the age of AI, it is important to remember that as the definition of who is *skilled* is being redefined, the consequence is that the definition of who is *unskilled* is also redefined.

Acknowledgements The authors are grateful to all of the attendees of the NII Shonan Meeting, "The Future of Education with AI," in March 2024. The discussions proved a valuable inspiration and launching point for this chapter. We also appreciate those who reviewed our manuscript, which we feel is much improved as a result. However, any errors remaining in the paper are our sole responsibility. We also wish to thank Hannah R. Nolasco for helping to improve the style of our spiral staircase visual in this chapter.

References

1. Abdelwahab, H.R., Rauf, A., Chen, D.: Business students' perceptions of Dutch higher educational institutions in preparing them for artificial intelligence work environments. Ind. High. Educ. **37**(1), 22–34 (2023)
2. Acemoglu, D.: The simple macroeconomics of AI. Technical Report, National Bureau of Economic Research (2024)

3. AI Technology, S.C.: Artificial intelligence technology strategy. Report of Strategic Council for AI Technology, Japan (2017). https://www.nedo.go.jp/content/100865202.pdf
4. Aoun, J.E.: Robot-proof. (No Title) (2017)
5. Atanasoski, N., Vora, K.: Surrogate humanity: posthuman networks and the (racialized) obsolescence of labor. Catal. Feminism, Theory, Technosci. **1**(1), 1–40 (2015)
6. Athaluri, S.A., Manthena, S.V., Kesapragada, V.K.M., Yarlagadda, V., Dave, T., Duddumpudi, R.T.S.: Exploring the boundaries of reality: investigating the phenomenon of artificial intelligence hallucination in scientific writing through ChatGPT references. Cureus **15**(4) (2023)
7. Attwell, G., Bekiaridis, G., Deitmer, L., Perini, M., Roppertz, S., Tütlys, V.: Artificial intelligence in policies, processes and practices of vocational education and training. Institut Technik und Bildung (ITB) (2020)
8. Australian Government Department of Industry, Science, Energy and Resources: Australia's AI Action Plan. Commonwealth of Australia (2021). https://webarchive.nla.gov.au/awa/20220816053410/. https://www.industry.gov.au/data-and-publications/australias-artificial-intelligence-action-plan
9. Autor, D.H.: Why are there still so many jobs? the history and future of workplace automation. J. Econ. Perspect. **29**(3), 3–30 (2015)
10. Balart, T.S., Shryock, K.J.: A framework for integrating artificial general intelligence into engineering education: enhancing human-centric approaches for industry 5.0. techrxiv (2024). https://doi.org/10.36227/techrxiv.171778881.15802086/v1
11. Bates, T., Cobo, C., Mariño, O., Wheeler, S.: Can artificial intelligence transform higher education? Int. J. Educ. Technol. High. Educ. **17** (2020). https://doi.org/10.1186/s41239-020-00218-x
12. Baumard, N.: Psychological origins of the industrial revolution. Behav. Brain Sci. **42**, e189 (2019)
13. Beudt, S., Blanc, B., Feichtenbeiner, R., Kähler, M.: Critical reflection of AI applications for persons with disabilities in vocational rehabilitation. In: Schumacher, C. (ed.) Proceedings of DELFI Workshop 2020. DeLFI Workshops (DeLFI-WS), pp. 137–146 (2020)
14. Bloom, B.S.: Taxonomy of Educational Objectives, Handbook I: The Cognitive Domain. David McKay Co Inc, New York (1956)
15. Boettcher, J.V.: Design levels for distance and online learning. In: Distance Learning and University Effectiveness: Changing Educational Paradigms for Online Learning, pp. 21–54. IGI Global (2004)
16. Boettcher, J.V.: Ten core principles for designing effective learning environments: Insights from brain research and pedagogical theory. Innov. J. Online Educ. **3**(3) (2007)
17. Buiten, M., de Streel, A., Peitz, M.: The law and economics of AI liability. Comput. Law Secur. Rev. **48**, 105794 (2023). https://doi.org/10.1016/j.clsr.2023.105794. https://www.sciencedirect.com/science/article/pii/S0267364923000055
18. Burger, B., Kanbach, D.K., Kraus, S., Breier, M., Corvello, V.: On the use of AI-based tools like ChatGPT to support management research. Eur. J. Innov. Manag. **26**(7), 233–241 (2023)
19. Camilleri, P.: Robot-proof: higher education in the age of artificial intelligence (2018)
20. Cazzaniga, M., Jaumotte, F., Li, L., Melina, G., Panton, A.J., Pizzinelli, C., Rockall, E.J., Tavares, M.M.: Gen-AI: Artificial intelligence and the future of work. In: IMF Staff Discussion Note SDN2024/001, International Monetary Fund, Washington, DC (2024). https://www.imf.org/en/Publications/Staff-Discussion-Notes/Issues/2024/01/14/Gen-AI-Artificial-Intelligence-and-the-Future-of-Work-542379?cid=bl-com-SDNEA2024001
21. Černý, M.: Ai literacy in higher education: theory and design. In: Tomczyk, Ł. (ed.) New Media Pedagogy: Research Trends, Methodological Challenges, and Successful Implementations, pp. 364–379. Springer Nature Switzerland, Cham (2024). https://doi.org/10.1007/978-3-031-63235-8_24
22. Chen, Y.H., Ceccarelli, M., Yan, H.S.: A historical study and mechanical classification of ancient music-playing automata. Mech. Mach. Theory **121**, 273–285 (2018)
23. Cordasco, F.: A Brief History of Education: A Handbook of Information on Greek, Roman, Medieval, Renaissance, and Modern Educational Practice. No. 67, Rowman & Littlefield (1976)

24. Cornerstone OnDemand: 2024 global state of the skills economy. Technical Report, Cornerstone OnDemand (2024). https://www.cornerstoneondemand.com/resources/article/global-state-skills-economy-2024/
25. Crawford, K., Paglen, T.: Excavating AI: the politics of images in machine learning training sets. Ai & Soc. **36**(4), 1105–1116 (2021)
26. Danaher, J.: Technological change and human obsolescence (2022)
27. Dellermann, D., Calma, A., Lipusch, N., Weber, T., Weigel, S., Ebel, P.: The future of human-AI collaboration: a taxonomy of design knowledge for hybrid intelligence systems (2021). arXiv preprint arXiv:2105.03354
28. Desta, F., Brown, E.J.: Facial recognition for deepfake detection. In: 2022 IEEE Integrated STEM Education Conference (ISEC), pp. 364–364 (2022). https://doi.org/10.1109/ISEC54952.2022.10025295
29. Dominici, P.: Educating for the future in the age of obsolescence. In: 2019 IEEE 18th International Conference on Cognitive Informatics & Cognitive Computing (ICCI* CC), pp. 278–285. IEEE (2019)
30. Floridi, L., Cowls, J.: A unified framework of five principles for AI in society. Harv. Data Sci. Rev. **1**(1) (2019). https://hdsr.mitpress.mit.edu/pub/l0jsh9d1
31. Frank, M.R., Autor, D., Bessen, J.E., Brynjolfsson, E., Cebrian, M., Deming, D.J., Feldman, M., Groh, M., Lobo, J., Moro, E., Wang, D., Youn, H., Rahwan, I.: Toward understanding the impact of artificial intelligence on labor. Proceed. Natl. Acad. Sci. **116**(14), 6531–6539 (2019). https://doi.org/10.1073/pnas.1900949116
32. Fui-Hoon Nah, F., Zheng, R., Cai, J., Siau, K., Chen, L.: Generative AI and ChatGPT: applications, challenges, and AI-human collaboration (2023)
33. Gibney, E.: Ai models fed AI-generated data quickly spew nonsense. Nature **632**(8023), 18–19 (2024)
34. Glikson, E., Woolley, A.W.: Human trust in artificial intelligence: review of empirical research. Acad. Manage. Ann. **14**(2), 627–660 (2020)
35. Green, A., Salvi del Pero, A., Verhagen, A.: Artificial intelligence, job quality and inclusiveness. In: OECD Employment Outlook 2023: Artificial Intelligence and the Labour Market, pp. 128–154. OECD Publishing, Paris, France (2023). https://doi.org/10.1787/99c4c123-en
36. Guarnieri, M.: The roots of automation before mechatronics [historical]. IEEE Ind. Electron. Mag. **4**(2), 42–43 (2010)
37. Hazan, E., Madgavkar, A., Chui, M., Smit, S., Maor, D., Singh Dandona, G., Huyghues-Despointes, R.: A new future of work: The race to deploy generative AI in Europe and beyond. Online article at McKinsey.com web site (2024). https://www.mckinsey.com/mgi/our-research/a-new-future-of-work-the-race-to-deploy-ai-and-raise-skills-in-europe-and-beyond
38. Hornberger, M., Bewersdorff, A., Nerdel, C.: What do university students know about artificial intelligence? development and validation of an ai literacy test. Comput. Educ. Artif. Intell. **5**, 100165 (2023). https://doi.org/10.1016/j.caeai.2023.100165. https://www.sciencedirect.com/science/article/pii/S2666920X23000449
39. Hosseini, M., Rasmussen, L.M., Resnik, D.B.: Using AI to write scholarly publications (2023)
40. Jobin, A., Ienca, M., Vayena, E.: The global landscape of AI ethics guidelines. Nat. Mach. Intell. **1**(9), 389–399 (2019). https://doi.org/10.1038/s42256-019-0088-2
41. Kim, T.: Confucianism, modernities and knowledge: China, South Korea and Japan. In: International Handbook of Comparative Education, pp. 857–872. Springer (2009)
42. Kincl, T., Štrach, P.: Born digital: Is there going to be a new culture of digital natives? J. Glob. Sch. Market. Sci. **31**(1), 30–48 (2021). https://doi.org/10.1080/21639159.2020.1808811
43. Kingston, J.K.C.: Artificial intelligence and legal liability. In: Bramer, M., Petridis, M. (eds.) Research and Development in Intelligent Systems XXXIII. pp. 269–279. Springer International Publishing, Cham (2016). https://doi.org/10.1007/978-3-319-47175-4_20
44. Knight, P.T., Yorke, M.: Employability and good learning in higher education. Teach. High. Educ. **8**(1), 3–16 (2003)

45. Kochhar, R.: Which U.S. Workers are More Exposed to AI on Their jobs? Pew Research Center online report (2023). https://www.pewresearch.org/social-trends/2023/07/26/which-u-s-workers-are-more-exposed-to-ai-on-their-jobs/
46. Laupichler, M.C., Aster, A., Schirch, J., Raupach, T.: Artificial intelligence literacy in higher and adult education: a scoping literature review. Comput. Educ. Artif. Intell. **3**, 100101 (2022). https://doi.org/10.1016/j.caeai.2022.100101. https://www.sciencedirect.com/science/article/pii/S2666920X2200056X
47. Lawler, D.: Flood of 'junk': how Ai is changing scientific publishing. Phys. Org. (2024). https://phys.org/news/2024-08-junk-ai-scientific-publishing.html
48. Li, M.D., Little, B.P.: Appropriate reliance on artificial intelligence in radiology education. J. Am. Coll. Radiol. **20**, 1126–1130 (2023). https://doi.org/10.1016/j.jacr.2023.04.019
49. Lintner, T.: A systematic review of AI literacy scales. NPJ Sci. Learn. **9** (2024). https://doi.org/10.1038/s41539-024-00264-4
50. Lochrin, É.: The role of the automaton from ancient Greece to the modern day. Ph.D. thesis, Institute of Art, Design+Technology (2024)
51. Luckin, R., Cukurova, M., Kent, C., du Boulay, B.: Empowering educators to be AI-ready. Comput. Educ. Artif. Intell. **3**, 100076 (2022). https://doi.org/10.1016/j.caeai.2022.100076. https://www.sciencedirect.com/science/article/pii/S2666920X22000315
52. Maillard, D.: The obsolescence of man in the digital society. Int. J. Appl. Inf. Manage. **1**(3), 99–124 (2021)
53. Marques-Silva, J., Huang, X.: Explainability is not a game. Commun. ACM **67**(7), 66–75 (2024)
54. Martinez, D., Malyska, N., Streilein, B., Caceres, R., Campbell, W., Dagli, C., Gadepally, V., Greenfield, K., Hall, R., King, A., Lippmann, R., Miller, B., Reynolds, D., Richardson, F., Sahin, C., Tran, A., Trepagnier, P., Zipkin, J., Roeser, C., Hennighausen, K., Mohindra, S., Thornton, J.: Artificial intelligence: short history, present developments, and future outlook. Tech. rep., Massachusets Institution of Technology (2019). https://www.ll.mit.edu/r-d/publications/artificial-intelligence-short-history-present-developments-and-future-outlook
55. Masters, K., Herrmann-Werner, A., Festl-Wietek, T., Taylor, D.: Preparing for artificial general intelligence (AGI) in health professions education: Amee guide no. 172. Med. Teach. **0**(0), 1–14 (2024). https://doi.org/10.1080/0142159X.2024.2387802, pMID: 39115700
56. Mayr, O.: The origins of feedback control. Sci. Am. **223**(4), 110–119 (1970). http://www.jstor.org/stable/24927641
57. McGrath, S., Yamada, S.: Skills for development and vocational education and training: current and emergent trends. Int. J. Educ. Dev. **102**, 102853 (2023)
58. Memarian, B., Doleck, T.: Teaching and learning artificial intelligence: insights from the literature. Educ. Inf. Technol. (2024). https://doi.org/10.1007/s10639-024-12679-y
59. Ministry of Science, Technology, and Innovations: Summary of the Brazilian Artificial Intelligence Strategy-EBI. Government of Brazil (2021)
60. Minsky, M.: Steps toward artificial intelligence. Proc. IRE **49**(1), 8–30 (1961)
61. Minsky, M., et al.: A Framework for Representing Knowledge (1974)
62. Montgomery, R.M.: The Obsolescence of Traditional Peer Review: Why AI Should Replace Human Validation in Scientific Research (2024)
63. Moran, N., Ackerman, D.: Can Ai really help me land a job? student reactions to the use of artificial intelligence in career preparation. J. Educ. Bus. **99**(2), 103–112 (2024). https://doi.org/10.1080/08832323.2023.2275205
64. Müller, C.J.: Prometheanism: Technology, Digital Culture and Human Obsolescence. Rowman & Littlefield (2016)
65. Müller, V.C.: Philosophy of AI: a structured overview. In: Smuha, N.A. (ed.) Cambridge Handbook on the Law, Ethics and Policy of Artificial Intelligence, pp. 1–25. Cambridge University Press (2024)
66. Murphy, T.E.: A Road for Prometheus: Technological Disruptions and Infrastructure Investment in History (2020)

67. Ng, D.T.K., Leung, J.K.L., Chu, S.K.W., Qiao, M.S.: Conceptualizing AI literacy: an exploratory review. Comput. Educ. Artif. Intell. **2**, 100041 (2021). https://doi.org/10.1016/j.caeai.2021.100041. https://www.sciencedirect.com/science/article/pii/S2666920X21000357
68. NITI Aayog: National strategy for artificial intelligence #AIforAll. Discussion paper of Ministry of Electronics and Information Technology (NITI Aayog), Government of India (2018). https://www.niti.gov.in/sites/default/files/2019-01/NationalStrategy-for-AI-Discussion-Paper.pdf
69. Nixon, J.: Higher education and the public good. In: Teixeira, P.N., Shin, J.C. (eds.) The International Encyclopedia of Higher Education Systems and Institutions, pp. 637–643. Springer Netherlands, Dordrecht (2020). https://doi.org/10.1007/978-94-017-8905-9_15
70. OECD.AI: powered by EC/OECD (2021), database of national AI policies. Accessed on 19 Oct 2024. https://oecd.ai
71. Introducing ChatGPT (2022). https://openai.com/index/chatgpt/
72. O'Rourke, K.H., Rahman, A.S., Taylor, A.M.: Luddites, the industrial revolution, and the demographic transition. J. Econ. Growth **18**, 373–409 (2013)
73. Panthalookaran, V.: A revised taxonomy of educational objectives for AI-natives: reimagining thinking skills in the age of AI. High. Educ. Future **0**(0), 23476311241285100 (2025). https://doi.org/10.1177/23476311241285100
74. Patil, L.: Education governance and digitization: inherent conflicts and potential safeguards for a new social contract. PROSPECTS **54**, 323–329 (2024). https://doi.org/10.1007/s11125-023-09668-3
75. Roser, M.: The brief history of artificial intelligence: the world has changed fast—what might be next? Our World in Data (2022). https://ourworldindata.org/brief-history-of-ai
76. Rožman, M., Tominc, P., Vrečko, I.: Building skills for the future of work: Students' perspectives on emerging jobs in the data and AI cluster through artificial intelligence in education. Environ. Soc. Psychol. **8**(2) (2023). https://doi.org/10.54517/esp.v8i2.1670
77. Salami, E.: AI-generated works and copyright law: towards a union of strange bedfellows. J. Intell. Prop. Law Pract. **16**(2), 124–135 (2020). https://doi.org/10.1093/jiplp/jpaa189
78. Santomartino, S.M., Siegel, E., Yi, P.H.: Academic radiology departments should lead artificial intelligence initiatives. Acad. Radiol. **30**, 971–974 (2023). https://doi.org/10.1016/j.acra.2022.07.011
79. Sarkar, A.: Exploring perspectives on the impact of artificial intelligence on the creativity of knowledge work: Beyond mechanised plagiarism and stochastic parrots. In: Proceedings of the 2nd Annual Meeting of the Symposium on Human-Computer Interaction for Work, pp. 1–17 (2023)
80. Savage-Smith, E., Smith, M.B.: Islamic geomancy and a thirteenth-century divinatory device: another look. In: Magic and Divination in Early Islam, pp. 211–276. Routledge (2021)
81. Selenko, E., Bankins, S., Shoss, M., Warburton, J., Restubog, S.L.D.: Artificial intelligence and the future of work: a functional-identity perspective. Curr. Dir. Psychol. Sci. **31**(3), 272–279 (2022). https://doi.org/10.1177/09637214221091823
82. Seufert, S.: Artificial Intelligence in Vocational Education and Training (VET): Evaluating Vet Leaders' Acceptance of Ai in Switzerland (2024) (under review); pre-print downloaded from Research Square
83. Shah, P.: AI and the Future of Education: Teaching in the Age of Artificial Intelligence. Wiley (2023)
84. Southworth, J., Migliaccio, K., Glover, J., Glover, J., Reed, D., McCarty, C., Brendemuhl, J., Thomas, A.: Developing a model for AI across the curriculum: transforming the higher education landscape via innovation in AI literacy. Comput. Educ. Artif. Intell. **4**, 100127 (2023). https://doi.org/10.1016/j.caeai.2023.100127. https://www.sciencedirect.com/science/article/pii/S2666920X23000061
85. Sowa, K., Przegalinska, A., Ciechanowski, L.: Cobots in knowledge work: human-AI collaboration in managerial professions. J. Bus. Res. **125**, 135–142 (2021)

86. Sun, W., Shi, Z., Gao, S., Ren, P., de Rijke, M., Ren, Z.: Contrastive learning reduces hallucination in conversations. In: Proceedings of the Thirty-Seventh AAAI Conference on Artificial Intelligence and Thirty-Fifth Conference on Innovative Applications of Artificial Intelligence and Thirteenth Symposium on Educational Advances in Artificial Intelligence. AAAI'23/IAAI'23/EAAI'23, AAAI Press (2023). https://doi.org/10.1609/aaai.v37i11.26596
87. Tejani, A.S., Elhalawani, H., Moy, L., Kohli, M., Kahn, C.E.: Artificial intelligence and radiology education. Radiol. Artif. Intell. **5**(1), e220084 (2023). https://doi.org/10.1148/ryai.220084
88. Thakkar, D., Kumar, N., Sambasivan, N.: Towards an AI-powered future that works for vocational workers. In: Proceedings of the 2020 CHI Conference on Human Factors in Computing Systems, pp. 1–13 (2020)
89. Toukan, E., Tawil, S.: A new social contract for education: rebuilding trust in education as a common good. PROSPECTS **54**, 259–275 (2024). https://doi.org/10.1007/s11125-024-09702-y
90. Tyler, R.: Basic Principles of Curriculum and Instruction. University of Chicago Press, Chicago, IL (1949)
91. UNESCO: Curriculum Revision and Research. No. 28 in Education Studies and Documents, UNESCO, Paris, France (1958)
92. UNESCO: Recommendation on the Ethics of Artificial Intelligence. UNESCO, Paris, France (2022)
93. UNESCO: Guidance for Generative AI in Education and Research. UNESCO, Paris, France (2023)
94. United Nations Educational, Scientific and Cultural Organization: Understanding the Impact of AI on Skills Development. UNESCO-UNEVOC International Centre for Technical and Vocational Education and Training, Bonn, Germany (2021). https://unevoc.unesco.org/pub/understanding_the_impact_of_ai_on_skills_development.pdf
95. US Government: H.r. 9567 (89th): An act to strengthen the educational resources of our colleges and universities and to provide financial assistance for students in post-secondary and higher education. US Law (1965)
96. Venkatesh, V.: Adoption and use of AI tools: a research agenda grounded in UTAUT. Ann. Oper. Res. **308**(1), 641–652 (2022)
97. Vössing, M., Kühl, N., Lind, M., Satzger, G.: Designing transparency for effective human-AI collaboration. Inf. Syst. Front. **24**(3), 877–895 (2022)
98. Walter, Y.: Embracing the future of artificial intelligence in the classroom: the relevance of AI literacy, prompt engineering, and critical thinking in modern education. Int. J. Educ. Technol. High. Educ. **21** (2024). https://doi.org/10.1186/s41239-024-00448-3
99. Wang, C., Cai, J., Gao, C., Ye, X.: History, status, and development of AI-based learning science. SN Comput. Sci. **4**(3) (2023). https://doi.org/10.1007/s42979-023-01778-1
100. Wang, D., Churchill, E., Maes, P., Fan, X., Shneiderman, B., Shi, Y., Wang, Q.: From human-human collaboration to human-AI collaboration: designing AI systems that can work together with people. In: Extended Abstracts of the 2020 CHI Conference on Human Factors in Computing Systems, pp. 1–6 (2020)
101. Weber, L., Berga, S. (eds.): The public responsibility for higher education and research (2005). Council of Europe higher education series No. 2, Council of Europe (2005). https://book.coe.int/en/higher-education-and-research/3301-the-public-responsibility-for-higher-education-and-research-council-of-europe-higher-education-series-no-2.html
102. Wei, J., Karina, N., Chung, H.W., Jiao, Y.J., Papay, S., Glaese, A., Schulman, J., Fedus, W.: Measuring short-form factuality in large language models. Technical Report, OpenAI (2024)
103. Wen, H., Lin, X., Liu, R., Su, C.: Enhancing college students' AI literacy through human-AI co-creation: a quantitative study. In: Proceedings of the 2024 International Conference on Digital Society and Artificial Intelligence, p. 123–129. DSAI '24, Association for Computing Machinery, New York, NY, USA (2024). https://doi.org/10.1145/3677892.3677913
104. Westman, S., Kauttonen, J., Klemetti, A., Korhonen, N., Manninen, M., Mononen, A., Niittymäki, S., Paananen, H.: Artificial intelligence for career guidance-current requirements and prospects for the future. IAFOR J. Educ. **9**(4), 43–62 (2021)

105. Wheeler, D.: Curriculum Process. University of London Press (1967)
106. Wizner, S.: Beyond skills training. Clin. L. Rev. **7**, 327 (2000)
107. Xing, X., Shi, F., Huang, J., Wu, Y., Nan, Y., Zhang, S., Fang, Y., Roberts, M., Schönlieb, C.B., Del Ser, J., et al.: When AI eats itself: on the caveats of data pollution in the era of generative AI (2024). arXiv preprint arXiv:2405.09597
108. Zech, H.: Liability for AI: public policy considerations. ERA Forum **22**, 147–158 (2021). https://doi.org/10.1007/s12027-020-00648-0
109. Zhang, Y., Li, Y., Cui, L., Cai, D., Liu, L., Fu, T., Huang, X., Zhao, E., Zhang, Y., Chen, Y., et al.: Siren's song in the AI ocean: a survey on hallucination in large language models (2023). arXiv preprint arXiv:2309.01219

Affective Computing and the Future of Education

Benjamin Tag and Nan Gao

Abstract Emotions are critical in learning, influencing focus, motivation, and resilience. Recent advances in machine learning, artificial intelligence, and digital technologies enable new ways to measure and support peoples' emotional experiences. In education, these tools promise to offer personalized emotional support, helping students manage challenges and maintain engagement. However, alongside these benefits are significant ethical concerns, particularly regarding privacy and the potential for emotional manipulation. This chapter explores the opportunities and challenges of Affective Computing in education, examining how AI can enhance emotional support while addressing privacy risks and ethical considerations.

Keywords Affective Computing · Education · Artificial intelligence

1 Introduction

The intersection of technology and education is undergoing a paradigm shift, with *Affective Computing* technology [51]—designed to sense, interpret, and respond to human emotions—promising to play a pivotal role. As education moves toward a more personalized and adaptive format, the ability to understand and respond to students' emotional states has become a critical issue. Emotions, after all, are deeply intertwined with learning, shaping attention, motivation, resilience, enjoyment, and overall cognitive performance [62].

Recent breakthroughs in artificial intelligence and machine learning and the COVID-19 pandemic have put a spotlight on our reliance on digital technology and emotional well-being [60] and have reignited the interest in Affective Computing, offering promising opportunities to transform classrooms into emotion-aware learn-

B. Tag (✉)
University of New South Wales, Sydney, Australia
e-mail: benjamin.tag@unsw.edu.au

N. Gao
Nankai University, Tianjian, China
e-mail: nan.gao@nankai.edu.cn

A. Dengel et al. (eds.), *The Future of Education with AI*,
https://doi.org/10.1007/978-981-95-1622-3_6

ing environments. Using tools capable of real-time emotion recognition, educators and digital platforms allow educators to gain nuanced insights into students' engagement, well-being, and readiness to learn [7, 40]. This promises to benefit both educators and students by fostering academic achievement and emotional intelligence—an essential skill for thriving in an increasingly complex world.

While systems detect student attention and engagement [27], emotions pose different challenges due to their complexity and persistent challenges to detect them accurately. Today, however, we can imagine an AI-driven system that detects signs of frustration in a student—based on a multitude of signals—tackling a challenging problem. Such a system could dynamically adapt to the detected frustration by simplifying the task, offering alternative explanations, additional definitions, encouragement, or suggesting a short break. Conversely, recognizing excitement might signal readiness for more complex challenges, enhancing motivation and deepening engagement. This could lead to the system enriching the content with additional information or providing extra tasks. These personalized interventions promise to create a learning experience that is both academically rigorous and emotionally supportive [15].

However, as with any transformative technology, Affective Computing raises pressing ethical and practical questions. How can we ensure the privacy and security of emotion-based data, probably the most intimate data we humans have? What safeguards are necessary to prevent misuse or bias in emotion-sensing systems? And how do we balance the promise of emotional insights with the risk of over-surveillance in educational settings? Addressing these challenges will be vital to using the full potential of Affective Computing to build an emotionally intelligent educational environment—one where technology not only supports learning but also nurtures the whole student.

2 The Role of Emotion in Learning

Learning is not merely a cognitive activity but an equally emotional one. Emotions influence how information is processed, retained, and applied, acting as both enablers and blockages to learning success [62]. In this section, we briefly explore the core concepts of the role of emotions in learning, especially focusing on how they shape motivation, engagement, and resilience. We will introduce the intricate interplay between emotion and cognition in educational contexts, presenting a foundation for understanding how Affective Computing can enhance learning outcomes.

2.1 The Cognitive-Emotional Interconnection

Cognitive processes such as attention, memory, and decision-making are closely related to our emotional states. The main processing center for our emotions—the amygdala—also plays a critical role in modulating memory consolidation [45, 68]. Positive emotions have been shown to enhance creative thinking and problem-solving [32]. In contrast, negative emotions can hinder cognitive flexibility [55] and working memory capacity [36], highlighting the importance of considering emotions in educational practices. Studies using functional MRI (fMRI) have shown that positive emotional states enhance activation in regions associated with memory and attention, while negative emotions, such as anxiety, reduce this activation and increase stress-related cortisol levels, lowering cognitive performance [49].

Another part of our brain—the hippocampus—which is vital for encoding long-term memories, is more active when emotional stimuli are involved [13, 56]. This explains why emotionally charged experiences tend to be remembered more vividly than neutral ones, a phenomenon that can be strategically used in teaching methodologies. For example, students who feel excited about a topic are more likely to engage deeply and retain knowledge [39]. In contrast, chronic stress or anxiety can disrupt this process, emphasizing the need for emotional regulation strategies in education [34, 48].

Emotionally engaging content enhances student retention and understanding. For instance, storytelling in science education has been found to boost recall and application of concepts by invoking curiosity and excitement [54]. However, on the contrary, negative emotions, such as frustration during poorly scaffolded tasks, can lead to cognitive overload, where working memory is overwhelmed, creating obstacles to learning [11].

2.2 Motivation and Engagement

Motivation theories, such as *Self-Determination Theory* (SDT) [16] and *Expectation Value Theory* [16], prove the importance of emotions in sustaining effort and perseverance. SDT emphasizes that environments that foster positive emotions, such as satisfaction and interest, encourage intrinsic motivation, which describes a state where learners pursue a task for their inherent value rather than external rewards.

However, emotional states such as fear of failure can activate avoidance behaviors, reducing the student's willingness to engage in challenging tasks. It is vital for educators (and technology) to understand these dynamics because this enables them to create interventions that minimize negative emotional triggers and maximize positive emotional reinforcement.

Engagement is closely linked to emotional resonance. Students are more likely to engage deeply when they see personal relevance in the material or feel emotionally invested. For example, prior research has shown that a history lesson framed around the emotional struggles of individuals in a historical context captivates students more effectively than a purely factual recount of the past [38].

Technology offers opportunities to create this form of engagement. For example, Virtual reality (VR) and simulations can immerse students in emotionally charged scenarios, fostering empathy and a deeper connection to the subject matter [23]. The challenge, however, to avoid creating entertainment and not educational content persists.

2.3 Resilience and Academic Success

Resilience is defined as the capacity to recover from setbacks and persist despite difficulties. Emotional resilience is crucial in education, where challenges are inevitable. Emotion-focused interventions, such as mindfulness practices, journaling, and group discussions [57], have been successfully used in prior research to teach students strategies to manage stress and overcome other academic barriers.

Educational programs focusing on Social-Emotional Learning (SEL) [30] have demonstrated significant benefits, including reduced anxiety, improved self-regulation, and higher academic achievement. These programs teach skills such as recognizing and managing emotions, setting positive goals, and developing empathy.

The relationship between emotional well-being and **academic success** is well documented. Different meta-analyses on hundreds of studies have found that students with higher emotional intelligence (EI) not only perform better academically but also exhibit stronger interpersonal relationships and greater life satisfaction [19, 42], highlighting the importance of integrating emotional development into traditional academic curricula.

Furthermore, chronic emotional distress, such as that caused by bullying or family challenges, can lead to academic disengagement [35]. Addressing emotional well-being through school counsellors, peer-support programs, but also adaptive technologies promise to be essential for creating an inclusive and supportive learning environment.

3 What Is Affective Computing?

The concept of Affective Computing was first formalized by Rosalind Picard in her seminal 1997 book *Affective Computing* [51], where she argued for the necessity of endowing machines with the ability to recognize, interpret, and respond to human emotions. Picard proposed that for technology to interact effectively with humans, it must account for the emotional dimensions of human behavior. This foundational idea has since evolved into a multidisciplinary field encompassing computer science, psychology, neuroscience, and education. Affective Computing is built on the premise that emotions are central to human decision-making and interaction. By equipping systems with affective awareness, researchers and developers aim to create technologies that can better adapt to human needs, making them more intuitive, empathetic, and effective across domains such as healthcare, business, and education.

Affective Computing applications typically follow a three-step process involving:

1. **Emotion Detection**: Capturing emotional signals from users through physiological, behavioral, or textual inputs.
2. **Emotion Interpretation**: Using algorithms, often driven by machine learning or artificial intelligence (AI), to analyze and classify emotional states.
3. **Adaptive Responses**: Implementing changes based on detected emotions, such as adjusting interface difficulty, offering encouragement, or tailoring feedback.

The origins of Affective Computing can be traced to advancements in artificial intelligence and emotion theory during the 1990s [50, 51]. Foundational contributions from psychology, particularly Paul Ekman's pioneering research on universal facial expressions [21], provided a basis for computational models of emotion recognition. Today, the field combines insights from artificial intelligence, psychology, and neuroscience to develop emotion-sensing technologies, including facial recognition, physiological monitoring, and sentiment analysis [66]. While early systems focused on detecting emotions through single modalities, modern Affective Computing systems integrate multiple modalities—facial expressions [61], voice tone [43], physiological signals [66], and even contextual data [5]—to provide a holistic understanding of user emotions. This multimodal approach has become particularly relevant in education, where the emotional state of learners often fluctuates dynamically.

The aims of Affective Computing are broad and profoundly transformative and can be summarized as follows:

- Enhancing user experiences by making technology more responsive.
- Supporting mental and emotional well-being through monitoring and intervention.
- Improving learning environments by personalizing content based on emotional engagement.

In education, Affective Computing offers transformative tools, including emotion detection through cameras to recognize frustration or excitement [20, 61], wearable devices to monitor physiological signals like heart rate variability and skin conductance [17, 27], and sentiment analysis tools to interpret the emotional tone of written reflections [46]. These technologies enable adaptive learning environments, offering personalized feedback, dynamic task adjustments, and emotional support to enhance student engagement and resilience. As the field evolves, addressing ethical considerations such as data privacy, algorithmic fairness, and the appropriate use of emotion-sensing tools in sensitive (educational) contexts remains a critical challenge. Today, parts of the field, e.g., the reliance on Paul Ekman's assumption of universal expressions of emotion [21, 67], are widely discussed and even debunked by thought leaders like Picard.

4 The Promise of Personalized Education

Affective Computing offers several promising technologies tailored for educational environments. These tools are designed to identify and respond to students' emotional needs, enhancing engagement and learning outcomes.

Emotion Detection Through Cameras Facial expression analysis via cameras can identify signs of frustration, confusion, or excitement in students. By detecting these states, adaptive learning platforms can adjust instructional strategies, such as simplifying tasks or offering motivational prompts.

Wearable Devices for Physiological Data Wearables such as smartwatches and biofeedback sensors can monitor physiological indicators like heart rate variability (HRV), skin conductance, and temperature. These data points provide insights into stress levels and cognitive load, helping educators understand when students might need a break or additional support.

Sentiment Analysis in Written Work Natural language processing tools can analyze students' written reflections or assignments to detect sentiment. For example, identifying negative sentiment in journal entries might indicate a need for emotional support, while positive sentiment could reflect engagement and motivation.

Educational Applications These technologies enable a range of applications in education:

- **Personalized Learning**: Systems can adapt lesson difficulty, pacing, or instructional style based on students' emotional engagement.
- **Real-Time Feedback**: Teachers can receive live updates on the emotional states of their class, allowing them to adjust teaching strategies dynamically.
- **Supportive Interventions**: Automated systems can provide encouragement or suggest stress-relief techniques to students experiencing frustration or anxiety.

Several studies highlight the potential of affective technology to enhance engagement and improve classroom dynamics by adapting to students' emotional states. For instance, Gashi et al. [28] discovered that physiological synchrony among students, measured via electrodermal activity (EDA) [8], was associated with a positive emotional climate in the classroom. This finding enables teachers to monitor and influence the emotional atmosphere unobtrusively, potentially enhancing student well-being and academic performance. Similarly, Di et al. [17] demonstrated that wearable devices can reliably track emotional engagement, allowing teachers to identify disengaged students accurately. Such feedback mechanisms empower teachers to intervene promptly while also enabling students to self-monitor and adjust their engagement levels.

In a practical application, Gao et al. [27] conducted a 4-week study in a K-12 school, deploying a student engagement sensing system that utilized wearable sensors and environmental data to monitor student engagement during classes. Their findings emphasize the potential of integrating wearable and environmental sensors to create adaptive, responsive learning environments.

Further, research by Gao et al. [26] on classroom seating arrangements revealed that students seated closer together exhibited higher engagement levels, as indicated by physiological synchrony. This suggests that optimized, AI-supported seating arrangements could harness insights from Affective Computing to improve focus and collaboration, fostering more adaptive and responsive learning environments.

5 Technologies Enabling Affective Computing

Affective Computing is driven by various technologies designed to detect, interpret, and respond to human emotions in real time. These technologies, spanning emotion detection methods and data analysis platforms, hold significant potential in educational settings, where insights into emotional states can support the development of personalized learning experiences.

5.1 Emotion Detection Methods

Emotion detection lies at the heart of Affective Computing, providing the foundation for technologies to recognize and respond to human emotions. Various techniques are used to monitor emotional states based on physiological, behavioral, and psychological indicators.

Facial Expression Analysis utilizes computer vision and machine learning algorithms to decode facial movements, often using systems like the Facial Action Coding System (FACS) [22]. These systems can detect emotions such as frustration or engagement, allowing adaptive learning systems to respond accordingly. In educational settings, systems such as EduSense [6] monitor students' facial expressions and can detect emotional states such as frustration, confusion, or engagement, allowing adaptive learning systems to respond accordingly.

Voice Tone and Speech Pattern Recognition analyze the prosody (pitch, tone, rhythm) of speech to infer emotions. Advances in speech processing and natural language processing (NLP) enable systems to recognize emotions like anger or excitement through vocal cues. In educational settings, this can identify when students are disengaged or confused [6], prompting interventions.

Physiological Signals such as heart rate, electrodermal activity, and electromyography provide objective indicators of emotional arousal. In educational environments, these sensors can be integrated into wearable technology to monitor students' emotional responses and engagement levels [17, 27]. For example, a significant increase in heart rate or EDA can be an indicator of stress or anxiety, prompting the system to recommend a calming activity or adjust the difficulty of a task.

Mobile Sensing utilizes smartphones and wearable devices for continuous, non-intrusive monitoring of emotional states [25, 61, 65]. These technologies capture data such as physical activity, sleep patterns, and communication habits, which correlate with emotional well-being. In education, mobile sensing enables real-time tracking of students' emotions, facilitating personalized interventions without disrupting learning.

5.2 Software and Tools

Various software platforms and tools are available to facilitate and integrate emotion detection into educational systems. These tools are often built around machine learning models that can process data from sensors, cameras, and speech analysis to infer emotions.

Emotion Recognition Platforms like *Affectiva* [3], *EmoReact* [47], and *RealEyes* [53] apply facial recognition, voice analysis, and other sensor data to identify emotional states. These platforms are usually embedded in tools that monitor and respond to human emotions [61, 67], enhancing personalized experience in learning and other domains.

Adaptive learning systems, such as *DreamBox* [4] and *Knewton* [2], are AI-powered platforms that personalize educational content based on individual student performance and engagement. When combined with Affective Computing technologies, these systems can go beyond performance metrics, adjusting content in response to the emotional state of the student.

5.3 Data Collection and Analysis

Effective data collection and analysis are essential for emotion recognition in Affective Computing. These processes leverage diverse data sources, as mentioned above, including facial expressions, speech, and mobile and physiological signals, to infer emotional states. Open datasets play a critical role in advancing this field, particularly in educational settings, as they provide a basis for training intelligent models.

5.3.1 Open Datasets for Affective Computing in Education

Several open datasets have been specifically designed or adapted to capture emotional data relevant to educational contexts. These datasets provide rich multimodal data and have become key resources for researchers in Affective Computing. Notable examples include

- StudentLife Dataset [63]: StudentLife Dataset [63]: This dataset utilizes passive sensing data collected from the smartphones of 48 Dartmouth students over a 10-week term. It captures mental health indicators (e.g., depression, loneliness, stress), academic performance metrics (e.g., grades, term GPA, cumulative GPA), and behavioral trends (e.g., changes in stress, sleep, and gym visits) in response to academic workload. This dataset is widely employed to study university students' emotional and mental well-being through mobile sensing.

- En-Gage Dataset [24]: This multi-sensing dataset combines physiological and environmental sensing data from 23 students and 6 teachers in a 4-week cross-sectional study in a high school. Collected from Empatica E4 [1] wearable sensors, it logs physiological data (e.g., EDA, blood volume pulse, skin temperature) and collects daily surveys on thermal comfort, learning engagement, emotions, and seating positions. The dataset includes 488 survey responses and over 1,400 h of wearable data, offering valuable insights into emotional and engagement dynamics in classroom settings.
- Globem Dataset [64]: This multi-year dataset encompasses over 700 user-years of data from 497 unique participants, collected via smartphone and wearable sensors (e.g., Fitbits). It includes metrics on physical activity, sleep behavior, emotion regulation, social well-being, and mental health indicators such as depression. The dataset supports research on the interplay between long-term behavioral patterns and emotional well-being.

5.3.2 Data Collection

Data collection in Affective Computing often involves multimodal sensing, wherein data is gathered from various sources simultaneously. In an educational environment, this might include (1) Cameras. To capture facial expressions and gestures for emotion and engagement analysis. (2) Microphones: To analyze voice tone and speech patterns. (3) Wearable Sensors: To measure physiological signals such as heart rate, skin conductivity, and temperature. (4) Interaction Logs: To track engagement metrics such as time spent on tasks or participation in digital learning activities. By integrating these diverse data streams, systems can provide a comprehensive and nuanced understanding of students' emotional and cognitive states. This multimodal approach enhances the reliability and accuracy of emotion detection models.

5.3.3 Data Processing and Analysis

Once data is collected, it undergoes preprocessing and analysis using machine learning algorithms. These algorithms are trained to identify patterns in the data that correspond to specific emotional states. For instance, a model might be designed to detect frustration by analyzing a combination of increased heart rate, elevated skin conductivity, negative facial expressions, and changes in voice tone.

In educational contexts, such analyses enable the creation of personalized learning experiences. For example, if the system detects anxiety during a test, it could trigger adaptive interventions, such as displaying calming prompts, suggesting a brief break, or modifying the test environment. These insights foster a supportive and responsive educational experience, ultimately enhancing student learning outcomes. A relatively young discipline that focuses on intelligently adapting learning processes and understanding the nuances of learning behaviors is known as *Learning Analytics* [29, 31].

6 Key Challenges and Limitations

While Affective Computing holds great promise in transforming education, several challenges and limitations must be overcome before its implementation. These issues span technological constraints, the inherent complexity of emotions, and practical barriers within educational settings. They, thus, require careful consideration for successful adoption and meaningful outcomes.

6.1 Technological Limitations

A significant challenge lies in the *accuracy and reliability* of emotion detection systems. Current algorithms often struggle to interpret subtle or ambiguous emotional expressions, particularly in real-time educational contexts where emotional signals are dynamic and influenced by multiple factors. Many systems rely on data from limited modalities, such as facial expressions or physiological signals, which may not fully capture the complexity of emotions [10]. Moreover, the contextual sensitivity of these systems remains limited; for instance, a moving eyebrow might be misinterpreted as frustration when it may simply indicate concentration.

Achieving *real-time adaptation* is another hurdle, as the computational demands of processing multimodal emotional data at scale can exceed the capabilities of current hardware and software systems. Additionally, limitations in data quality, such as noise or missing data, can reduce the effectiveness of detection models. These issues are particularly pronounced in classroom settings, where environmental variables like lighting, noise, or device interference can further compromise data reliability.

Another critical limitation involves the *generalizability of emotion detection models* [44]. Many systems are trained on datasets that lack diversity, leading to biases in emotion recognition across different cultural, demographic, or contextual scenarios. Addressing these biases requires the collection of more representative datasets and the development of algorithms capable of accounting for individual and cultural variations in emotional expression [14].

6.2 *The Complexity of Emotions in Context*

One of the greatest challenges in emotion detection lies in the accurate interpretation of emotions, which demands a nuanced understanding of the user context—a capability that current systems often lack or struggle to compute. Physiological signals can indicate a range of states, from stress to excitement, making it difficult to assign definitive emotional labels without considering subjective input or additional contextual factors [52]. Moreover, emerging research highlights the complexity of experiencing multiple emotions simultaneously, such as feeling both anxious and motivated, which further complicates simplistic categorizations [37].

Cultural and individual differences further complicate emotion recognition, as expressions of emotions such as anger, happiness, or sadness vary significantly across cultures and personal tendencies. For instance, while a smile might universally indicate happiness, its intensity, frequency, or associated behavioral cues may differ greatly, leading to potential misinterpretations in diverse educational environments [9]. These differences can lead to potential misinterpretations in diverse educational environments, emphasizing the need for systems that adapt to individual and cultural variability. Addressing these challenges requires advancements in multimodal emotion detection methods and the integration of adaptive, context-aware algorithms capable of interpreting emotions more holistically [14].

To address some of these limitations, researchers increasingly turn to multimodal approaches, which combine data from multiple sources such as facial expressions, voice tone, posture, and physiological signals. These systems hold promise for improving the accuracy of emotion detection by providing a more comprehensive understanding of emotional states. However, multimodal systems introduce new challenges, including increased computational complexity and the integration of diverse data streams in real time [18]. Furthermore, inconsistencies between modalities can arise—for example, a student's facial expression might show boredom, while their physiological signals indicate engagement—making it difficult to synthesize these inputs into a coherent emotional profile.

6.3 *Educational Environment Constraints*

Even when technological challenges are addressed, practical barriers within educational environments can hinder the adoption of Affective Computing. Resistance from educators and institutions is common, stemming from concerns about the reliability of these technologies, potential disruptions to traditional teaching methods, or skepticism about their added value. Budgetary and resource limitations also play a significant role, particularly in public schools or underserved communities where funding for advanced technology is scarce. Furthermore, integrating Affective Computing tools into existing educational workflows often requires significant training for teachers and ongoing technical support, both of which add to implementation costs and complexity.

7 Ethical and Privacy Concerns

The integration of Affective Computing into educational environments introduces complex ethical and privacy concerns. While these technologies have the potential to enhance learning and emotional well-being, their deployment must be carefully managed to safeguard the rights, autonomy, and psychological safety of students and educators.

7.1 Privacy and Data Security

Affective Computing heavily relies on collecting sensitive data, such as facial expressions, physiological signals, and emotional responses, raising significant concerns about privacy and data security. In classroom settings, where students often do not have the opportunity to opt out of continuous data collection, the risk of misuse or unauthorized access to this data becomes particularly concerning. Emotional data, unlike traditional academic records, is deeply personal and could be exploited for purposes unrelated to education, such as profiling or targeted advertising. Since students, except for university students, are usually underage, this raises even more significant questions. Further questions are related to the data processing. Since data from relatively large groups of students (classrooms) are collected, the large amounts of data have to be processed in real time. It has to be investigated if this is possible locally or if the data has to be transferred to a large computing cluster. This would again pose an additional risk since connections to the Internet make the infrastructure vulnerable to attacks. The providers of affective technologies have to ensure robust encryption, limited data retention policies, and strict access controls in order to mitigate these risks.

7.2 Consent and Autonomy

Issues of consent are especially critical in educational environments, where students—many of whom are minors—may not have the legal capacity or knowledge to provide informed consent. Parents or guardians are often required to act on behalf of students, which can create ethical dilemmas about whose interests are being prioritized. Furthermore, students should retain autonomy over their emotional data, including the ability to access, review, or delete it. Systems must be designed to allow opt-in participation and provide clear, accessible explanations of how data will be used.

7.3 Potential for Manipulation and Bias

Affective Computing introduces risks of manipulation and bias that can undermine its benefits. Systems designed to detect and influence emotions could shape student behavior in ways that prioritize compliance over genuine learning, potentially stifling creativity or self-expression. Additionally, biased algorithms—trained on datasets that fail to represent the diversity of student populations—may disadvantage certain groups based on factors like race, gender, or cultural background. For example, facial recognition systems have been shown to exhibit lower accuracy for individuals with darker skin tones, potentially leading to unfair assessments or interventions [12]. The psychological impact of constant monitoring, including stress, anxiety, or feelings of surveillance, may also harm students' well-being and erode trust in student–teacher relationships.

7.4 Usability Challenges

Ensuring the accessibility and usability of Affective Computing technologies is critical for their successful integration. For educators, these systems must be intuitive and seamlessly integrated into existing workflows, minimizing additional cognitive or administrative burdens. For students, the technology should enhance learning rather than distract from it, avoiding over-reliance on digital tools that could detract from meaningful interpersonal interactions in the classroom. Striking a balance between leveraging technology and preserving the natural dynamics of learning environments is essential to avoid creating new barriers or inequalities.

These ethical and privacy challenges demand a proactive approach that places student rights, fairness, and inclusivity at the forefront of development and implementation. By prioritizing transparency, accountability, and equitable access, educational institutions can harness the benefits of these technologies while minimizing potential harms. Ultimately, ethical frameworks and robust policies must guide the integration of future Affective Computing applications, ensuring that it empowers students and educators rather than compromising their autonomy or trust.

8 Future Directions and Innovations

Affective Computing has gained renewed momentum with the advent of powerful large language models (LLMs), driving its continued maturation. The potential for smart, automated, and personalized feedback in diverse contexts positions Affective Computing to extend its role in education beyond providing emotional insights toward more comprehensive and transformative applications. Realizing this potential will require technological advancements, alignment with educational policies, and the integration of human expertise to ensure ethical and effective implementation.

8.1 Advances in Affective Computing and AI Models

The future of Affective Computing lies in the refinement and expansion of research methodologies [59] to account for new emotion-sensing technologies and artificial intelligence models. Advances in machine learning are expected to improve the accuracy, contextual sensitivity, and interpretive capabilities of these systems, enabling them to detect subtle or complex emotional states with greater reliability. For example, next-generation AI models may incorporate contextual cues—such as the learning environment, social interactions, and historical emotional patterns—allowing for more nuanced and personalized insights.

Emerging sensing technologies also hold great promise [33]. Innovations such as wearable devices with advanced biometrics, neural interfaces, or ambient sensors embedded in classroom environments could enable more seamless and continuous monitoring of emotional and physiological states. Multimodal approaches will likely become more robust, integrating data from facial expressions, voice, posture, and even behavioral patterns in real time. Furthermore, the incorporation of generative AI capabilities could allow these systems to provide adaptive feedback, suggest strategies for emotional regulation, and even simulate empathetic responses tailored to individual learners.

8.2 Integration with Educational Policy and Standards

For Affective Computing to achieve widespread impact, educational policies and standards must evolve to embrace the importance of emotional and social learning alongside academic performance. Policymakers could formalize frameworks that prioritize emotional intelligence, resilience, and self-awareness as essential components of a student's development. For instance, national curricula might integrate emotional literacy training supported by Affective Computing tools that monitor and foster these skills.

Standards for data privacy, algorithmic transparency, and ethical use will also need to be established, ensuring that the deployment of affective technologies aligns with societal values and legal requirements. Certification programs or guidelines for technology providers could help ensure that these tools meet stringent criteria for safety, equity, and inclusivity. Additionally, funding initiatives and resource allocation will play a key role in addressing disparities in access to these advanced tools, ensuring that all students—regardless of socioeconomic background—can benefit from the integration of emotional and academic learning.

8.3 The Role of Teachers and Human Oversight

Despite the advances in Affective Computing, the role of educators will remain irreplaceable in interpreting and leveraging these technologies effectively [51]. Emotional data, while insightful, requires human judgment to contextualize and respond appropriately. Teachers will need to act as mediators, using insights from Affective Computing tools to adapt their teaching strategies and support individual student needs without compromising the authenticity of the teacher–student relationship [41].

Human oversight will also be critical to prevent over-reliance on automated systems and to address ethical dilemmas as they arise [58]. Educators and administrators must be trained to understand the capabilities and limitations of Affective Computing, ensuring that its use enhances rather than detracts from the educational experience. Collaborative models, where teachers, students, and technology work in tandem, will likely emerge as the most effective approach, preserving the balance between digital innovation and human connection.

8.4 Toward a Future of Holistic Education

Looking ahead, the integration of Affective Computing into education offers the potential to redefine learning environments as spaces that nurture not only intellectual growth but also emotional well-being. Advances in AI and emotion-sensing technologies will continue to shape how we understand and support learners while evolving policies and human-centric practices will ensure that these innovations are grounded in ethical and equitable principles. By focusing on the holistic development of students, educators and researchers can foster resilient, emotionally intelligent learners who are better prepared to navigate the complexities of the modern world.

9 Conclusion: Toward Emotionally Intelligent Education

Affective Computing offers transformative potential for education, enabling systems to adapt to students' emotional states and foster engagement, resilience, and learning. However, its implementation demands balance—leveraging technology to support, not control, the educational experience.

Advancing these tools requires prioritizing ethical considerations, equity, and transparency while integrating them thoughtfully into pedagogy. By focusing on holistic development, we can create learning environments that nurture both academic success and emotional intelligence, empowering students to thrive in an increasingly complex world.

References

1. E4 wristband | real-time physiological signals | wearable PPG, EDA, temperature, motion sensors, https://www.empatica.com/research/e4/
2. (2021), https://d3.harvard.edu/platform-digit/submission/knewton-personalizes-learning-with-the-power-of-ai/
3. (2024), https://www.affectiva.com/
4. (2024), https://www.dreambox.com/
5. Abbas, R., Ni, B., Ma, R., Li, T., Lu, Y., Li, X.: Context-based emotion recognition: a survey. Neurocomputing **618**, 129073 (2025). https://doi.org/10.1016/J.NEUCOM.2024.129073
6. Ahuja, K., Kim, D., Xhakaj, F., Varga, V., Xie, A., Zhang, S., Townsend, J.E., Harrison, C., Ogan, A., Agarwal, Y.: Edusense: Practical classroom sensing at scale. Proc. ACM Interact. Mob. Wearable Ubiquit. Technol. **3**(3), 1–26 (2019)
7. Avital, N., Egel, I., Weinstock, I., Malka, D.: Enhancing real-time emotion recognition in classroom environments using convolutional neural networks: a step towards optical neural networks for advanced data processing. Inventions **9**(6), 113 (2024)
8. Babaei, E., Tag, B., Dingler, T., Velloso, E.: A critique of electrodermal activity practices at chi. In: Proceedings of the 2021 CHI Conference on Human Factors in Computing Systems, pp. 1–14 (2021)
9. Barrett, L.F.: The theory of constructed emotion: an active inference account of interoception and categorization. Soc. Cogn. Affect. Neurosci. **12**, 1–23 (2017). https://doi.org/10.1093/scan/nsw154
10. Barrett, L.F., Russell, J.A. (eds.): The Psychological Construction of Emotion. Guilford Press (2014)
11. Basudan, S., Binanzan, N., Alhassan, A.: Depression, anxiety and stress in dental students. Int. J. Med. Educ. **8**, 179 (2017). https://doi.org/10.5116/IJME.5910.B961, https://pmc.ncbi.nlm.nih.gov/articles/PMC5457790/
12. Buolamwini, J., Gebru, T.: Gender shades: Intersectional accuracy disparities in commercial gender classification (2018), https://proceedings.mlr.press/v81/buolamwini18a.html
13. Buzsáki, G., Moser, E.I.: Memory, navigation and theta rhythm in the hippocampal-entorhinal system. Nat. Neurosci. **16**, 130–138 (2013). https://doi.org/10.1038/nn.3304, https://www.nature.com/articles/nn.3304
14. Calvo, R.A., D'Mello, S.: Affect detection: an interdisciplinary review of models, methods, and their applications. IEEE Trans. Affect. Comput. **1**, 18–37 (2010). https://doi.org/10.1109/T-AFFC.2010.1
15. Calvo, R.A., Peters, D.: Positive computing: Technology for wellbeing and human potential. Posit. Comput. (2014). https://doi.org/10.7551/MITPRESS/9764.001.0001, https://direct.mit.edu/books/monograph/4026/Positive-ComputingTechnology-for-Wellbeing-and
16. Deci, E.L., Ryan, R.M.: Self-determination theory. Handbook of Theories of Social Psychology **1**(20), 416–436 (2012)
17. Di Lascio, E., Gashi, S., Santini, S.: Unobtrusive assessment of students' emotional engagement during lectures using electrodermal activity sensors. Proc. ACM Interact. Mob. Wearable Ubiquit. Technol. **2**(3), 1–21 (2018)
18. D'Mello, S.K., Kory, J.: A review and meta-analysis of multimodal affect detection systems. ACM Comput. Surv. (CSUR) **47** (2015). https://doi.org/10.1145/2682899, https://dl.acm.org/doi/10.1145/2682899
19. Durlak, J.A., Weissberg, R.P., Dymnicki, A.B., Taylor, R.D., Schellinger, K.B.: The impact of enhancing students' social and emotional learning: a meta-analysis of school-based universal interventions. Child Dev. **82**(1), 405–432 (2011)
20. Dzedzickis, A., Kaklauskas, A., Bucinskas, V.: Human emotion recognition: review of sensors and methods. Sensors **20**(3), 592 (2020)
21. Ekman, P.: Universality of emotional expression? a personal history of the dispute; Darwin, C.: The Expression of the Emotions in Man and Animals, 3rd edn. Oxford University Press, New York, pp. 363–393 (1998)

22. Ekman, P., Friesen, W.V.: Facial action coding system. Environ. Psychol. & Nonverb. Behav. (1978)
23. G., R., Correia, A.F.L.S.M., Bilro: Creating memories and engagement in college student through virtual reality. In: Augmented Reality and Virtual Reality, pp. 167–179. Springer International Publishing (2021)
24. Gao, N., Marschall, M., Burry, J., Watkins, S., Salim, F.D.: Understanding occupants' behaviour, engagement, emotion, and comfort indoors with heterogeneous sensors and wearables. Sci. Data **9**(1), 261 (2022)
25. Gao, N., Nolan, S., Ji, K., Rumi, S.K., Heinisch, J.S., Anderson, C., David, K., Salim, F.D.: Living within four walls: exploring emotional and social dynamics in mobile usage during home confinement (2024), https://arxiv.org/abs/2310.13304
26. Gao, N., Rahaman, M.S., Shao, W., Ji, K., Salim, F.D.: Individual and group-wise classroom seating experience: effects on student engagement in different courses. Proc. ACM Interact. Mob. Wearable Ubiquit. Technol. **6**(3), 1–23 (2022)
27. Gao, N., Shao, W., Rahaman, M.S., Salim, F.D.: n-gage: Predicting in-class emotional, behavioural and cognitive engagement in the wild. Proc. ACM Interact. Mob. Wearable Ubiquitous Technol. **4**(3), 1–26 (2020)
28. Gashi, S., Di Lascio, E., Santini, S.: Using students' physiological synchrony to quantify the classroom emotional climate. In: Proceedings of the 2018 ACM International Joint Conference and 2018 International Symposium on Pervasive and Ubiquitous Computing and Wearable Computers, pp. 698–701 (2018)
29. Gašević, D., Dawson, S., Siemens, G.: Let's not forget: learning analytics are about learning. TechTrends **59**, 64–71 (2015). https://doi.org/10.1007/S11528-014-0822-X/METRICS, https://link.springer.com/article/10.1007/s11528-014-0822-x
30. Husaj, S.: Social emotional learning (sel). Eur. J. Multidiscip. Stud. **1**(3), 168–171 (2016)
31. Hwang, G.J., Xie, H., Wah, B.W., Gašević, D.: Vision, challenges, roles and research issues of artificial intelligence in education. Comput. Educ. Artif. Intell. **1**, 100001 (2020). https://doi.org/10.1016/J.CAEAI.2020.100001
32. Isen, A.M., Daubman, K.A., Nowicki, G.P.: Positive affect facilitates creative problem solving. J. Pers. Soc. Psychol. **52**(6), 1122 (1987)
33. Jiang, W., Yang, K., Windl, M., Chiossi, F., Tag, B., Mayer, S., Sarsenbayeva, Z.: Current challenges of using wearable devices for online emotion sensing (2022). https://doi.org/10.48550/arXiv.2208.05206
34. Jiménez-Mijangos, L.P., Rodríguez-Arce, J., Martínez-Méndez, R., Reyes-Lagos, J.J.: Advances and challenges in the detection of academic stress and anxiety in the classroom: a literature review and recommendations. Educ. Inf. Technol. **28**, 3637–3666 (2023). https://doi.org/10.1007/S10639-022-11324-W/TABLES/11, https://link.springer.com/article/10.1007/s10639-022-11324-w
35. Juvonen, J., Graham, S.: Bullying in schools: the power of bullies and the plight of victims. Annual Rev. Psychol. **65**, 159–185 (2014). https://doi.org/10.1146/ANNUREV-PSYCH-010213-115030, https://pubmed.ncbi.nlm.nih.gov/23937767/
36. Kensinger, E.A., Corkin, S.: Effect of negative emotional content on working memory and long-term memory. Emotion **3**(4), 378 (2003)
37. Kreibig, S.D., Gross, J.J.: Understanding mixed emotions: paradigms and measures. Curr. Opin. Behav. Sci. **15**, 62–71 (2017)
38. Levstik, L.S., Barton, K.C.: Doing history: investigating with children in elementary and middle schools. Doing Hist. (2005). https://doi.org/10.4324/9781410613387, https://www.taylorfrancis.com/books/mono/10.4324/9781410613387/history-linda-levstik-keith-barton
39. Li, J., Xue, E.: Dynamic interaction between student learning behaviour and learning environment: meta-analysis of student engagement and its influencing factors. Behav. Sci. **13**, 59 (2023).https://doi.org/10.3390/BS13010059, https://pmc.ncbi.nlm.nih.gov/articles/PMC9855184/
40. Llurba, C., Palau, R.: Real-time emotion recognition for improving the teaching-learning process: a scoping review. J. Imag. **10**(12), 313 (2024)

41. Luckin, R., Holmes, W.: Intelligence unleashed: an argument for AI in education (2016)
42. MacCann, C., Jiang, Y., Brown, L.E., Double, K.S., Bucich, M., Minbashian, A.: Emotional intelligence predicts academic performance: a meta-analysis. Psychol. Bull. **146**(2), 150 (2020)
43. Madanian, S., Chen, T., Adeleye, O., Templeton, J.M., Poellabauer, C., Parry, D., Schneider, S.L.: Speech emotion recognition using machine learning—a systematic review. Intell. Syst. Appl. **20**, 200266 (2023). https://doi.org/10.1016/J.ISWA.2023.200266
44. McDuff, D., Czerwinski, M.: Designing emotionally sentient agents. Commun. ACM **61**, 74–83 (11 2018).https://doi.org/10.1145/3186591, https://dl.acm.org/doi/10.1145/3186591
45. McGaugh, J.L.: The amygdala modulates the consolidation of memories of emotionally arousing experiences. Annu. Rev. Neurosci. **27**(1), 1–28 (2004)
46. Nandwani, P., Verma, R.: A review on sentiment analysis and emotion detection from text. Soc. Netw. Anal. Min. **11**(1), 81 (2021)
47. Nojavanasghari, B., Baltrušaitis, T., Hughes, C.E., Morency, L.P.: Emoreact: a multimodal approach and dataset for recognizing emotional responses in children. In: Proceedings of the 18th ACM International Conference on Multimodal Interaction, pp. 137–144 (2016)
48. Nolan, K., Bergin, S.: The role of anxiety when learning to program: a systematic review of the literature. ACM Int. Conf. Proc. Seri. 61–70 (2016). https://doi.org/10.1145/2999541.2999557, https://dl.acm.org/doi/10.1145/2999541.2999557
49. Ochsner, K.N., Silvers, J.A., Buhle, J.T.: Functional imaging studies of emotion regulation: a synthetic review and evolving model of the cognitive control of emotion. Ann. N. Y. Acad. Sci. **1251**(1), E1–E24 (2012)
50. Picard, R.W.: Affective computing. M.I.T Med. Lab. Percept. Comput. Sect. Tech. Rep. **321** (1995), http://www.media.mit.edu/picard/
51. Picard, R.W.: Affective Computing. MIT Press (1997)
52. Picard, R.W.: Emotion research by the people, for the people. Emot. Rev. **2**, 250–254 (2010). https://doi.org/10.1177/1754073910364256
53. Realeyes: Realeyes | ad testing for the attention economy (2024), https://www.realeyesit.com/
54. Reyes, E.P., Blanco, R.M.F.L., Doroon, D.R.L., Limana, J.L.B., Torcende, A.M.A.: Feynman technique as a heutagogical learning strategy for independent and remote learning. Recoletos Multidiscip. Res. J. **9**(2), 1–13 (2021)
55. Sacharin, V.: The influence of emotions on cognitive flexibility. Ph.D. thesis, University of Michigan (2009)
56. Santangelo, V., Cavallina, C., Colucci, P., Santori, A., Macrì, S., McGaugh, J.L., Campolongo, P.: Enhanced brain activity associated with memory access in highly superior autobiographical memory. Proc. Natl. Acad. Sci. USA. **115**, 7795–7800 (2018). https://doi.org/10.1073/pnas.1802730115, https://www.pnas.org/doi/abs/10.1073/pnas.1802730115
57. Schwind, J.K., McCay, E., Beanlands, H., Martin, L.S., Martin, J., Binder, M.: Mindfulness practice as a teaching-learning strategy in higher education: a qualitative exploratory pilot study. Nurse Educ. Today **50**, 92–96 (2017)
58. Selwyn, N.: Should robots replace teachers? AI and the future of education, p. 145 (2019), https://www.wiley.com/en-gb/Should+Robots+Replace+Teachers%3F%3A+AI+and+the+Future+of+Education-p-9781509528967
59. Tag, B., Goncalves, J., Webber, S., Koval, P., Kostakos, V.: A retrospective and a look forward: Lessons learned from researching emotions in-the-wild. IEEE Pervasive Comput. **21** (2022). https://doi.org/10.1109/MPRV.2021.3106272
60. Tag, B., Berkel, N., Vargo, A.W., Sarsenbayeva, Z., Colasante, T., Wadley, G., Webber, S., Smith, W., Koval, P., Hollenstein, T., et al.: Impact of the global pandemic upon young people's use of technology for emotion regulation. Comput. Hum. Behav. Rep. **6**, 100192 (2022)
61. Tag, B., Sarsenbayeva, Z., Cox, A.L., Wadley, G., Goncalves, J., Kostakos, V.: Emotion trajectories in smartphone use: towards recognizing emotion regulation in-the-wild. Int. J. Hum. Comput. Stud. **166**, 102872 (2022)
62. Tyng, C.M., Amin, H.U., Saad, M.N., Malik, A.S.: The influences of emotion on learning and memory. Front. Psychol. **8**, 235933 (2017)

63. Wang, R., Chen, F., Chen, Z., Li, T., Harari, G., Tignor, S., Zhou, X., Ben-Zeev, D., Campbell, A.T.: Studentlife: assessing mental health, academic performance and behavioral trends of college students using smartphones. In: Proceedings of the 2014 ACM International Joint Conference on Pervasive and Ubiquitous Computing, pp. 3–14 (2014)
64. Xu, X., Zhang, H., Sefidgar, Y., Ren, Y., Liu, X., Seo, W., Brown, J., Kuehn, K., Merrill, M., Nurius, P., et al.: Globem dataset: multi-year datasets for longitudinal human behavior modeling generalization. Adv. Neural Inf. Process. Syst. **35**, 24655–24692 (2022)
65. Yang, K., Tag, B., Wang, C., Gu, Y., Sarsenbayeva, Z., Dingler, T., Wadley, G., Goncalves, J.: Survey on emotion sensing using mobile devices. IEEE Trans. Affect. Comput. (2022)
66. Yang, K., Wang, C., Gu, Y., Sarsenbayeva, Z., Tag, B., Dingler, T., Wadley, G., Goncalves, J.: Behavioral and physiological signals-based deep multimodal approach for mobile emotion recognition. IEEE Trans. Affect. Comput. (2021)
67. Yang, K., Wang, C., Sarsenbayeva, Z., Tag, B., Dingler, T., Wadley, G., Goncalves, J.: Benchmarking commercial emotion detection systems using realistic distortions of facial image datasets. Vis. Comput. **37**, 1447–1466 (2021)
68. Zotev, V., Krueger, F., Phillips, R., Alvarez, R.P., Simmons, W.K., Bellgowan, P., Drevets, W.C., Bodurka, J.: Self-regulation of amygdala activation using real-time fMRI neurofeedback. PLOS ONE **6**, e24522 (2011). https://doi.org/10.1371/JOURNAL.PONE.0024522, https://journals.plos.org/plosone/article?id=10.1371/journal.pone.0024522

Ethics and AI in Education

Laurence Devillers

Abstract Ethical technologies in education must support, not hinder, human autonomy. We need a paradigm shift from talking about augmenting human intelligence with Artificial Intelligence (AI), to enhancing intelligence with AI in order to develop new skills, enrich our tastes, and expand our faculties and imagination. Interdisciplinary collaboration between science and the humanities is essential to ensure that AI advances truly benefit everyone. With this in mind, there is an urgent need to strengthen education in computer science and the sciences in general, in order to build our free will in the face of the massive arrival of AI.

Keywords AI · Education · Children · Generative AI · Vulnerability · Mental representations · Critical thinking skills · Dopamine reward system · Risks and opportunities of AI · Ethics · Long-term effects of AI

1 Introduction

An increasing number of studies have highlighted how AI technologies can enhance children's development across various areas, including creativity, attention, language acquisition, socio-emotional well-being, and science education [1]. While these educational tools differ in design, they all utilize AI to foster personalized and interactive learning experiences. The incorporation of AI into educational and divertissement tools offers then opportunities but also potential risks, especially for children and young adults whose brains are still developing [2]. Your cognitive, emotional, and social growth is shaped by your interactions with the world. Moreover, children's interactions with technology start early, with more than one-third of American parents reporting in 2020 that their child began interacting with smartphones before age 5 [3]. AI-based technologies facilitate also enhanced monitoring capabilities, from devices that track temperature and breathing of babies to tracking tools and home-monitoring systems.

L. Devillers (✉)
Sorbonne University/LISN-CNRS, Paris, France
e-mail: Laurence.devillers@lisn.fr

A. Dengel et al. (eds.), *The Future of Education with AI*,
https://doi.org/10.1007/978-981-95-1622-3_7

Furthermore, increasingly advanced AI agents are being incorporated into industries like video games, where their role extends beyond functionality: they actively help create emotional connections, enhancing player immersion and, consequently, increasing their dependency. Children already rely on digital assistants like ChatGPT or Alexa to ask questions and find information. Due to their ability to mimic human interactions, AI agents can foster manipulative behaviors, particularly in younger children. This can result in unhealthy attachments to these agents, potentially hindering their emotional and social development [4]. Children are increasingly engaging with AI-powered technologies through immersive experiences. By the age of 14, they spend more than half of their waking hours using these technologies. The well-known negative effects of excessive screen time [5] include sleep disorders, worsening eyesight (with myopia already affecting nearly 33% of Europeans and potentially reaching 50% by 2050), and a rise in sedentary behaviors.

AI has the potential to support children's cognitive, emotional, and social development, but it can also pose risks. Our collective ability to address the ethical challenges we face today will determine our future. The main goal of this chapter is to explore the benefits and risks of children's interactions with AI in education, with a particular focus on ethical considerations.

2 AI Enhancing Solutions in Education

There is currently a consensus that AI tools should be used with caution in education. Recent research investigating education technology, video gaming, and emerging technologies and their influence on children's development are well developed in [1]. AI holds great potential to personalize education, assist in learning, and improve the inclusion of children with disabilities. Intelligent tutoring systems powered by AI allow content to be customized to meet individual learning needs. Additionally, AI tutors can help ensure that children worldwide have access to education. These applications draw on a diverse range of AI technologies, including speech recognition, computer vision, and generative AI with Transformers. Affective computing also develops systems that recognize or influence the aspects of human life related to emotions, including feelings and moods. Even technologies such as social robots and virtual reality headsets have recently become more widely available and are beginning to be present in children's homes and classrooms [6].

We carried out tests with my research team on nudge strategies in children's oral interactions with different agents (a NAO or Pepper robot, a voice speaker or a human). We compared the reactions of children aged 8–10 in an adaptation of The Dictator Game, a psycho-economics experiment. Here, each agent (human, speaker, or robot) gives a child 10 marbles, which he divides between himself and the other children. The agent then gives a nudge by saying "The others gave more" or "I'll give less." Our test results show that children are more inclined to follow incentives to change their minds from machines than from humans. Machines represent a kind of authority. Young people are vulnerable to AI assistants. We need to understand how they react to systems that talk to them like a human being.

We've developed AI and ethics capsules on the uses and ethics of AI for elementary school, on attention-grabbing, harassment, computer does my homework, you'll find a few examples on our site in English.

I've also carried out tests with my first-year students at the Sorbonne in computer science and languages, and found that they can lose rationality in their decisions and follow what ChatGPT4 says, whereas without ChatGPT they would respond correctly. The machine makes mistakes!

The immense potential for both positive and negative outcomes, particularly for children, makes affective computing and AI, in general, ethically complex [4] and challenging to navigate. However, their use presents risks, including the negative effects on children's ability to manage gratification, develop executive skills, and engage in critical thinking. It is also important to exercise caution regarding the over-gamification of education. There are a lot of vulnerable cognitive abilities in the digital age [7], such as sensory integration, language, attention, executive functioning, memory, mental representations, critical thinking skills, intrinsic motivation and dopamine reward system and also a lot of vulnerable socio-emotional development, such as attachment and relationship, social isolation, anxiety and stress, and empathy.

AI must be used to ensure children's safety, privacy and well-being. It should be employed to educate but also to protect children both online and offline. In the era of rapidly advancing artificial intelligence, the long-term effects on child development are still largely unknown and often ignored. For instance, children born after 2020 will grow up in a vastly different environment compared to previous generations. Despite young children often having access to and using these technologies, they remain underrepresented in research on emerging technologies. To enhance both the short-term safety and long-term benefits of children's use of emerging AI technologies in education, developers must focus on responsible, child-appropriate design. Longitudinal studies that track behavioral patterns over the course of childhood and into adulthood are essential to better understand the long-term effects of technology use.

3 Generative AI and Voice Assistants as Information Sources

Generative AI systems have quickly become "valuable" tools in education due to their ability to generate syntactically correct and often semantically plausible natural language texts. Generative AI could significantly enhance these benefits for vocabulary expansion, as evidenced by studies demonstrating increased learning and retention with interactive AI [8]. Generative AI systems can be used by students to write texts for them, to answer questions for an assignment, or by teachers to produce summaries or descriptions of their lectures, or to generate MCQs. However, these systems can also produce inaccurate information or present false facts, known as "hallucinations." Specifically, large language models (LLMs) sometimes provide incorrect details about spatial or temporal aspects of the real world [9].

Children are especially vulnerable to voice assistants and generative AI. They often perceive these assistants as trustworthy sources of information, while ChatGPT becomes the ideal confidant—always available, non-judgmental, and ready to listen to their innermost thoughts. Childhood and adolescence are critical stages when their brains undergo significant changes. During this time, they are constantly developing new skills, gaining knowledge, and shaping their understanding of the world through interactions with their environment. These transitional periods, when their identity is being formed and redefined, make them particularly sensitive to external influences, including the technologies that shape their digital experiences. As individuals, we are all exposed to technologies designed to capture our attention, keep us connected, and, over time, foster dependence. Rather than offering simple support, these AI agents create a dynamic where we are continuously drawn back, fueling a cycle of emotional and psychological dependency. This raises important questions about the role of technology in our personal development and the ethical implications of our interactions with these unconscious entities.

Human learning is a process. The understanding of concepts, the assimilation of knowledge, and the acquisition of know-how are achieved through reflection, reformulation, analysis, and synthesis. If the aim of education is to train minds and teach them to reason rigorously, the risk of replacing this objective with that of acquiring knowledge, the accuracy of which is not guaranteed, through the intermediary of the machine is obvious. Replacing human reasoning with machine-generated texts would run counter to our traditional approach to school learning, which we must preserve. It's not a question of banning these new tools, but it is necessary to supervise their use and teach children the underlying concepts.

4 Children's Understanding of AI

This challenge is further compounded by the fact that many AI products aimed at children are designed to mimic humans and encourage children to view technologies as trainers or companions, often without disclosing their inner workings. The study [10] shows for example that the more 5-year-old children tend to anthropomorphize the robot, the better their second-language vocabulary learning outcomes are. This combination of factors could amplify children's tendency to anthropomorphize AI, which has been shown to correlate positively with children's acceptance of information presented by AI. However, children's tendency to anthropomorphize AI may also lead to unrealistic expectations about AI's capabilities, which could affect their perception of AI in the future. It's important to explain how AI works to children with different levels of concepts at different ages to avoid naive beliefs about these tools.

To address these issues, experts have emphasized the importance of fostering children's accurate understanding of AI so they can effectively interact with AI technologies. Students are exposed to digital worlds from an early age. At the French Blaise Pascal national Foundation, we built 10 ethics AI video capsules to enable 8–10-year children to gain new knowledge and awareness of digital issues, AI tool and to talk about your experiences, discuss them with the class and the teacher, and avoid the preconceived ideas and pitfalls associated with the various aspects of AI and digital technology [11]. One of these AI video capsules explains the capture of attention by the providers of the tool (e.g., video game) and the dopamine effect which is a natural reaction of the body. Children are then more able to understand why they are attached to their phone or video game.

We also carried out tests on nudge strategies (R. Thaler, Nobel Prize in 2017) in children's oral interactions with different agents (a NAO or Pepper robot, a voice speaker, or a human) [12]. We compared the reactions of children aged 5–10 in an adaptation of The Dictator Game, a psycho-economics experiment. Here, each agent (human, speaker, or robot) gives a child 10 marbles, which he divides between himself and the other children. The agent then gives a nudge by saying "The others gave more" or "I'll give less." Our test results show that children are more inclined to follow incentives to change their minds from machines than from humans. Machines represent a kind of authority. Young people are vulnerable to AI assistants. We need to understand how they react to systems that talk to them like a human being.

Various frameworks have been developed to teach what has been called AI literacy [13] which can be viewed as a set of skills that enable individuals to critically evaluate, communicate, and collaborate effectively with AI as a tool. This includes distinguishing between machine and human or animal intelligence, recognizing technological artifacts that use AI, and understanding the strengths and limitations of AI.

5 Ethical Concerns

Although children's privacy laws, such as the Children's Online Privacy Protection Act (COPPA), have been in place for many years, they need to be updated and extended to take account of emerging technologies. The AI Act, approved by the European Parliament on March 23, 2024, creates a comprehensive regulatory framework to oversee the development, deployment, and use of artificial intelligence in European countries. This framework focuses specifically on children, reflecting the EU's proactive approach to regulation and protection.

Interdisciplinary collaboration between science and the humanities is essential to ensure that advances in AI truly benefit everyone. Ethical technology must support and not hinder human autonomy. We need a paradigm shift from talking about increasing human intelligence with AI to improving intelligence to develop new skills, enrich our tastes, expand our faculties, and our imaginations. With this in mind, we reiterate the urgent need to strengthen mathematics education and our free will in the face of the massive arrival of AI.

Examining the literature on emerging technologies also raises important ethical questions about the place of technology such as AI in the lives of children. The lack of distinction between a text written by a human being and one generated by an AI system is a major ethical problem. Children must confuse a result produced by a machine with one created by a human author. A main concept in child development is how the use of AI might reshape learning and interactions during sensitive periods of development [14]. It is also unclear who should be responsible for regulating children's access to emerging technologies and ensuring that the content those technologies present is appropriate for children. AI used in social media can lead to children and young people feeling addicted to social media, affecting their mental states. Although additional research on children's interactions with virtual agents is necessary, it is important to keep in mind that as this technology continues evolving, new questions and challenges may arise.

It's crucial to make children aware of the challenges of responsible and ethical digital technology, and to encourage them to take up mathematical and computer sciences to understand and shape current and future technologies. There is an urgent need to arouse interest in these disciplines, to help them discover their richness and the pleasures they offer, while at the same time promoting a digital world that is sober, at the service of society and respectful of the environment. The ethical dimension must also be emphasized, as an essential safeguard to ensure that digital developments make a genuine contribution to progress, while preserving the fundamental values of our society. Last but not least, it's vital to understand the steps involved in scientific reasoning, including the role of doubt and the right to make mistakes. "To act with reason in the face of uncertainty," Pascal [15].

References

1. Christakis, A., Hale, L.: Handbook of Children and Screens (2025)
2. Neugnot-Cerioli, M., Muss Laurenty, O.: The Future of Child Development in the AI Era: Cross-Disciplinary Perspectives Between AI and Child Development Experts (2024)
3. Auxier, B., Anderson, M., Perrin, A., Turner, E.: Parenting Children in the Age of Screens (2020)
4. Devillers, L., Cowie, R.: Ethical considerations on affective computing: an overview. Proc. IEEE **111**(10), 1445–1458 (2024)
5. Muppalla, S., Vuppalapati, S., Reddy Pulliahgaru, A., et al.: Effects of excessive screen time on child development: an updated review and strategies for management. Cureus **15**(6), e40608 (2023)
6. Rideout, V., Peebles, A., Mann, S., Robb, M.: The common sense census: media use by tweens and teens (2021)
7. International Coalition: Beneficial AI for Children. AI Summit (2025). https://everyone.ai/research/
8. Xu, Y., Aubele, J., Vigil, V., Bustamante, A.S., Kim, Y.S., Warschauer, M.: Dialogue with a conversational agent promotes children's story comprehension via enhancing engagement. Child Dev. **93**(2), e149–67 (2022). https://doi.org/10.1111/cdev.13708.2021
9. Chatila, R., Devillers, L., Grinbaum, A.: Opinion N°7, ethical issues of generative artificial intelligence systems. CNPEN. https://www.ccne-ethique.fr/sites/default/files/2024-08/CNPEN%20Opinion%207.pdf (2024)

10. van den Berghe, R., de Haas, M., Oudgenoeg-Paz, O., et al.: A toy or a friend? children's anthropomorphic beliefs about robots and how these relate to second-language word learning. J. Comput. Assist. Learn. **37**(2), 396–410 (2021). https://doi.org/10.1111/jcal.12497
11. Devillers, L.: President of Foundation Blaise Pascal. Capsules AI Ethics. https://www.fondation-blaise-pascal.org/
12. Ali Mehenni, H., Kobylyanskaya, S., Vasilescu, I., Devillers, L.: Nudges with conversational agents and social robots: a first experiment with children at a primary school. Convers. Dialogue Syst. Next Decade, 257–270 (2020)
13. Long, D., Magerko, B.: What is AI literacy? competencies and design considerations. In: Proceedings of the 2020 CHI Conference on Human Factors in Computing Systems, pp. 1–16. ACM, New York (2020). https://doi.org/10.1145/3313831.3376727
14. Banich, M., Compton, R.: Cognitive Neuroscience, 5th edn. Cambridge University Press (2023)
15. Pascal, B.: Les Pensées (1670)

Beyond the Interface: Augmenting Meta-Skills for Long-Term Cognitive Enhancement

Shoya Ishimaru

Abstract In this chapter, we explore how technology can enhance human cognition in ways that foster lasting development. Central to our discussion is the concept of the *Meta-Augmented Human*, an approach that aims to permanently amplify cognitive abilities by cultivating skills that transcend specific tools or interfaces. Our exploration covers sensing technologies that detect learning states, actuation systems that provide timely support, and AI-driven knowledge transfer mechanisms. We examine how smart sensors can recognize cognitive and affective states to deliver personalized assistance that builds lasting capabilities rather than creating dependency. The chapter addresses key challenges in this emerging field, including accurately recognizing cognitive/affective states, and designing interventions that strike the right balance between immediate help and long-term skill development. We conclude by examining future directions for human–AI collaboration in learning environments, highlighting the importance of technologies that enhance human potential while preserving autonomy and fostering skills that remain even when the technology is absent.

Keywords Human–AI collaboration · Intelligence amplification · Cognitive Augmentation · Affective computing · Intelligent Learning Assistant

1 Introduction

One of the fundamental roles of technology is to extend human capabilities across various dimensions. From optical eyeglasses that enhance vision to computers that support cognitive tasks including memory and calculation, technological innovations have consistently aimed to augment human capabilities and improve our daily lives. The field of augmented human has demonstrated that human beings and technologies perform better when they collaborate rather than work individually [10]. This concept—often termed *augmented intelligence* or *intelligence amplification*—stands

S. Ishimaru (✉)
Osaka Metropolitan University, Sakai, Japan
e-mail: ishimaru@omu.ac.jp

A. Dengel et al. (eds.), *The Future of Education with AI*,
https://doi.org/10.1007/978-981-95-1622-3_8

in contrast to the notion of fully autonomous AI. Instead of aiming to supersede human intelligence, the goal is to build systems that leverage the complementary strengths of humans and machines. However, there remains a significant challenge: the more people depend on technologies, the more their original performances may deteriorate over time. This phenomenon, described as the *Glass Cage* effect [6], highlights the need for a more nuanced approach to human augmentation, one that enhances abilities permanently rather than temporarily by focusing on meta-skills that transcend specific interfaces or tools.

In this chapter, we explore the concept of *Meta-Augmented Human* [12], which aims to amplify human abilities not only while using external devices but permanently, even when direct technological support is absent. We focus particularly on two critical areas: Cognitive Augmentation and Intelligent Learning Assistant. These domains represent the frontier of research in enhancing human cognitive capabilities and learning experiences through technology. By understanding the current state, challenges, and future directions of these fields, we can develop more effective approaches to augmenting human cognition and learning in the age of artificial intelligence (AI). The result is a symbiotic relationship that goes beyond the interface: humans provide context, values, and creative insight, while AI contributes speed, memory, and analytical power, ultimately enhancing the meta-skills that enable long-term cognitive growth.

The relationship between humans and technology is evolving rapidly, with significant implications for how we learn, work, and interact with the world. As Arthur C. Clarke noted, "The old idea that Man invented tools is therefore a misleading half-truth; it would be more accurate to say that tools invented Man" [8]. This reciprocal relationship between humans and technology underscores the importance of designing augmentation systems that not only enhance immediate performance but also contribute to long-term cognitive development. Through the lens of Meta-Augmented Human, we examine how technologies can assist meta-skills—skills to master new skills—such as reading and learning, thereby providing lasting augmentation of human capabilities that persists beyond the interface. This notion is closely related to what Licklider envisioned as *Man-Computer Symbiosis* [28], and what Engelbart termed *Augmentation of Human Intellect* [10].

In the following sections, we delve into the current state of Cognitive Augmentation, exploring sensing technologies for understanding cognitive activities and affective states. We then examine Intelligent Learning Assistant, discussing how this system can recognize learners' behaviors and provide personalized support. Throughout the chapter, we highlight the challenges in developing these technologies and propose directions for future research and development. By addressing these challenges, we can create augmentation systems that truly enhance human cognitive abilities while avoiding the pitfalls of over-dependence on technology.

2 Sensing Human Cognition

Cognitive Augmentation and Intelligent Learning Assistant encompass a broad spectrum of technologies and approaches aimed at enhancing human cognitive abilities and learning experiences. The current state of these fields reflects significant advancements in sensing technologies, activity recognition, and intervention methods. In this section, we explore the key developments in these areas, focusing on the recognition of cognitive activities, assessment of affective states, and the conceptual foundations that underpin these technologies.

2.1 Cognitive Activity Recognition

The recognition of cognitive activities, such as reading, writing, and problem-solving, represents a fundamental challenge in Cognitive Augmentation. Unlike physical activities that involve substantial bodily movements, cognitive activities often occur with minimal external manifestations, making them difficult to detect using conventional sensing approaches. Researchers have addressed this challenge by developing innovative sensing methodologies that can capture subtle indicators of cognitive engagement.

Eye-tracking has emerged as a particularly promising approach for cognitive activity recognition. The relationship between eye movements and cognitive tasks has been well established in cognitive science and psychology [34]. During reading, for example, eye movements consist of a series of rapid movements (saccades) and short stops (fixations), with occasional movements in the opposite direction (regressions) to aid comprehension [25]. By analyzing these patterns, researchers can gain insights into the cognitive processes underlying reading and other activities. Systems like the Wordometer have demonstrated the feasibility of estimating reading volume in everyday life using commercial EOG glasses [18], providing a foundation for quantifying cognitive activities in natural settings.

Various eye-tracking methodologies have been developed, ranging from high-precision search coil eye trackers to more accessible electrooculography (EOG) and corneal reflection approaches. Recent advancements have made eye-tracking more affordable and less obtrusive, enabling its use in everyday settings. For instance, commercial EOG glasses like JINS MEME provide a lightweight, visually familiar, and relatively inexpensive option for tracking eye movements throughout the day [19]. These devices can detect specific eye movements, such as blinks and saccades, which can be used to recognize cognitive activities like reading.

Beyond eye-tracking, researchers have explored the use of other sensing modalities for cognitive activity recognition. Head-mounted cameras can capture the user's field of view, providing context for activity recognition [29]. Inertial measurement units (IMUs) can detect head movements, which, when combined with eye movement data, can improve the accuracy of activity recognition [21]. By integrating multiple sensing modalities, researchers have achieved promising results in recognizing various cognitive activities, including reading, watching videos, and solving mathematical problems.

Despite these advancements, significant challenges remain in cognitive activity recognition. One major challenge is the distinction between controlled activities in laboratory settings and natural activities in real-world environments. Natural reading, for instance, involves various devices, document layouts, and reading styles, resulting in irregular eye movements that may not match the patterns observed in controlled experiments. Recent research has addressed this challenge by collecting large-scale datasets of natural activities and developing deep learning-based approaches for activity recognition [16]. These approaches have shown promise in detecting natural reading activities, although their accuracy still falls short of that achieved in controlled settings.

2.2 Cognitive and Affective State Recognition

Human internal states, including attention, interest, and self-confidence, play crucial roles in cognitive processes and learning. Recognizing these states is essential for providing appropriate support and intervention. Researchers have developed various approaches for assessing cognitive and affective states, leveraging physiological signals, eye movements, and other behavioral indicators.

Eye movements provide valuable insights into affective states. Fixation duration and fixation rate, for example, can indicate increased attention on a task [7]. The pattern of blinks can reveal information about cognitive engagement, with reduced blink rates associated with increased concentration [2]. Pupil diameter changes in response to cognitive load, with larger pupils indicating higher mental effort [23]. By analyzing these and other eye movement features, researchers can assess various affective states, including comprehension, interest, and mental workload.

Physiological sensing offers another approach to affective state assessment. The autonomic nervous system (ANS) provides insights into hidden mental processes [33], with various physiological signals reflecting changes in affective states. Electrodermal activity (EDA), for instance, measures the electrical conductance of the skin, which increases with sympathetic nervous system activation. EDA can be decomposed into tonic and phasic components, with the tonic component reflecting baseline skin conductance and the phasic component capturing short-term responses to stimuli. These components have been associated with cognitive activity, stress, and emotional responses [5].

Other physiological signals, such as blood volume pulse (BVP) and nose temperature, also provide information about affective states. BVP can be monitored using photoplethysmography (PPG), with changes in heart rate and heart rate variability associated with frustration and anxiety [27]. Nose temperature decreases with sympathetic nervous system activation, making it a potential indicator of cognitive load and stress [1]. By combining multiple physiological signals, researchers can develop more robust approaches to affective state assessment.

Recent advancements in wearable sensing technologies have made physiological sensing more accessible for everyday use. Devices like the E4 wristband can measure EDA and BVP continuously throughout the day, enabling long-term monitoring of affective states. Infrared thermal cameras can capture nose temperature changes, providing another modality for affective state assessment. These technologies, when combined with appropriate analysis methods, offer promising approaches for understanding the affective dimensions of cognitive activities.

Despite these advancements, affective state assessment still faces significant challenges. Individual differences in physiological responses, environmental factors, and the complexity of affective states all contribute to the difficulty of accurate assessment. Moreover, the relationship between physiological signals and affective states is not always straightforward, requiring sophisticated analysis methods to extract meaningful information. Addressing these challenges remains an active area of research in Cognitive Augmentation.

3 Actuating Human Cognition

The application of Cognitive Augmentation and Intelligent Learning Assistant spans various domains, from educational settings to workplace environments to everyday life. These technologies aim to enhance human cognitive capabilities and learning experiences by providing personalized support based on recognized cognitive and affective states. In this section, we explore how these technologies are applied in practice, focusing on their implementation in learning, reasoning, and communication contexts.

3.1 Learning

Learning represents a fundamental cognitive process that can be significantly enhanced through augmentation technologies. At its core, intelligent learning systems seek to understand the learner's cognitive and affective state and provide appropriate support to enhance learning outcomes. This understanding typically involves sensing technologies that capture behavioral, physiological, or performance indicators, combined with models that interpret these indicators in terms of relevant learning constructs.

One key aspect in learning augmentation is the recognition of learners' affective states. Research has shown that affective states such as interest, confusion, frustration, and boredom significantly influence learning processes and outcomes [31]. By recognizing these states, intelligent systems can provide interventions that address not only cognitive but also affective dimensions of learning. Recent advances in this area include the development of appearance-based confidence detection systems that evaluate gaze behavior using deep learning [3] and frameworks for recognizing various learning abilities [15].

Interactive eye-tracking applications represent a powerful approach to intervention in reading and learning. Systems like iDict provide translations for comprehension problems detected in the reader's gaze patterns [11]. The eyeBook creates an interactive and entertaining reading experience by displaying images, translations, and other supplementary materials based on eye movements [4]. These systems demonstrate how eye-tracking can be used to enhance reading experiences by providing timely and relevant support.

Content adaptation represents one form of intervention, adjusting the material presented to the learner based on their state and characteristics. This adaptation can involve selecting appropriate content difficulty, providing additional explanations or examples, or offering alternative representations of concepts. Intelligent digital textbooks like HyperMind exemplify this approach, displaying supplementary materials when the learner appears to have difficulty understanding the content [13, 14, 20]. These systems can also visualize the learner's affective states in real time, enabling teachers to monitor progress and identify areas where intervention may be needed [17]. Recent advancements have further integrated these systems with large language models to generate personalized questions based on eye-tracking data [22] and provide adaptive summaries of content [32].

Interface adaptations offer another form of intervention, adjusting how content is presented or how the learner interacts with the system. Adaptive scrolling algorithms can adjust the presentation of text based on the reader's eye movements, facilitating more fluid reading experiences [26]. By aligning the scrolling with the reader's natural reading pace, these systems can enhance reading fluency and reduce the cognitive load associated with manual scrolling. Haptic feedback can augment reading experiences by providing tactile sensations that complement the visual information [39], while virtual reality offers new possibilities for immersive learning experiences [9].

In reading and language learning, augmentation technologies have shown promise in enhancing comprehension and vocabulary development. Recent innovations include systems that leverage social media images and large language models to build personalized vocabulary in context [38], and tools that monitor facial expressions and body language during web browsing to provide insights into learning behaviors [35].

3.2 Reasoning

Reasoning augmentation focuses on enhancing human cognitive processes involved in problem-solving, decision-making, and critical thinking. These systems aim to support higher order cognitive functions by providing relevant information, suggesting alternative perspectives, or guiding analytical processes.

One approach to reasoning augmentation involves the development of systems that can detect cognitive load and adapt accordingly. When a user is engaged in complex reasoning tasks, these systems can monitor indicators of cognitive strain, such as pupil dilation, eye movement patterns, or physiological signals, and adjust the presentation of information to reduce unnecessary cognitive burden. For instance, a system might simplify visualizations, highlight key information, or suggest breaks when cognitive overload is detected.

The concept of scaffolding, providing temporary support that is gradually removed as competence develops, informs the design of reasoning augmentation systems. These systems can offer varying levels of support depending on the user's expertise and the complexity of the reasoning task. For novices, the system might provide more explicit guidance; for experts, it might offer more subtle cues or advanced analytical tools.

Another important aspect of reasoning augmentation is the support for metacognitive processes. Metacognition, thinking about one's own thinking, plays a crucial role in effective reasoning and problem-solving. Augmentation systems can promote metacognitive awareness by providing feedback on reasoning strategies, highlighting potential biases, or suggesting alternative approaches. By making implicit cognitive processes more explicit, these systems help users develop more effective reasoning strategies.

3.3 Communicating

Communication represents a fundamental aspect of human cognition that can be significantly enhanced through augmentation technologies. These systems aim to improve the effectiveness, efficiency, and accessibility of communication processes, both for individuals and groups.

In the context of knowledge transfer, communication augmentation technologies can help identify and analyze key micro-behaviors that influence the effectiveness of information exchange. As highlighted in recent research [37], camera-based systems can detect subtle communication signals such as speaking patterns and nodding behaviors, providing valuable insights into the dynamics of group discussions. These technologies enable the quantitative evaluation of communication patterns, helping participants understand how they engage in discussions.

Engagement detection represents another important dimension of communication augmentation. Systems like EnGauge [36] can estimate participants' engagement levels during online meetings by analyzing facial expressions through deep neural networks. This real-time feedback allows speakers to adjust their communication approach based on audience engagement, potentially leading to more effective knowledge transfer.

The integration of avatars in communication contexts offers another promising approach to augmentation. Digital representations can facilitate more natural and engaging interactions, particularly in remote or virtual environments. These avatars can be designed to convey social cues, express emotions, and adapt to different communication contexts, enhancing the richness of digital interactions.

Group communication represents a particularly rich area for augmentation. Technologies that visualize speaking time, turn-taking patterns, or topic coverage can help groups become more aware of their communication dynamics and address potential imbalances. Systems that detect when certain participants are being excluded or when the discussion is becoming dominated by a few voices can prompt more inclusive participation patterns.

4 Discussion

As research in Cognitive Augmentation and Intelligent Learning Assistant continues to advance, several promising directions and persistent challenges emerge. In this section, we explore these future directions and challenges, considering both technological developments and broader implications for human cognition and learning. We also address the ethical, social, and methodological considerations that must be navigated to realize the full potential of these technologies.

Designing effective interventions remains a significant challenge. Interventions must be timely, relevant, and non-disruptive to be effective. They must also balance immediate support with long-term meta-skill development, avoiding the pitfalls of over-dependence on technology. The goal is to go beyond the interface to create lasting cognitive enhancement that persists even when the technology is not present. Moreover, the effectiveness of interventions may vary across individuals, contexts, and tasks, requiring adaptive approaches that can accommodate this variability. Addressing these challenges is essential for realizing the full potential of Cognitive Augmentation.

4.1 Technical and Methodological Challenges

One of the primary technical challenges in Cognitive Augmentation is the development of sensing technologies that are both accurate and unobtrusive. Current sensing approaches often involve trade-offs between precision and usability. High-precision sensors, such as medical-grade EEG or fMRI, can provide detailed information about cognitive processes but are typically bulky, expensive, and limited to laboratory settings. More accessible sensors, such as commercial EOG glasses or wristbands, offer greater usability but may sacrifice some precision. Bridging this gap requires innovations in sensor design, signal processing, and data analysis to extract meaningful information from noisy, real-world data.

Another technical challenge lies in the integration of multiple sensing modalities. Different sensors capture different aspects of cognitive activities and affective states, and combining these diverse data sources can provide a more comprehensive understanding. However, integrating multimodal data presents significant challenges in terms of synchronization, alignment, and fusion. Sensors may operate at different sampling rates, capture different time scales of phenomena, and exhibit varying levels of noise and reliability. Developing robust methods for multimodal integration remains an active area of research in Cognitive Augmentation.

The recognition of complex cognitive activities and affective states in natural settings represents another significant technical challenge. Laboratory studies often involve controlled tasks and environments, which may not reflect the complexity and variability of real-world cognitive activities. Natural reading, for example, encompasses a wide range of materials, devices, and contexts, each with its own characteristics and challenges. Developing recognition algorithms that can generalize across these diverse scenarios requires large-scale datasets, sophisticated machine learning approaches, and careful consideration of individual and contextual factors.

Beyond technical challenges, Cognitive Augmentation faces methodological challenges related to experimental design, evaluation, and validation. Studying cognitive augmentation often involves complex, multifaceted phenomena that are difficult to isolate and measure. Traditional experimental paradigms may not capture the richness and complexity of augmented cognitive experiences, requiring new methodological approaches that balance rigor with ecological validity.

One methodological challenge lies in the collection of ground truth data for cognitive activities and affective states. Unlike physical activities, which can often be observed directly, cognitive processes are internal and not directly observable. Researchers typically rely on self-reports, performance measures, or physiological correlates as proxies for cognitive states, each with its own limitations and biases. Developing more reliable and valid methods for assessing cognitive states is essential for advancing research in Cognitive Augmentation.

Another methodological challenge involves the evaluation of augmentation systems in terms of their impact on cognitive performance and experience. Traditional metrics such as task completion time or accuracy may not fully capture the benefits of cognitive augmentation, which could include enhanced understanding, creativity, or long-term skill development. Moreover, the effects of augmentation may vary across individuals, tasks, and contexts, requiring evaluation approaches that can accommodate this variability. Developing comprehensive, multidimensional evaluation frameworks remains an important methodological challenge in the field.

Longitudinal studies present particular methodological challenges in Cognitive Augmentation. The goal of Meta-Augmented Human is to enhance abilities permanently, not just temporarily while using technology. Assessing such long-term effects requires extended studies that track changes in cognitive abilities over time, both with and without technological support. These studies face challenges related to participant retention, controlling for confounding factors, and distinguishing between the effects of augmentation and natural development or learning. Despite these challenges, longitudinal research is essential for understanding the lasting impact of cognitive augmentation technologies.

4.2 Technological Advancements and Future Directions

Advances in sensing technologies promise to enhance the capabilities of Cognitive Augmentation systems. Miniaturization and integration of sensors will enable more unobtrusive monitoring of cognitive and affective states, reducing the burden on users and enabling long-term use in natural settings. Improvements in signal processing and noise reduction will enhance the quality of sensor data, enabling more accurate recognition of subtle cognitive and affective states. And the development of new sensing modalities, such as functional near-infrared spectroscopy (fNIRS) or advanced EEG, may provide more direct insights into brain activity and cognitive processes.

Machine learning and artificial intelligence will continue to play crucial roles in advancing Cognitive Augmentation. Deep learning approaches have already shown promise in recognizing complex patterns in multimodal sensor data, and further developments in these methods will enhance their accuracy and generalizability [30]. Reinforcement learning may enable systems to adapt their interventions based on observed outcomes, optimizing support strategies over time. And explainable AI approaches will be essential for developing systems that users can understand and trust, particularly in sensitive domains like education and healthcare. Recent work integrating large language models with eye-tracking data for generating personalized learning content [22] and predicting student difficulties in mathematics [24] demonstrates the potential of these approaches.

Advances in human–computer interaction will also shape the future of Cognitive Augmentation. Mixed reality technologies, combining elements of virtual and augmented reality, offer new possibilities for immersive learning experiences and cognitive support. Natural language interfaces may enable more intuitive interaction with augmentation systems, reducing the cognitive load associated with system use. And advances in personalization and adaptation will enable systems to better accommodate individual differences and preferences, enhancing their effectiveness and acceptability.

4.3 Integration with Artificial Intelligence

The integration of Cognitive Augmentation with artificial intelligence represents a particularly promising direction for future research and development. AI systems can complement human cognition in various ways, from performing routine cognitive tasks to providing insights and recommendations based on large-scale data analysis. By combining the strengths of human and artificial intelligence, integrated systems can achieve performance levels that neither could reach alone.

One approach to human–AI integration involves the development of cognitive assistants that work alongside humans, providing information, suggestions, or feedback as needed. These assistants can leverage AI capabilities such as natural language processing, knowledge representation, and machine learning to enhance human cognitive processes. For example, a cognitive assistant might monitor a learner's progress, identify areas where they are struggling, and suggest resources or strategies to address these challenges. By providing timely and relevant support, these assistants can enhance human cognitive performance while promoting skill development.

Collaborative human–AI reasoning systems represent another approach to integration. Rather than a one-on-one human assistant scenario, these systems scale augmentation to groups and complex tasks. For instance, swarm intelligence platforms can connect groups of humans through an AI mediator to make collective decisions. By using real-time feedback loops, groups can produce answers (e.g., predictions, diagnoses) more accurate than individuals or traditional votes. This can be seen as augmenting group cognition, essentially creating a *hive mind* that is smarter than its parts through AI facilitation. Such hybrid collective intelligence systems blur the line between human intelligence amplification and algorithmic guidance, opening new ways to tackle complex, uncertainty-laden problems by pooling knowledge effectively.

Another approach involves the use of AI for cognitive offloading, delegating certain cognitive tasks to artificial systems to free up human cognitive resources for other activities. This offloading can range from simple memory aids (such as digital calendars or note-taking systems) to more complex cognitive supports (such as automated summarization or information filtering). By reducing cognitive load in some areas, offloading can enable humans to focus their attention and effort on tasks that require uniquely human capabilities, such as creative thinking or ethical judgment. This concept is related to the extended mind hypothesis from cognitive science, which argues that external artifacts (notebooks, devices, software) can become integral parts of an individual's cognitive process. In the augmented cognition perspective, the computer (and AI algorithms it runs) essentially functions as an extension of the user's mind, offloading certain cognitive tasks and providing information or computation that the brain alone could not easily accomplish.

The concept of intelligence augmentation, as distinct from artificial intelligence, emphasizes the enhancement of human intelligence through technological means rather than the creation of autonomous intelligent systems. This approach recognizes the unique strengths of human cognition, such as contextual understanding, creativity, and ethical reasoning, while acknowledging the potential for technology to address limitations in areas such as memory, attention, or processing capacity. By focusing on augmentation rather than replacement, this approach seeks to develop technologies that enhance human capabilities while preserving human agency and autonomy.

A very recent wave in this field is the integration of generative AI models into knowledge work. Large language models (LLMs) have shown the ability to generate human-like text, summarize information, and even perform basic reasoning tasks. They are being deployed as writing assistants, coding copilots, and conversational research aides. Early studies have found that such AI assistance can significantly improve productivity for tasks like writing documents or code, but the best outcomes occur when the human remains actively involved—guiding the AI with prompts, reviewing and editing its outputs, and steering it away from errors or inappropriate content. Instead of expecting the AI to do a task completely, many researchers argue for designing interactions where the AI helps the user do the task themselves, for example, by generating suggestions, filling in routine parts, or providing inspirations that the human can build upon. This way the AI acts as a thought partner and amplifier of the human's own ideas, rather than a replacement.

4.4 Ethical and Social Considerations

As Cognitive Augmentation technologies become more sophisticated and widespread, ethical and social considerations will become increasingly important. Privacy concerns will continue to be significant, as these technologies collect and analyze sensitive data about cognitive processes and affective states. Augmented cognition systems often rely on sensitive data about the user: their behaviors, physiological signals, perhaps even direct neural data. Brain signals, for example, could potentially reveal a person's emotional state or certain pathologies; misuse of such data (or even the fear of misuse) could harm users. Similarly, a cognitive assistant that reads all your emails and messages to provide context is effectively privy to your private life. Developing robust privacy frameworks, transparent data practices, and user control mechanisms will be essential for addressing these concerns while enabling effective augmentation. In some cases, on-device processing can mitigate risks (so raw data never leaves the user's control, only the assistance comes back).

Questions of autonomy and agency will also become more pressing as augmentation systems become more proactive and influential. How much control should these systems have over cognitive processes? How can we ensure that augmentation enhances rather than diminishes human agency? There is also the risk of manipulation. A system that deeply understands your cognitive patterns could subtly nudge your decisions. This could be benign (nudging toward healthier habits) or maleficent (steering purchases, opinions, or even political views). The extended mind perspective heightens this concern: if part of your cognition is externalized to software, someone who controls that software has a pathway to influence your thought process. Addressing these questions requires careful consideration of the balance between technological assistance and human autonomy, as well as the development of design principles that prioritize user control and transparency.

Another fundamental challenge is calibrating user trust in AI assistance. If the user trusts the system too much (over-reliance), they may follow AI suggestions blindly, potentially leading to errors if the AI is wrong (automation bias). On the other hand, too little trust (underutilization) means the powerful capabilities of the augmentation are wasted because the user ignores or second-guesses the AI even when it is correct. Achieving appropriate trust is tricky because AI systems, especially learned ones, can make mistakes in unpredictable ways. Transparency and explainability are often cited as solutions: if the AI can explain why it suggests something, the user can make an informed judgment.

Closely related is the issue of reliance and cognitive atrophy. If a particular cognitive function is consistently offloaded to AI, humans might lose practice or even ability in that domain. Just as the ubiquity of GPS navigation has arguably reduced people's innate wayfinding skills, or as reliance on search engines has reduced rote memorization, one can ask: will constant use of writing autocompletion erode our writing skill? Some argue that cognitive offloading is not new (writing itself offloads memory), and humans will always adapt by focusing on higher level skills. However, research has found that people who are more prone to cognitive offloading (immediately turning to their smartphone for answers) engage in less analytical thinking on their own, suggesting a "use it or lose it" effect on cognitive effort. In augmented cognition, if a system handles all arithmetic, information retrieval, and even basic decisions, the human user may become a passive operator.

Equity and access represent another critical ethical consideration. As cognitive augmentation technologies become more powerful and widespread, ensuring equitable access becomes increasingly important. If these technologies provide significant advantages in learning, work, or daily life, inequitable access could exacerbate existing social disparities. Moreover, the design of these technologies may reflect the biases and assumptions of their creators, potentially limiting their effectiveness for diverse populations. Developing inclusive design approaches and addressing barriers to access are essential for ensuring that the benefits of cognitive augmentation are widely shared. Another aspect is user diversity. People have different cognitive styles and needs; an augmentation that helps one person might overwhelm or mislead another. HCI research emphasizes inclusive design: cognitive augmentation should adapt to the individual and be customizable. For instance, some users might want very proactive assistance, others might prefer a minimalist approach. Ethically, people should have the right to "dial down" or turn off augmentation at times, lest they feel coerced by an ever-present AI.

The broader societal implications of Cognitive Augmentation raise questions about the changing relationship between humans and technology. As cognitive tasks are increasingly shared between humans and machines, how will this affect human cognitive development, social interaction, and cultural practices? Will increased reliance on cognitive augmentation lead to atrophy of certain cognitive skills, as suggested by the *Glass Cage* effect, or will it enable new forms of cognitive development and expression? This is especially concerning in high-skill professions: for example, pilots under advanced autopilot regimes can suffer skill fade, so that in rare emergency cases where they must take over, they perform worse (the classic "automation irony" where automation increases demands on the human at the worst times). Designers of augmentation systems are thus urged to keep the human in an active role, perhaps by occasionally requiring manual engagement or by using the AI in a centaur mode where it provides options but the human must do the final step. Addressing these questions requires interdisciplinary dialogue involving not only technologists but also psychologists, educators, ethicists, and policymakers.

When human and AI work jointly on a task, accountability becomes blurred. If an AI-driven clinical decision support suggests a treatment that a doctor follows and it has bad outcomes, who is responsible—the doctor (user) or the AI tool (developer)?

Legally and ethically, this is complex. In most current practice, the human is expected to be the final authority, essentially supervising the AI. This aligns with the principle of human-in-the-loop control. However, as AI systems grow more autonomous and confident, there is a risk that humans become rubber stamps, merely executing AI recommendations. To keep accountability clear, some have proposed requiring AI systems to indicate uncertainty and requiring human confirmation on critical decisions.

4.5 Balancing Technological Assistance and Human Development

A fundamental challenge in Cognitive Augmentation and Intelligent Learning Assistant is balancing immediate technological assistance with long-term human development. While technology can provide valuable support for cognitive tasks, overreliance on this support may impede the development of independent cognitive abilities. This tension is particularly evident in educational contexts, where the goal is not only to help learners complete tasks but to develop their capabilities for future learning and problem-solving.

The concept of Meta-Augmented Human offers a promising approach to this challenge, focusing on the enhancement of meta-skills—skills that enable the acquisition of other skills. By supporting the development of reading, learning, and metacognitive strategies, augmentation technologies can enhance human capabilities in ways that persist even when the technology is not present. This approach recognizes that the ultimate goal of cognitive augmentation is not to replace human cognition but to enhance it in ways that promote autonomy and growth. It embodies the core principle of going beyond the interface to create lasting cognitive enhancement that transforms how people learn and think.

Designing for this balance requires careful consideration of when and how to provide support. Adaptive scaffolding, which adjusts the level of assistance based on the learner's needs and progress, represents one approach to this challenge. By providing more support when needed and gradually reducing it as the learner develops competence, adaptive scaffolding can facilitate learning while promoting independence. Similarly, metacognitive support, which helps learners understand and regulate their own cognitive processes, can enhance learning while developing skills that transfer to new contexts.

5 Conclusion

Cognitive Augmentation and Intelligent Learning Assistant represent promising approaches to enhancing human cognitive capabilities and learning experiences. By leveraging sensing technologies, activity recognition, and adaptive interventions, these systems can provide personalized support that addresses individual needs and preferences. The concept of Meta-Augmented Human, which aims to enhance abilities permanently rather than temporarily, offers a framework for developing augmentation technologies that contribute to long-term cognitive development by focusing on meta-skills that transcend specific interfaces or tools.

The journey from early visions of human–computer symbiosis to today's sophisticated augmentation systems reflects our ongoing quest to transcend our cognitive limitations. If we navigate the challenges wisely, augmented cognition systems could help solve pressing global problems by enabling humans to process complexity and volume of information far beyond our un-augmented capacity. They could personalize education and healthcare in transformative ways, and they might even help us better understand ourselves by externalizing parts of our mind in interactive mirrors. By uniting advances in AI with insights from HCI and cognitive science, augmented cognition strives to fulfill the timeless quest to transcend our innate limitations. The coming years will no doubt bring new breakthroughs in this quest, ensuring that as our machines get smarter, so do we—not just while using them, but through the lasting enhancement of our meta-skills for long-term cognitive growth that persists beyond the interface.

References

1. Abdelrahman, Y., Velloso, E., Dingler, T., Schmidt, A., Vetere, F.: Cognitive heat: exploring the usage of thermal imaging to unobtrusively estimate cognitive load. Proc. ACM Interact. Mob. Wearable Ubiquit. Technol. **1**(3), 33 (2017)
2. Acosta, M.C., Gallar, J., Belmonte, C.: The influence of eye solutions on blinking and ocular comfort at rest and during work at video display terminals. Exp. Eye Res. **68**(6), 663–669 (1999)
3. Bhatt, A., Watanabe, K., Santhosh, J., Dengel, A., Ishimaru, S.: Abcde: appearance-based confidence detection by evaluating gaze behavior using deep learning (2025), in press
4. Biedert, R., Buscher, G., Dengel, A.: The eyebook-using eye tracking to enhance the reading experience. Informatik-Spektrum **33**(3), 272–281 (2010)
5. Boucsein, W.: Electrodermal Activity. Springer Science & Business Media (2012)
6. Carr, N.: The Glass Cage: Automation and US. WW Norton & co (2014)
7. Chen, S., Epps, J., Ruiz, N., Chen, F.: Eye activity as a measure of human mental effort in HCI. In: Proceedings of the 16th International Conference on Intelligent User Interfaces, pp. 315–318. ACM (2011)
8. Clarke, A.C.: Profiles of the Future. Pan Books (1964)
9. Dingler, T., Kunze, K., Outram, B.: Vr reading uis: Assessing text parameters for reading in VR. In: Extended Abstracts of the 2018 CHI Conference on Human Factors in Computing Systems, p. LBW094. ACM (2018)
10. Engelbart, D.C.: Augmenting human intellect: a conceptual framework (1962)
11. Hyrskykari, A., Majaranta, P., Aaltonen, A., Räihä, K.J.: Design issues of idict: a gaze-assisted translation aid. In: Proceedings of the 2000 Symposium on Eye Tracking Research & Applications, pp. 9–14. ACM (2000)
12. Ishimaru, S.: Meta-Augmented Human: From Physical to Cognitive Towards Affective State Recognition. Ph.D. thesis, Technische Universität Kaiserslautern (2020)

13. Ishimaru, S., Bukhari, S.S., Heisel, C., Großmann, N., Klein, P., Kuhn, J., Dengel, A.: Augmented learning on anticipating textbooks with eye tracking. In: Positive Learning in the Age of Information, pp. 387–398. Springer (2018)
14. Ishimaru, S., Bukhari, S.S., Heisel, C., Kuhn, J., Dengel, A.: Towards an intelligent textbook: eye gaze based attention extraction on materials for learning and instruction in physics. In: Proceedings of the 2016 ACM International Joint Conference on Pervasive and Ubiquitous Computing: Adjunct Publication, pp. 1041–1045. ACM (2016)
15. Ishimaru, S., Dengel, A.: Arfled: ability recognition framework for learning and education. In: Proceedings of the 2017 ACM International Joint Conference on Pervasive and Ubiquitous Computing: Adjunct Publication, pp. 339–343. ACM (2017)
16. Ishimaru, S., Hoshika, K., Kunze, K., Kise, K., Dengel, A.: Towards reading trackers in the wild: detecting reading activities by EEG glasses and deep neural networks. In: Proceedings of the 2017 ACM International Joint Conference on Pervasive and Ubiquitous Computing and Proceedings of the 2017 ACM International Symposium on Wearable Computers, pp. 704–711. ACM (2017)
17. Ishimaru, S., Jacob, S., Roy, A., Bukhari, S.S., Heisel, C., Großmann, N., Thees, M., Kuhn, J., Dengel, A.: Cognitive state measurement on learning materials by utilizing eye tracker and thermal camera. In: Proceedings of the 14th IAPR International Conference on Document Analysis and Recognition, pp. 32–36 (2017)
18. Ishimaru, S., Kunze, K., Kise, K., Dengel, A.: The wordometer 2.0: Estimating the number of words you read in real life using commercial EGG glasses. In: Proceedings of the 2016 ACM International Joint Conference on Pervasive and Ubiquitous Computing: Adjunct Publication, pp. 293–296. ACM (2016)
19. Ishimaru, S., Kunze, K., Tanaka, K., Uema, Y., Kise, K., Inami, M.: Smart eyewear for interaction and activity recognition. In: Proceedings of the 33rd Annual ACM Conference Extended Abstracts on Human Factors in Computing Systems, pp. 307–310 (2015)
20. Ishimaru, S., Watanabe, K., Großmann, N., Heisel, C., Klein, P., Arakawa, Y., Kuhn, J., Dengel, A.: Hypermind builder: pervasive user interface to create intelligent interactive documents. In: Proceedings of the 2018 ACM International Joint Conference on Pervasive and Ubiquitous Computing: Adjunct Publication, pp. 357–360. ACM (2018)
21. Ishimaru, S., Weppner, J., Kunze, K., Bulling, A., Kise, K., Dengel, A., Lukowicz, P.: In the blink of an eye: combining head motion and eye blink frequency for activity recognition with google glass. In: Proceedings of the 5th Augmented Human International Conference, pp. 150–153. ACM (2014)
22. Iwatsuru, K., Ishimaru, S., Vargo, A., Kise, K.: Enhancing text comprehension for language learning by generating questions with eye-tracking and LLM (2025), in press
23. Kahneman, D., Beatty, J.: Pupil diameter and load on memory. Science **154**(3756), 1583–1585 (1966)
24. Kennel, K., Ishimaru, S., Küchemann, S., Steinert, S., Kuhn, J., Ruzika, S.: Gaze-based prediction of students' math difficulties—a time dynamic machine learning approach to enable early individual assistance, pp. 1–25 (2025)
25. Kliegl, R., Nuthmann, A., Engbert, R.: Tracking the mind during reading: the influence of past, present, and future words on fixation durations. J. Exp. Psychol. Gen. **135**(1), 12 (2006)
26. Kunze, K., Shiga, Y., Ishimaru, S., Kise, K.: Reading activity recognition using an off-the-shelf EEG—detecting reading activities and distinguishing genres of documents. In: Proceedings of the 2013 12th International Conference on Document Analysis and Recognition, pp. 96–100. IEEE Computer Society (2013)
27. Kushki, A., Fairley, J., Merja, S., King, G., Chau, T.: Comparison of blood volume pulse and skin conductance responses to mental and affective stimuli at different anatomical sites. Physiol. Meas. **32**(10), 1529 (2011)
28. Licklider, J.C.: Man-computer symbiosis. IRE Trans. Hum. Factors Electron. **1**, 4–11 (1960)
29. Ma, M., Fan, H., Kitani, K.M.: Going deeper into first-person activity recognition. In: Proceedings of the IEEE Conference on Computer Vision and Pattern Recognition, pp. 1894–1903 (2016)

30. Morita, R., Watanabe, K., Zhou, J., Dengel, A., Ishimaru, S.: Genaireading: Augmenting human cognition with interactive digital textbooks using large language models and image generation models. In: Proceedings of the Augmented Human International Conference 2025 (2025), to appear
31. Rudmann, D.S., McConkie, G.W., Zheng, X.S.: Eyetracking in cognitive state detection for HCI. In: Proceedings of the 5th International Conference on Multimodal Interfaces, pp. 159–163. ACM (2003)
32. Santhosh, J., Dengel, A., Ishimaru, S.: Gaze-driven adaptive learning system with ChatGPT-generated summaries 173714–173733 (2024)
33. Sapolsky, R.M.: Why Zebras Don't Get Ulcers. WH Freeman New York (1994)
34. Spache, G.D.: Is this a breakthrough in reading? Read. Teach. **15**(4), 258–263 (1962)
35. Watanabe, K., Dengel, A., Ishimaru, S.: Metacognition-engauge: real-time augmentation of self-and-group engagement levels understanding by gauge interface in online meetings. In: Proceedings of the 15th Augmented Human International Conference (2024)
36. Watanabe, K., Sathyanarayana, T., Dengel, A., Ishimaru, S.: Engauge: Engagement gauge of meeting participants estimated by facial expression and deep neural network. IEEE Access **11**, 52886–52898 (2023)
37. Watanabe, K., Soneda, Y., Matsuda, Y., Nakamura, Y., Arakawa, Y., Dengel, A., Ishimaru, S.: Discaas: Micro behavior analysis on discussion by camera as a sensor. Sensors **21**(17), 5719 (2021)
38. Watanabe, K., Tanaka, S., Vargo, A., Kise, K., Ishimaru, S.: Trackthink camera: a tool for tracking facial and body information while web browsing. In: AIED' 23 Workshop: Automated Assessment and Guidance of Project Work, pp. 7–14 (2023)
39. Yannier, N., Israr, A., Lehman, J.F., Klatzky, R.L.: Feelsleeve: haptic feedback to enhance early reading. In: Proceedings of the 33rd Annual ACM Conference on Human Factors in Computing Systems, pp. 1015–1024. ACM (2015)

Learning in the Loop: AI, Feedback, and the Future of Human Thought

Tilman Dingler

Abstract This chapter explores the evolving relationship between humans and artificial intelligence (AI) as partners in learning. Grounded in Douglas Engelbart's vision of man–machine symbiosis, we outline the development of AI-powered learning systems capable of personalizing feedback, adapting to cognitive states, and enhancing knowledge retention. In addition to these promises, the chapter critically examines the risks our current technology landscape poses to learners, such as device dependency, information overload, distraction, and cognitive manipulation. In response to these challenges, the chapter challenges designers and creators of information systems to prioritize deep engagement, learner autonomy, and critical reflection. Shifting from passive information consumption to active knowledge construction is a prerequisite for a future in which AI systems are not just tools of efficiency, but trusted partners in our lifelong learning journey.

Keywords Cognitive augmentation · AI-augmented learning · Man–machine intelligence

1 How We Got Here?

In 1968, Douglas Engelbart stood before a crowd at the Fall Joint Computer Conference in San Francisco and unveiled what would later be known as the "Mother of All Demos." In a 90-min live demonstration, he introduced the computer mouse, hypertext, windowed interfaces, real-time collaborative editing, and video conferencing—decades before any of these technologies made it into consumer products.

But Engelbart's vision was not just technological, but also deeply philosophical and educational. He believed that humans could not keep up with the complexity of modern problems using the capacity of their unaided minds alone. What he proposed was a system of "augmenting human intellect"—not replacing it with machines, but

T. Dingler (✉)
Delft University of Technology, Delft, Netherlands
e-mail: t.dingler@tudelft.nl

A. Dengel et al. (eds.), *The Future of Education with AI*,
https://doi.org/10.1007/978-981-95-1622-3_9

enhancing our ability to understand, solve, and learn through symbiotic relationships with computers [1].

Transitioning into a digital society entailed virtually unlimited access to information. Today's computing devices act as a portal to that information through which we perceive the digital and increasingly also our physical world. The sheer amount of information available requires us to develop strategies to sift through that information effectively and separate the relevant from the redundant. This has led us to information environments, where a great number of devices, apps, and services compete for our attention. The resulting battle for engagement comes at the cost of users' perceptual and cognitive capacities, and rather than engaging in deep learning activities, users often employ shortcuts to sift through the sheer amount of available information and compromise on deeper engagement or critical reflection [2].

While commercial interests of these platforms often contradict meaningful interaction and even well-being [3], recent research has been exploring some promising avenues of deepening engagement, creating new learning opportunities, and supporting well-being. With that regard, Chapter "Sensing and Actuation for Learning" explored AI-powered sensing and actuation technologies to understand and enhance various aspects of the learning process, from reading comprehension to knowledge consolidation and the impact of physical well-being. In previous research, we applied thermal sensors to monitor facial temperature changes and train machine learning models to determine real-time cognitive load [4, 5]. This information paired with data on users' gaze patterns can be used to estimate how focused and engaged they are during a task [6] or how deeply they read [7]. With such sensing methods, technology can move beyond providing mere access to information and toward more adaptive information interfaces that take users' cognitive load into account and hence adapt their presentation and content accordingly.

The research outlined in Chapter "AI-Driven Approaches to Knowledge Acquisition and Skill Mastery: an Application to Second-Language Learning" shows how speech processing and eye tracking can be effectively applied to second language learning, including pronunciation and reading comprehension. This aligns with Engelbart's vision by demonstrating how technology can augment learners' abilities to acquire and master a new language through personalized feedback, deeper insights into their learning processes, and adaptive learning experiences. Language learning can further be integrated into everyday activities, thereby allowing users to pick up a language complementing dedicated study sessions [8, 9]. And while Chapter "Knowledge Transfer with AI" focuses on understanding, estimating, and accelerating the transmission of knowledge, it highlights the role AI plays in analyzing facial features, speech, and nonverbal behaviors. Contactless sensors may soon be ubiquitous and accompany learners in combination with a personal, AI-powered tutor, which focuses on advancing users' knowledge and mastering their high-density information environments. Chapter "Affective Computing and the Future of Education" gives a taste of what it would mean to give these tutors also access to their learners' emotional data. Such tutors could well enhance knowledge building by offering hyper-personalized, interactive, and engaging learning experiences for pupils, students, and lifelong learners. Rightfully, this may lead to a substantial shift in university education. New policy and curriculum development framework, as described in Chapter "Skills Training in the Age of AI," are needed to balance educational needs and real-world costs as both educators and students need to adapt to the evolving needs of Industry and academic research.

These developments collectively demonstrate how Engelbart's vision of human–computer symbiosis is increasingly being realized through AI-powered systems that perceive, adapt, and respond to learners in highly individualized ways. We are witnessing a convergence of sensing, affective computing, personalization, and AI-driven feedback that seems to reshape the way we acquire knowledge and develop skills. Yet, as promising as these current trajectories are, they may only scratch the surface of what lies ahead. If today's systems can personalize learning based on observable behavior and physiological cues, what might be possible when we are able to model and interact with the internal architecture of a learner's mind, i.e., their memory, biases, knowledge structures, and patterns of association? In the following section, we turn our attention to a more speculative but increasingly plausible future: one in which AI systems not only adapt to the learner's observable behavior, but are deeply attuned to their internal cognitive structures. The result may be symbiotic systems that optimize learning pathways, extend memory, and fundamentally reshape the relationship between devices, knowledge, and identity.

2 The Future of AI-Augmented Learning?

Let us imagine a device that records, encodes, and archives all information an individual is exposed to since the early beginnings of their mind development. It resembles a digital record of an individual's memory and takes into account encoding errors as well as the process of forgetting. It further learns the probabilities of certain memories being evoked according to the underlying topology of the individual's neural network and, therefore, is aware of chains of associations and biases. Such a system is capable of invoking the entirety of information and experiences a person has been exposed to over the course of their life and yields the ability to predict how memories are surfaced when certain cues are presented. Not only does such a system serve as a digital memory archive, but it can also inform about the most effective way to present new information so that new content is optimally embedded in existing knowledge structures. It does so by using existing preconceptions and biases the learner has and builds upon them. It constantly simulates the likelihood of new knowledge being connected in various ways and determines the most effective anchor points. The result is that information is being processed quicker by matching new information optimally with prior experiences, emotions, and interests and hence is longer retained due to building meaningful associations.

Sounds far-fetched? Let us consider recent developments in genome research that have dramatically brought down the costs of gene sequencing. When we fully understand an individual's genome, we are able to understand how to optimize the individual itself, including mapping the perfect diet to the individual, the drugs that work, and the optimal exercise regimen required. Understanding what microbiome types or gut flora are ideal for an individual will allow us to accurately predict how specific sedatives and medicines will impact an individual's body and will enable us to learn which disease an individual is most likely to develop and how to prevent it. Holistic, AI-powered learning systems attempt to achieve the same for the individual learning regimen: by understanding how an individual best learns in terms of content presentation, learning modality, and content connection, learning content can be adapted to the needs of the individual. By taking into account previous knowledge, preconceptions, and preferences, new learning items can be optimally integrated into a learner's web of knowledge and experiences.

While such a vision of hyper-personalized, knowledge-aware learning systems may seem futuristic, the trajectory toward technologies that support a continuous, lifelong learning process supported by AI is already evident. Data storage is abundant, and cloud services retain our information perpetually. Just as genome sequencing enables tailored healthcare, next-generation learning systems aim to provide tailored intellectual growth by adapting content, modality, and feedback to each individual's evolving interests and cognitive ability. Realizing this vision, however, requires more than technological innovation; it demands a reimagining of how we approach learning across an entire lifespan. In the next section, we explore how AI is already beginning to reshape the concept of lifelong learning, forging a new kind of cognitive partnership between humans and machines.

2.1 Toward a Lifelong Cognitive Partnership

While the influx of AI into education and workplaces has been dramatically accelerating, it is transforming not only job roles and in-demand skills but also the very nature of how we acquire, retain, and apply knowledge. In this context, lifelong learning is not just desirable—it is essential. As artificial intelligence reshapes industries, the ability to adapt continuously becomes a core human competency [10]. What we learn, how we learn, and when we learn are all undergoing a profound shift. AI plays a pivotal role in this evolution by being able to support learning across the lifespan through just-in-time knowledge delivery, contextualized feedback, and immediate access to global expertise [11]. Whether through interactive virtual assistants, intelligent tutoring systems, or curated content streams, AI systems are increasingly capable of personalizing learning pathways to suit individual needs, goals, and learning styles [12].

The central idea of lifelong learning in the age of AI is also explored in Chapter "AI-Driven Approaches to Knowledge Acquisition and Skill Mastery: an Application to Second-Language Learning," which highlights how educational trajectories are moving beyond the fixed curricula of institutional structures. Instead, learners are beginning to design their own educational experiences, curated dynamically and shaped by the ever-changing demands of society and work [13]. This democratization of learning is promising yet demanding: it places agency into the hands of individuals while also requiring continuous cognitive engagement. Learning can now happen anywhere, at any time—while commuting, exercising, or sports. Devices have become increasingly multimodal, allowing for voice interaction, haptic feedback, eye tracking, and even brain–computer interfaces [14]. These interfaces are no longer restricted by the machine's capabilities but by the limitations of the human–computer interface and our ability to absorb, process, and reflect on new information. In our recent research, we have looked into building passively collected memory stores, inviting users to reflect on their daily activities in an effort to deepen experiences and consolidate episodic memory [15]. Such reflections yielded positive effects on remembering events and their surrounding details. A cognitive support system could subsequently extract cues from such data in order to dynamically build reviews and trigger just-in-time reminders [16].

In the utopian vision that framed this chapter, we imagined a world where learning experiences are recorded from early childhood, namely, by building a dynamic, evolving digital twin of an individual's knowledge and memory. This digital twin would allow us to query our understanding, track knowledge gaps, and develop memory reinforcement strategies. The challenge of the future is not just to make AI work *for* us, but to ensure that it works *with* us, i.e., to enhance human agency rather than diminish it. Lifelong learning in an AI-augmented world is not just a matter of access or efficiency, but of designing systems that truly support human flourishing [17]. Apart from the critical questions of privacy and potential of unauthorized access breaches, AI-augmented learning systems should raise critical questions about how they would interact with our attention, autonomy, and cognitive limitations. The same technologies that support our learning can also undermine it if not carefully designed and ethically governed.

2.2 Trouble in Tech Paradise

Engelbart envisioned a future where machines would act as partners in thinking, thereby helping us to perpetually learn, navigate complexity, and improve our collective intelligence. While his vision fell short of being fully adopted in his lifetime, more than 50 years later, some parts of it have been implemented in the form of intelligent, interactive systems like AI tutors and augmented writing assistants [18]. His vision was largely rooted in optimism for the ability to pair human intellect with digital tools in order to meet the increasing complexity of the modern world. He believed that if we could build systems that allowed people to interact with information more effectively, we could amplify human capability and ultimately build a more intelligent, responsive society. In his framework, technology was less about convenience and more about collective problem-solving, and computers were a medium for extending cognition rather than replacing it [1, 19].

In recent years, however, it has become increasingly clear that rather than building tools for deep engagement and critical thinking, dominant technology platforms have prioritized engagement, entertainment, and influence [20]. The very systems designed to support learning and collaboration became pipelines for information overload, covering users in data, notifications, updates, and recommendations, most of which demand immediate but shallow attention. What Engelbart could not have foreseen is the rise of algorithmically curated content ecosystems, driven by attention economies. Platforms that once promised democratized access to knowledge are now criticized for fragmenting attention, encouraging dopamine-driven behaviors, and even shaping public opinion through opaque algorithmic processes. In this sense, we have moved from augmenting intellect to splintering it, i.e., distributing our focus across so many channels and stimuli that deeper engagement and learning become increasingly difficult [21].

Modern AI systems, especially recommender systems, large language models (LLMs), and adaptive feeds, are far from being neutral tools. They make choices on our behalf: what information to surface, how to frame such information, and which perspectives to prioritize. This introduces significant risks of manipulation, not only through mis- and disinformation, but through the subtle shaping of how we think, decide, and prioritize our choices and actions [22]. Additionally, in educational contexts, students increasingly rely on AI not just for scaffolding their understanding but for generating their arguments, paraphrasing their ideas, or summarizing complex texts. The question here is what happens to the process of thinking itself? Writing, after all, is a form of cognition. When that process is outsourced, learners are at risk of becoming passive recipients of AI-structured knowledge, rather than active constructors of meaning [23]. The promise of AI-augmented learning must, therefore, be viewed critically. Technologies that extend cognition must be designed to enhance attention, not fracture it; to promote critical engagement, not blind acceptance; and to support long-term memory and reflection, not just entertainment and short-term performance. If we fail to address these challenges, we risk building systems that do not serve our growth as learners and thinkers, but rather systems that train us to be efficient yet distracted and compliant.

3 Threats to Enlightenment

While AI-powered learning systems promise to enhance how we learn, what we know, and how we connect new knowledge, there is a growing concern that the very foundations of independent thinking and intellectual autonomy are being quietly undermined. The hyper-personalized nature of these technologies may very well discourage the kind of deliberate reflection, deep inquiry, and critical thinking that democratic societies depend upon. The subtle features of social media, in particular, including likes, swipes, autoplaying videos, and infinite scroll, encourage users to consume information reactively, often without noticing how their attention is being guided in the process. Technology does not merely mediate thought but rather conditions users toward immediacy, emotionality, and confirmation, while eroding the slower, effortful processes required for critical analysis, skepticism, and independent judgment. In the following, we confront the challenges that accompany our constant connection with AI-powered technology, most prominent risks being device dependency, information overload, constant distraction, and the growing potential for manipulation through algorithmic persuasion. These risks do not necessarily emerge from malice, but from the very design of systems optimized for perpetual user engagement.

3.1 Device Dependency

As AI-powered systems become part of everyday live, questions of dependency and autonomy arise. Just like navigation apps that help us get from A to B, new learning technologies undeniably enhance our capabilities in the moment, but they may also lead to a decline in our own cognitive skills, a phenomenon also referred to as *offloading*. Studies have shown that offloading can be detrimental to memory and thinking [24, 25]. Hence, the question is raised whether we are still as capable without the use of our devices? Access to these tools can be revoked rather suddenly, be that through technical failure, power outages, or corporate restriction. Economic or regulatory barriers can further keep such technologies out of the hands of marginalized groups. As reliance on external systems increases, so too does our vulnerability to their absence. When building such technologies, it is thus critical to envision how they can create and bolster innate cognitive skills and intelligence that reside within their users rather than in a form of distributed cognition [26].

Further, technologies increasingly guide our patterns of attention and shape the rhythms of our thought. What begins as momentary engagement (through the receipt of a notification) often becomes habitual checking, and eventually a felt need to remain constantly connected. This dependence on digital devices, especially smartphones, extends beyond convenience. It becomes a psychological tether, where the absence of the device can induce discomfort, anxiety, or even a sense of disorientation [25]. Rather than simply using apps and services as needed, our devices themselves begin to structure how we allocate time, how we process information, and how we relate to ourselves and others. Technology does not just seem to compete for our attention, but rather condition us to need it, creating a loop in which distraction and engagement reinforce one another. With such current role models, realizing the risk of dependency may very well hinder users from adopting of AI-powered learning technology, as benign as they may be.

3.2 Information Overload

Following the invention of the printing press in the sixteenth century, scholars expressed their unease about the potentially rapid dissemination of information. Swiss humanist Conrad Gesner warned of a "*confusing and harmful abundance of books*" and the overwhelming task of discerning truth [27]. Instead of liberating intellect, he feared that the flood of printed material might drown it. This anxiety echoed through the centuries: Enlightenment thinkers like Diderot and Leibniz wrestled with the challenge of organizing the subsequent explosion of knowledge into coherent systems. Turing award winner Herbert Simon famously voiced his growing concern about the risk of attention scarcity directly following the abundance of information stating: "*A wealth of information creates a poverty of attention*" [28].

Today, as AI systems accelerate content creation and curation, the dilemma has only intensified. In 2011, it was estimated that the average U.S. adult consumes about 34 gigabytes of information on a daily basis [29]. This includes television, radio, digital media, reading, and video games and amounts to about 100,000 words per day. This number is expected to have only gone up, especially when taking into account multitasking with multiple screens and platforms. Unfortunately, the mere abundance and acc essibility of information does not make us any smarter. In contrast, all this additional information exposure has been shown to correlate with reduced attention control, inhibited working memory, and lower task-switching efficiency [30].

3.3 Distraction

In this increasingly connected world of ours, we are constantly accompanied by a chorus of pings, vibrations, pop-ups, and algorithmically curated feeds. Each app, service, and notification competes for our attention. Smartphones sit within arm's reach at nearly every waking moment [31] and create a state of perpetually divided attention. The engagement with a single train of thought often seems like a rare luxury. Instead, our focus tends to drift from notification to notification, rarely settling long enough to think critically or reflect. Our downtime, as short as it may be, is quickly filled by automatic glances at our mobile screens [32]. This environment not only cultivates distraction, but also fosters malleability: when individuals are repeatedly prompted, nudged, and rewarded for quick responses over careful consideration, their cognitive habits begin to shift. Deep thinking, reflection, and creative pondering are replaced by scrolling infinitely through endorphine-inducing feed snippets.

Over several decades, psychologist Gloria Mark has compiled empirical evidence that our ability to maintain attention on a single task has been steadily declining. Drawing from years of observational and experimental research, Mark argues that the average attention span on digital tasks has shrunk from around 2.5 min in the early 2000s to just 47s today [33]. She argues that this may very well be a direct consequence of having to deal with both physical and online environments that tend to fragment our attention. Constant context switching, multitasking, and digital interruptions condition our minds for short bursts of engagement, which make it increasingly difficult to enter or sustain states of deep work or reflection. Such loss of attentional control directly affects our productivity, well-being, sense of agency, and learning ability.

3.4 Manipulation and Play on Cognitive Biases

As our attentional capacities erode, so does our ability to properly scrutinize the information we encounter. In fragmented digital environments, we are not only distracted, we are also susceptible to various forms of cognitive manipulation. People have been characterized as *cognitive misers* as we constantly strive for conserving our cognitive energy [34]. After all, our ability to process information is limited and, hence, we often adopt strategies for simplifying complex problems by applying excessive use of what Kahneman called system 1 thinking, i.e., an automatic, intuitive, and often unconscious mode of thinking as opposed to deliberate, effortful, and analytical (system 2) [35].

Modern propaganda promotes the use of system 1 thinking and is designed to take advantage of the limited processing capabilities of the cognitive misers resulting in adoption of simple messaging and biased memorization [36]. We saw this in our own experiments, in which we exposed participants to biased news feeds while recording their brain oxygenation levels using Functional Near-Infrared Spectroscopy (FNIR) [37]. When participants' interest levels on a given topic were low, we saw reduced brain activity, hinting at lower cognitive exertion while processing the new information. When they had a strong interest or strong personal stake, however, they would be much more inclined in cognitively processing the information, as shown by increased blood flow to the cerebrum.

In a follow-up study, we examined what makes individuals prone to falling victim to their biases when consuming online news feed media [38]. In the study, we asked participants to skim through a news feed filled with controversial topics. After a short break, we asked them to freely recall everything they could remember from the items they had just read. We then cross-referenced what they remembered with where they stood in terms of their own opinions and subscribed ideologies, finding that lower effortful thinking, strong political beliefs, and the perception of content as strongly opinionated amplified their own biases, leading to skewed information processing. The study showed that both individual and contextual factors make users susceptible to confirmation bias during information consumption. Low-effortful (system 1) thinking, strong political beliefs, and content's perceived issue strength are key contributors to confirmation bias. In practice, understanding who is more susceptible to confirmation bias and in what situations can lead to concrete changes in how we design and interact with information.

Consequently, if an individual generally tends toward over-applying system 1 thinking, they may need to be more mindful when encountering information that aligns with their beliefs. They could consciously try to engage in more deliberate (system 2) thinking to evaluate information more critically, especially on topics they feel strongly about. If they hold strong political beliefs, they might be more inclined to favor information confirming those beliefs. Being aware of this tendency can encourage them to actively seek out and consider diverse perspectives, even if they challenge their own. When they encounter content that feels very strongly opinionated, regardless of whether it aligns with their views, it might be more likely to trigger their confirmation bias. Recognizing this could prompt them to be more cautious in accepting this information without further scrutiny.

Learning systems but also social media and news platforms could potentially help with this by tailoring the feeds according to these susceptibility factors. They could, for example, consider strategies to reduce the prevalence or impact of extremely polarized content and integrate media literacy-building mechanisms directly into their interfaces to encourage more critical evaluation of information. Platforms could actively work to ensure a diversity of viewpoints are presented on debated topics, which would make it easier for users to encounter information that challenges their existing beliefs.

In conclusion, the threats of device dependency, information overload, perpetual distraction, and the exploitation of cognitive biases highlight a growing tension at the heart of our digital learning environments. While technologies are often designed to empower learners, they risk undermining the innate cognitive abilities, intellectual skills, and learners' autonomy that education seeks to cultivate. Going forward requires thoughtful design, ethical awareness, and a renewed commitment to building AI systems that reinforce rather than replace our capacity to think, reflect, and grow.

4 Opportunities for Optimists

Current characteristics of online information spaces, including information-dense environments, short-form content, and people's tendency to be caught in extended sessions of system 1 thinking, make it increasingly more difficult for users to think deeply about important issues and decisions. This gives algorithmic curation of news feeds and the manipulators behind those free rein to ever so slowly sway their users' opinions and value systems. As a result, Jaron Lanier, Computer Scientist and Virtual Reality pioneer, has long called for the need to remove ourselves from social media's reign of influence [22]. He argues that these systems use subtle forms of behavioral modification to gradually shape opinions and actions without users realizing it. By prioritizing sensationalism, misinformation, and emotionally charged content over factual or nuanced information, social media seems to play toward shallow yet continuous engagement, suppressing critical analysis and reflection. He concludes that withdrawing participation is the most direct way individuals can reclaim their autonomy, and potentially pressure the Industry toward taking more responsibility for a healthy societal discourse.

Democratic societies rest on the foundational belief that free speech, open discussion, and the exchange of ideas lead to more just and effective decision-making. Yet, as *cognitive misers*, individuals often engage in shallow information processing, making them more susceptible to simplistic persuasive tactics than to thoughtful analysis and scrutiny. There is no easy remedy for this dilemma. It requires individuals to develop self-awareness about their cognitive biases, the ways they process information, and the influence of digital platforms on their opinion formation. At present, many platforms lack meaningful incentives to encourage deeper engagement or critical reflection. In response, governments may consider stricter regulations on the behavioral steering of users—though such efforts remain deeply politically contentious.

As researchers, we should therefore focus on building up the body of empirical evidence that could inform such regulation with the goal of balancing individual, corporate, and societal needs. To that end, we set out to understand how cognitive biases are currently studied through the lens of human–computer interaction (HCI) as a discipline [39]. In this scoping review, we synthesized 127 articles, which evidenced a wide range of cognitive biases studied in various HCI contexts, including information interaction, recommender systems, human–AI interaction, and social computing. We identified five key ways HCI, in which researchers study cognitive biases:

- **Investigating Effects** covers studies that provide evidence on how cognitive biases manifest and impact users' behavior and decision-making in digital environments, informing the potential harms that regulation might aim to address.
- **Mitigating Biases** research explores the effectiveness of various techniques (nudging, boosting, cognitive aids) in counteracting negative effects. This offers potential solutions that regulation could encourage or mandate.
- **Utilizing Biases** studies examine how cognitive biases are leveraged to steer user behavior, raising ethical concerns about manipulation that regulation might need to address to protect individual autonomy.
- **Quantifying Biases** research focuses on developing tools and methods to detect and measure cognitive biases. Such tools could be essential for monitoring the effectiveness of regulations.
- **Observing Biases** research documents the real-world occurrences and unintended consequences of cognitive biases in human–computer interaction, further justifying the need for interventions.

Cognitive biases are not just quirks of the mind, but can be considered influencing factors that determine engagement and interaction. Thus far, only limited work has explored how cognitive biases can be harnessed for the greater good. By understanding how cognitive biases affect human behaviors, designers and architects of AI-powered learning systems can take them into account when building interactive systems as design elements can prioritize positive behaviors, such as critical engagement, over shallow information processing. Current commercial platforms rarely incentivize critical thinking or deliberate engagement, leaving users exposed to subtle behavioral steering that gradually reshapes their views. While regulatory action may provide some long-term structural guardrails, we must also consider more immediate, user-centered strategies. If we are to preserve autonomy and support democratic discourse in the digital age, we need to cultivate users' capacity for critical evaluation and bias awareness. This calls for educational interventions and learning environments that help individuals recognize and reflect on their own cognitive tendencies—ideally through short, actionable feedback cycles that reinforce effortful thinking in real time.

Shortening the Feedback Loop: Learning, at its core, is shaped by the distance between action and consequence. When feedback is delayed or ambiguous, it becomes difficult to establish clear causal relationships between what we do and what outcomes we experience. This is particularly evident in complex and wicked problems, such as climate change, where the environmental consequences of individual behavior may only become visible after years or decades. Similarly, in domains like nutrition, medicine, or behavioral change, long feedback cycles make it difficult for individuals to learn what truly works for them. By contrast, short feedback loops enhance learning by providing timely, specific, and personalized information about the effects of one's actions, making it easier to adapt and encourage experimentation [40].

The use of sensors, AI, and adaptive learning technologies can play a transformative role in shortening these loops. Physiological sensing (e.g., eye tracking, EEG, heart rate variability), combined with machine learning models that adapt to the user's state and behavior, can provide learners with immediate and context-sensitive feedback on performance, attention, comprehension, and emotional engagement. In the field of education, formative assessment and feedback theory have long shown that effective learning environments rely on continuous feedback that is integrated into the learning process itself [41]. AI-powered systems can further deeply personalize the learning experience and allow for experimentation where learners test different strategies, formats, or content types, and immediately see how these changes translate into learning outcomes. Over time, these systems can help individuals build a dynamic and personalized understanding of what works best for them, effectively becoming co-investigators in their own learning journey. AI-powered systems can further deeply personalize the learning experience and allow for experimentation where learners test different strategies, formats, or content types, and immediately see how these changes translate into learning successes. Over time, these systems can help individuals build a holistic understanding of what works best for them, effectively becoming co-investigators in their own learning journey.

Such systems hold promise beyond formal education and reach far into the premise of lifelong learning. They may help users better understand the consequences of our health decisions, our carbon footprint, and the cognitive impacts of our daily routines. The same infrastructure that powers today's attention-hungry information environments could be reimagined as a feedback-rich, curiosity-driven ecosystem, where exploration, reflection, and learning are central to the experience. In doing so, AI-powered learning technologies could augment learners in ways that cultivate deeper knowledge and more critical engagement as well as make us more attuned to the connections between our choices and the world we shape.

Acknowledgements The ideas expressed in this chapter are partly inspired by the work on *bias-aware computing* with my Ph.D. candidate Nattapat Boonprakong. Our conversations on bias detection, mitigation, and user agency have shaped this chapter. AI tools, such as ChatGPT and NotebookLM, helped me put these ideas into a stringent, written argument.

References

1. Engelbart, D.C., English W.K.: Proceedings of the December 9–11, 1968, Fall Joint Computer Conference, Part I, pp. 395–410 (1968)
2. Simon, H.A.: Q. J. Econ. **69**(1), 99 (1955)
3. Przybylski, A.K., Orben, A., Weinstein, N.: J. Am. Acad. Child Adolesc. Psychiatry **59**(9), 1080 (2020)
4. Abdelrahman, Y., Velloso, E., Dingler, T., Schmidt, A., Vetere, F.: Proc. ACM Interact. Mob. Wearable Ubiquitous Technol. **1**(3) (2017). https://doi.org/10.1145/3130898. URL https://doi.org/10.1145/3130898
5. Zhou, Q., Newn, J., Srivastava, N., Dingler, T., Goncalves, J., Velloso, E.: Extended Abstracts of the 2019 CHI Conference on Human Factors in Computing Systems. Association for Computing Machinery, New York, NY, USA, pp. 1–6 (2019). https://doi.org/10.1145/3290607.3313010. https://doi.org/10.1145/3290607.3313010
6. Babaei, E., Srivastava, N., Newn, J., Zhou, Q., Dingler, T., Velloso, E.:Proceedings of the 2020 CHI Conference on Human Factors in Computing Systems. Association for Computing Machinery, New York, NY, USA, pp. 1–13 (2020). https://doi.org/10.1145/3313831.3376566. https://doi.org/10.1145/3313831.3376566
7. Chen, X., Srivastava, N., Jain, R., Healey, J., Dingler, T.: Proceedings of the 2023 CHI Conference on Human Factors in Computing Systems. Association for Computing Machinery, New York, NY, USA (2023). https://doi.org/10.1145/3544548.3581174. https://doi.org/10.1145/3544548.3581174
8. Cai, C.J., Ren, A., Miller, R.C.: ACM Trans. Comput. Hum. Interact. **24**(1) (2017). https://doi.org/10.1145/3044534. https://doi.org/10.1145/3044534
9. Dingler, T., Weber, D., Pielot, M., Cooper, J., Chang, C.C., Henze, N.: Proceedings of the 19th International Conference on Human-Computer Interaction with Mobile Devices and Services. Association for Computing Machinery, New York, NY, USA (2017). https://doi.org/10.1145/3098279.3098565. https://doi.org/10.1145/3098279.3098565
10. Brynjolfsson, E., McAfee, A.: The Second Machine Age: Work, Progress, and Prosperity in a Time of Brilliant Technologies. W. W. Norton & Company, New York (2014)
11. Luckin, R., Holmes, W., Griffiths, M., Forcier, L.B.: Intelligence unleashed: an argument for AI in education (2016). https://www.pearson.com/content/dam/one-dot-com/one-dot-com/global/Files/about-pearson/innovation/open-ideas/Intelligence-Unleashed-Publication.pdf. Accessed 28 Mar 2025
12. Holmes, W., Bialik, M., Fadel, C.: Artificial Intelligence in Education: Promises and Implications for Teaching and Learning. Center for Curriculum Redesign, Boston, MA (2019). Accessed 28 Mar 2025
13. Peters, M.A., Jandrić, P., Hayes, S.: Postdigital Dialogue: Postdigital Science and Education. Springer, Cham (2020). https://doi.org/10.1007/978-3-030-43620-9
14. Zander, T.O., Kothe, C.: J. Neural Eng. **8**(2), 025005 (2011). https://doi.org/10.1088/1741-2560/8/2/025005
15. Rzayev, R., Dingler, T., Henze, N.: Proceedings of the 17th International Conference on Mobile and Ubiquitous Multimedia. Association for Computing Machinery, New York, NY, USA, pp. 285–291 (2018). https://doi.org/10.1145/3282894.3282907. https://doi.org/10.1145/3282894.3282907
16. Dingler, T., El Agroudy, P., Viet Le, H., Schmidt, A., Niforatos, E., Bexheti, A., Langheinrich, M.: IEEE MultiMed. **23**(2), 4 (2016). https://doi.org/10.1109/MMUL.2016.31
17. Floridi, L., Cowls, J., Beltrametti, M., Chatila, R., Chazerand, P., Dignum, V., Luetge, C., Madelin, R., Pagallo, U., Rossi, F., Schafer, B., Valcke, P., Vayena, E.: Mind. Mach. **28**(4), 689 (2018). https://doi.org/10.1007/s11023-018-9482-5
18. Lee, M., Gero, K.I., Chung, J.J.Y., Shum, S.B., Raheja, V., Shen, H., Venugopalan, S., Wambsganss, T., Zhou, D., Alghamdi, E.A., August, T., Bhat, A., Choksi, M.Z., Dutta, S., Guo, J.L., Hoque, M.N., Kim, Y., Knight, S., Neshaei, S.P., Shibani, A., Shrivastava, D., Shroff, L.,

Sergeyuk, A., Stark, J., Sterman, S., Wang, S., Bosselut, A., Buschek, D., Chang, J.C., Chen, S., Kreminski, M., Park, J., Pea, R., Rho, E.H.R., Shen, Z., Siangliulue, P.: Proceedings of the 2024 CHI Conference on Human Factors in Computing Systems. Association for Computing Machinery, New York, NY, USA (2024). https://doi.org/10.1145/3613904.3642697. https://doi.org/10.1145/3613904.3642697
19. Schmidt, A.: IEEE Pervasive Comput. **16**(1), 6 (2017)
20. Boonprakong, N., Tag, B., Dingler, T.: IEEE Pervasive Comput. **22**(3), 8 (2023). https://doi.org/10.1109/MPRV.2023.3275514
21. Carr, N.: The Shallows: What the Internet Is Doing to Our Brains. W. W. Norton & Company, New York (2010)
22. Lanier, J.: Ten Arguments for Deleting Your Social Media Accounts Right Now. Random House (2018)
23. Perfors, A.: The Work of Creation in the Age of AI (2024). https://perfors.net/blog/creation-ai/. Accessed 29 Mar 2025
24. Barr, N., Pennycook, G., Stolz, J.A., Fugelsang, J.A.: Comput. Hum. Behav. **48**, 473 (2015). https://doi.org/10.1016/j.chb.2015.02.029
25. Pielot, M., Rello, L.: Proceedings of the 33rd Annual ACM Conference Extended Abstracts on Human Factors in Computing Systems. Association for Computing Machinery, New York, NY, USA, pp. 1761–1766 (2015). https://doi.org/10.1145/2702613.2732704. https://doi.org/10.1145/2702613.2732704
26. Hollan, J., Hutchins, E., Kirsh, D.: ACM Trans. Comput. Hum. Interact. (TOCHI) **7**(2), 174 (2000). https://doi.org/10.1145/353485.353487
27. Gesner, C.: Bibliotheca Universalis: sive catalogus omnium scriptorum locupletissimus, in tribus linguis, Latinâ, Graecâ, & Hebraicâ: extantium & non extantium veterum & recentiorum, publicatorum & in bibliothecis latentium. Christoph Froschauer, Zurich, 1545. Originally published in Latin
28. Simon, H.A.: Brookings Institute Lecture (1969)
29. Hilbert, M., López, P.: Science **332**(6025), 60 (2011)
30. Wilmer, H.H., Sherman, L.E., Chein, J.M.: Frontiers in Psychology **8**, 605 (2017). https://doi.org/10.3389/fpsyg.2017.00605. https://www.frontiersin.org/articles/10.3389/fpsyg.2017.00605/full
31. Dingler, T., Pielot, M.: Proceedings of the 17th International Conference on Human-Computer Interaction with Mobile Devices and Services. Association for Computing Machinery, New York, NY, USA, pp. 1–5 (2015). https://doi.org/10.1145/2785830.2785840. https://doi.org/10.1145/2785830.2785840
32. Pielot, M., Dingler, T., Pedro, J.S., Oliver, N.: Proceedings of the 2015 ACM International Joint Conference on Pervasive and Ubiquitous Computing. Association for Computing Machinery, New York, NY, USA, pp. 825–836 (2015). https://doi.org/10.1145/2750858.2804252. https://doi.org/10.1145/2750858.2804252
33. Mark, G.: Attention Span: A Groundbreaking Way to Restore Balance, Happiness and Productivity. Hanover Square Press, Toronto, Canada (2023). https://gloriamark.com/attention-span/
34. Waller, B.N.: Analysis **59**(4), 223 (1999). https://doi.org/10.1093/analys/59.4.223, https://academic.oup.com/analysis/article-abstract/59/4/223/173241
35. Kahneman, D.: Thinking, Fast and Slow. Farrar, Straus and Giroux, New York (2011)
36. Pratkanis, A.R., Aronson, E.: Age of Propaganda: The Everyday Use and Abuse of Persuasion. W.H. Freeman, New York (2001). https://www.amazon.com/Age-Propaganda-Everyday-Abuse-Persuasion/dp/0805074031
37. Boonprakong, N., Chen, X., Davey, C., Tag, B., Dingler, T.: Proceedings of the 2023 CHI Conference on Human Factors in Computing Systems. Association for Computing Machinery, New York, NY, USA, (2023). https://doi.org/10.1145/3544548.3580917. https://doi.org/10.1145/3544548.3580917
38. Boonprakong, N., Pareek, S., Tag, B., Goncalves, J., Dingler, T.: Proceedings of the 2025 CHI Conference on Human Factors in Computing Systems (2025). https://doi.org/10.1145/3706598.3713873. URL https://doi.org/10.1145/3706598.3713873

39. Boonprakong, N., Tag, B., Goncalves, J., Dingler, T.: Proceedings of the 2025 CHI Conference on Human Factors in Computing Systems (2025). https://doi.org/10.1145/3706598.3713450. URL https://doi.org/10.1145/3706598.3713450
40. Kluger, A.N., DeNisi, A.: Psychol. Bull. **119**(2), 254 (1996)
41. Shute, V.J.: Rev. Educ. Res. **78**(1), 153 (2008). https://doi.org/10.3102/0034654307313795

MIX
Papier aus verantwortungsvollen Quellen
Paper from responsible sources
FSC® C105338

If you have any concerns about our products,
you can contact us on
ProductSafety@springernature.com

In case Publisher is established outside the EU,
the EU authorized representative is:
Springer Nature Customer Service Center GmbH
Europaplatz 3, 69115 Heidelberg, Germany

Printed by Libri Plureos GmbH
in Hamburg, Germany